LAW AND RELIGION

Essays on the Place of the Law in Israel and Early Christianity
by members of the Ehrhardt Seminar
of Manchester University

edited by
Barnabas Lindars SSF

James Clarke & Co
Cambridge

James Clarke & Co
P.O. Box 60
Cambridge CB1 2NT

British Library Cataloguing in Publication Data
Law and religion: essays on the place of
the law in Israel and early Christianity.
1. Bible. Special subjects: Christian
doctrine. Divine law. Exegetical studies
I. Linders, Barnabas
241′.2

ISBN 0–227–67907–3

First published 1988 by James Clarke & Co

Typeset by Wyvern Typesetting Ltd, Bristol

Printed in Great Britain by
Billing & Sons Ltd, Worcester

CONTENTS

vi / *Contents*

ABBREVIATIONS

APOCRYPHA AND PSEUDEPIGRAPHA

Apoc. Abr.	*Apocalypse of Abraham*
Arist. (or *Ep. Arist.*)	*Epistle of Aristeas*
Bar (or 1 Bar)	Baruch
2 Bar.	Syriac *Apocalypse of Baruch*
4 Bar.	*4 Baruch*
Gos. Pet.	*Gospel of Peter*
Jdt	Judith
Jub.	*Jubilees*
1-2-3-4 Macc	1-2-3-4 Maccabees
Pss. Sol.	*Psalms of Solomon*
Sib. Or.	*Sibylline Oracles*
Sir	Sirach (Ecclesiasticus)
Thomas	*Gospel of Thomas*
T. Levi	*Testament of Levi*
Wis	Wisdom of Solomon

DEAD SEA SCROLLS

CD	Cairo text of the *Damascus Document*
1QapGen	*Genesis Apocryphon* from Cave 1
1QSa	Appendix A (*Rule of the Congregation*) to the *Manual of Discipline* (1QS) from Cave 1
4QDeut^q	Fragment q of Deuteronomy from Cave 4
4Q (XQ) Phyl	Phylacteries from Cave 4 and other caves
4QPss^a	The Psalms Scroll from Cave 4
4QtgLev	Targum of Leviticus from Cave 4
11QT	The Temple Scroll from Cave 11

RABBINIC WORKS

b.	*Babylonian Talmud* (followed by name of tractate in full; so also:–)
j.	*Jerusalem Talmud*
m.	*Mishnah*
p.	*Palestinian Talmud*
t.	*Tosephta*
Exod. Rab.	*Exodus Rabbah*
Num. Rab.	*Numbers Rabbah*
Lam. Rab.	*Lamentations Rabbah*
Mek.	*Mekilta*

OTHER ANCIENT WRITERS

Apos. Con.	*The Apostolic Constitutions*
Dionysius, *RA*	*Roman Antiquities* of Dionysius of Halicarnassus

Josephus, *Ant.*	Josephus' *Antiquities of the Jews*
Ap.	*Against Apion*
BJ	*Jewish War*
Vita	*The Life of Flavius Josephus*
Justin, *Dial.*	Justin's *Dialogue with Trypho*
Philo, *Leg. Gaium*	Philo's *Legation to Gaius*
Spec. Leg.	*On the Special Laws*

GENERAL

AB	The Anchor Bible
ANET	J. B. Pritchard (ed.), *Ancient Near Eastern Texts* (2nd edn), 1955
AV	Authorised Version
BA	*Biblical Archaeologist*
BASOR	*Bulletin of the American Schools of Oriental Research*
BBB	Bonner biblische Beiträge
BCE	Before the Christian Era
BETL	Bibliotheca Ephemeridum Theologicarum Lovaniensium
BGBE	Beiträge zur Geschichte der biblischen Exegese
Bib	*Biblica*
BJRL	*Bulletin of the John Rylands University Library of Manchester*
BJS	Brown Judaic Studies
BWANT	Beiträge zur Wissenschaft vom Alten und Neuen Testament
BZ	*Biblische Zeitschrift*
BZAW	Beihefte zur *ZAW*
CBQ	*Catholic Biblical Quarterly*
CE	Of the Christian Era
ConBNT	Coniectanea Biblica, New Testament
CRINT	Compendia Rerum Iudaicorum ad Novum Testamentum
CTA	A. Herdner, *Corpus des tablettes en cunéiforme alphabétiques*
D	Writings of the Deuteronomic school
DJD	Discoveries in the Judaean Desert
E	Elohistic strand of the Pentateuch
ET	English translation
EV(V)	English version(s)
ExpT	*Expository Times*
Frag.	Fragment
FRLANT	Forschungen zur Religion und Literatur des Alten und Neuen Testaments
H	The Holiness Code (Lev 17–26)
HeyJ	*Heythrop Journal*

HTKNT	Herders Theologischer Kommentar zum Neuen Testament
HTR	*Harvard Theological Review*
HUCA	*Hebrew Union College Annual*
HUCM	Hebrew Union College Monographs
ICC	International Critical Commentary
Int	*Interpretation*
J	Yahwistic strand of the Pentateuch
JANESCU	*Journal of the Ancient Near Eastern Society of Columbia University*
JAOS	*Journal of the American Oriental Society*
JBL	*Journal of Biblical Literature*
JJS	*Journal of Jewish Studies*
JNES	*Journal of Near Eastern Studies*
JPOS	*Journal of the Palestine Oriental Society*
JSHRZ	Jüdische Schriften aus hellenistisch-römischer Zeit
JSJ	*Journal for the Study of Judaism in the Persian, Hellenistic and Roman Period*
JSNT	*Journal for the Study of the New Testament*
JSNTSup	*JSNT Supplement Series*
JSOT	*Journal for the Study of the Old Testament*
JSOTSup	*JSOT Supplement Series*
JSS	*Journal of Semitic Studies*
JTS	*Journal of Theological Studies*
LCL	Loeb Classical Library
LXX	Septuagint
MT	Massoretic Text
NCB	New Century Bible
NEB	*New English Bible*
NIDNTT	*New International Dictionary of New Testament Theology*
NovT	*Novum Testamentum*
NovTSup	Supplements to *Novum Testamentum*
NT	New Testament
NTS	*New Testament Studies*
OT	Old Testament
OTL	Old Testament Library
P	Writings of the Priestly School
P^g	*Grundschrift* of the Priestly Code
par	parallel(s)
Q	Source material common to Matthew and Luke
R	Redactor
RA	*Revue d'Assyriologie et d'Archéologie Orientale*
RB	*Revue Biblique*

RevQ	*Revue de Qumran*
RS	Ras Shamra
RSV	Revised Standard Version
SBLDS	Society of Biblical Literature Dissertation Series
SBT	Studies in Biblical Theology
SCS	Septuagint and Cognate Studies
SJLA	Studies in Judaism in Late Antiquity
SJT	*Scottish Journal of Theology*
SNTSMS	Society for New Testament Studies Monograph Series
SNTU	*Studien zum neuen Testament und seiner Umwelt*
TDNT	G. Kittel und G. Friedrich (eds.), *Theological Dictionary of the New Testament*
UF	*Ugarit-Forschungen*
VT	*Vetus Testamentum*
VTSup	Supplements to *Vetus Testamentum*
WMANT	Wissenschaftliche Monographien zum Alten und Neuen Testament
WUNT	Wissenschaftliche Untersuchungen zum Neuen Testament
ZAW	*Zeitschrift für die Alttestamentliche Wissenschaft*
ZNW	*Zeitschrift für die Neutestamentliche Wissenschaft*
ZTK	*Zeitschrift für Theologie und Kirche*

INTRODUCTION

A connection between law and religion is almost universal in human history and society, but the relationship between them is not always easily determined, and this became a major issue in the emergence of Christianity from the cradle of Judaism. By the time of Jesus the law comprised in the books of the Pentateuch had become central to Jewish self-definition, and was the focus of the deepest religious feelings of devout Jews. Half a century later the movement which sprang from Jesus had largely thrown off allegiance to the Jewish law and had become predominantly Gentile in its membership. It is possible to regard this as an ironic quirk of history. But it is profoundly serious for all that, because it has left scars on subsequent religious history which remain even today. Bitterness between believers and non-believers starts within the New Testament period itself, and the subsequent hostility between Christians and Jews is a sad and shaming story, which has been responsible for centuries of injustice. Within Christianity itself the plight of the Jewish–Christian groups in the early centuries can only add to the impression of disquiet. Moreover the Church quickly developed, one should perhaps say inevitably developed, its own new brand of reliance on law, creating a tension in its own self-understanding which inevitably erupted in the Reformation. That, too, has its own after-history of irreconcilable differences between Christians in which the perpetual problem of law and religion is constantly arising.

With such a devastating inheritance it is difficult for the modern Christian or Jew to look at the story of the rise of Christianity without a measure of distortion where this issue is concerned. But recent scholarship has greatly improved our knowledge of Judaism in the time of Christ. We shall never overcome our inherited prejudices unless we look afresh at the causes of them, and we are now much better placed to do so. It is the purpose of this book to draw together some of the many facets of the issue of law and religion which have to be taken into account in any attempt at renewed understanding of the phenomenon of the rise of Christianity.

The essays collected in this volume are the fruit of the 1985–6 session of the Ehrhardt Seminar in the Department of Biblical Studies of the Faculty of Theology in the University of Manchester. The Seminar, named after the late Dr Arnold A. T. Ehrhardt, is a forum where staff and research students, and other biblical specialists working outside the University, meet for papers and discussion on biblical subjects. Law and Religion was chosen as the focus of study for the session because of the changing attitudes that have been taking place in this area in recent years. The most spectacular change has been in connection with the understanding of Paul's attitude to the law, set in motion by E. P. Sanders in his large-scale work on *Paul and Palestinian Judaism* (1977). Modern critical scholarship, especially in Germany, has tended to work with a stereotype, in which the Pharisees have been represented as unyielding legalists and Paul has been regarded as opposed to the law as fundamentally incompatible with authentic religion. Sanders questioned both these assumptions, and thereby aroused a controversy which has proved to have wide ramifications. We are grateful to Professor Bruce, who returned to the Seminar of which he had long been the chairman during his tenure of the Rylands Professorship, for his contribution on 'Paul and the law in recent research', in which the main lines of the current discussion have been drawn together.

In fact, as is shown by Barnabas Lindars in 'Paul and the law in Romans 5–8: an actantial analysis', the question for Paul is not separable from the Judaistic controversy in which he was the principal figure. But the issue compelled him to think more deeply about the place of the law in religion in a wider context. He could not disregard the sense in which something comparable to the Jewish law operates in pagans too, so that converts from among the Gentiles have similar moral and spiritual problems to face as a result of their innate consciousness of good and evil and awareness of the insidious character of sin. There is thus a tension in these chapters between Paul's involvement in the arguments concerning the rights and wrongs of imposing the Jewish law on the Gentile converts, and his attempt to see the positive place of the law in a larger understanding of religion which embraces both Jews and Gentiles. The autobiographical section in Rom 7:7–25 is especially liable to misinterpretation because of the ambiguity which arises from this tension, with the result that its real importance for Paul's understanding of religion can be easily missed.

The reappraisal of Paul's attitude to the law leads inevitably to further questions. In the first place, the significance of the law in the religion of Judaism at the time needs to be reconsidered. We are now more aware of the variety and fluidity of Jewish religious ideas in the intertestamental period than was possible before the discovery of the Dead Sea Scrolls. Jewish religion was the product of centuries of tradition, rolling on like a stream, but joined by many tributary influences on the way and subject to dramatic changes of environment. This is illustrated in the essays in Part I of this book. The ancient connection between rulers and gods, providing divine sanctions for the laws that ensure the good ordering of society, is displayed in the opening essay of Adrian Curtis on 'God as "judge" in Ugaritic and Hebrew thought'. It cannot be claimed that a law-book was central to Israelite religious consciousness in the period of the Judges and the Kings. This begins only with the use of a law-book (probably to be identified with the legal chapters of Deuteronomy) as the basis of the religious reform under Josiah at the very end of the period. Before this, laws were given divine sanctions, and law-codes included regulations for the conduct of worship, but the law as such was not perceived to be the focus of the relationship between the people and God. The essay by Arnold Anderson on 'Law in Old Israel: laws concerning adultery' shows in a practical way the difficulty of ascertaining the real status of laws in old Israel, but indicates at the same time the prominence of divine sanctions in laws relating to social customs.

The change in the relationship between law and religion must be attributed to the vast upheaval of the Babylonian exile. Now the conditions of life in a foreign land made the law not only a platform for reform, but the repository of a precious tradition that was in danger of being lost. In his essay on 'A perpetual statute throughout your generations' Roger Tomes shows how the writers of the Priestly School, who undertook a comprehensive revision and rationalisation of the ancient laws, attached this phrase especially to religious ordinances which were in danger of extinction under the conditions of exile and the restrictions imposed after the return to the Judea by the Persian overlords. The law now becomes the repository of the distinctive customs and beliefs of the Jewish people, and these are represented as unchangeable by divine decree. Thus the law is by this time central to Jewish self-definition, both religiously as defining Israel's relationship with God, and politically in defining Judaism over against other peoples. The law comprises the revelation of God, and corresponding with this there is a spirituality (expressed splendidly in Psalm 119) which consists in meditation on the law as the means of enlightening the mind and stirring the will and the emotions in the service of God (though Paul holds that, in the last analysis, the law fails at this point).

These developments not only explain the centrality of the law in the religion of Judaism in the NT period, but also suggest ample reasons for finalising the law in unalterable and fixed form. It has long been held that this is what was achieved by the Priestly School, when the Priestly Code reached its final form in the fourth/third century BCE. However, recent study shows that the matter is more complicated. For there is in our period an effort on the part of some deeply devout people to revise the law further, so as to make it more self-consistent in the light of the unchanging principles which it contains and to make it more workable as a code of religious practice. Thus the very seriousness with which the law is approached provides the motivation for further change. So Roger Tomes begins his article by pointing out the paradoxical way in which the 'perpetual statutes' of the law are claimed by the writer of *Jubilees* in his rewriting of Genesis and Exodus 1–12. *Jubilees* was known and used at Qumran, but should not be regarded as a product of the Qumran Sect itself. It belongs to a wider movement for reform in the period of the Maccabean Revolt and its aftermath, a movement which cannot be identified with certainty because of the scarcity of evidence, but seems certainly to have included the Essenes. The publication of the Temple Scroll from Qumran, after long delay, has added further relevant considerations. In 'The Temple Scroll: a law unto itself?', George Brooke argues that it is best regarded as a further work of revision of the law along the same lines as *Jubilees*, starting where *Jubilees* leaves off. Both books have a connection with the *Damascus Document*, which must also be reappraised in the light of them. The conclusion is drawn that the *Damascus Document* is not a distinctively Qumran work (like the Manual of Discipline) but the programme of reform of a comparable group with which the Qumran Sect had close sympathy. Qumran shared some of the reforms which are advocated in this literature, especially the *Jubilees* calendar. On the other hand, while possessing the Temple Scroll, and so being well aware of the revisions of the law which it contains, the Qumran sectaries made no direct use of it. Their *halakah*, or way of keeping the law, was derived from their unknown founder (the Teacher of Righteousness), who was revered as the definitive interpreter of the law.

It so comes about that, though the text of the Pentateuch is in process of fixation and standardisation all through our period, the interpretation of it is quite fluid, even extending to proposals for rewriting it on the part of a significant element of devout Jews. From this point of view the old tendency to divide Judaism between Pharisees and Sadducees, the former prepared to admit very considerable latitude of interpretation in order to promote faithful adherence to the law, and the latter opposed to all innovations, can be seen to be too simple. Philip Alexander's essay on 'Jewish law in the time of Jesus' helps to put the record straight. Though these groups did not accept further rewriting of the law, they were not immune from the need to update it in relation to changing circumstances. The rabbis developed rules of interpretation whereby points of the law could be legitimately extended to cover new conditions. The Targums also often show a modernising tendency, to enable the hearers to grasp the meaning of the law and to apply it in their own lives.

Christianity began as a movement within Judaism, and neither Jesus nor his followers intended to overthrow the law. The reappraisal of Paul's attitude to the law inevitably reopens the question of the attitude of Jesus himself, with the consequence that E. P. Sanders was constrained to follow up his books on Paul with a study of *Jesus and Judaism* (1985). The point is taken up in an essay on 'All foods clean: thoughts on Jesus and the law', in which Barnabas Lindars attempts to show that Jesus' references to the law are subordinate to the main purpose of his teaching, which concerns the imminent manifestation of the kingdom of God. Jesus did not introduce a new *halakah* as an alternative to the interpretations already on offer, but he would not allow the law to be used as a screen to evade the full impact of the claim of God upon the conscience. His use of irony, and what may almost be called shock-tactics (if one may so refer to the parables as 'language-events'), intrigued his audience, but rendered him liable to misunderstanding on the part of scribes and Pharisees. How this also affected the central authorities in Jerusalem and contributed to the movement to put him to death is the subject of the highly original essay of Richard Bauckham on 'Jesus' demonstration in the temple'. All the subsequent developments in early Christianity can be seen as consequences of Jesus' teaching. The most primitive preaching takes the continuance of the law for granted. Jewish Christianity eventually makes some modifications, using the remembered teaching of Jesus as the halakic basis of its position. Paul goes to the heart of Jesus' challenge to the conscience in order to cope with the new situation created by the admission of Gentiles into Christian fellowship. The fluidity of Christian attitudes to the law in the earliest period is illustrated further by the suggestion of Christopher Tuckett, in his article on 'Q, the law and Judaism', that the Q collection of sayings of Jesus was channelled through a group of Christian Pharisees, who felt that their position was supported by Jesus' teaching.

It seems, then, proper to think of a Christian dialectic in relation to the law. The teaching of Jesus can be taken to uphold the law, but it also undergirds Paul's radical critique. In the Johannine community there is the additional factor of Jewish Wisdom speculation with regard to the law, which is taken to support the Christian claims concerning Jesus as himself the embodiment of wisdom. Johannine Christianity thus entails a christological interpretation of the law itself, which was the cause of heated debate between the community and the synagogue. This is argued by George Brooke in his essay on 'Christ and the law in John 7–10', in which it is shown how the Jewish opposition to Jesus is regarded by John as equivalent to transgression of the decalogue. At this stage relations between Church and Synagogue are at breaking-point, and the interpretation of the law is a central issue in the dispute.

Meanwhile in the Gentile churches the position so strongly advocated by Paul eventually prevailed. Martin Kitchen, writing on 'The status of law in the Letter to the Ephesians', argues that the fall of Jerusalem was taken in the circles to which this letter belongs to be the vindication of Paul's policy of taking the Church beyond the confines of Judaism as constituted under the law to the new era, in which the Spirit is directly operative in enabling the Christians to produce good works. The law itself is no longer a burning issue for these Christians of the second generation. However, we must not be deceived by the single-minded enthusiasm of the writer to the Ephesians into supposing that the law played no further part in Gentile

Christianity. Gerald Downing, on 'Law and custom: Luke–Acts and late Hellenism', points out that law had long been perceived as essential to religion among the Greeks and Romans, and that the partial abandonment of the Jewish law (not amounting to denial of its moral value) on the part of the Christians was calculated to show them in the best possible light from a Gentile point of view – shedding the pointless and often barbarous requirements of the Jewish inheritance, but affirming its basic value by the high moral standard of their lives. This at least was Luke's hope as he wrote his account of earliest Christianity for the benefit of a sympathetic enquirer like Theophilus.

The dialectical understanding of law and religion is necessary, because of the ambiguous character of religion in the history of humanity. From a sociological point of view, religion often functions as a stabilising factor. It is thereby allied to law and tends towards conservatism and traditionalism. But religion is also characterised by charismatic outbursts, which make it a revolutionary force and a trenchant critic of established norms. Both aspects belong to the rise of Christianity. The profound impact of Jesus is due, partly at least, to the way in which they are combined in his teaching, which sets the issue firmly in the higher setting of the claim of God upon humankind.

Part I

The law in Israelite religion

1

GOD AS 'JUDGE' IN UGARITIC AND HEBREW THOUGHT

ADRIAN CURTIS

The many legal texts discovered at Ugarit make it clear that the king played an important legal role; although legal transactions could be carried out before witnesses, many were characterised by the dynastic seal and an indication that they were enacted 'before x (son of y) king of Ugarit' or that they record decrees, decisions or acts of the king.[1] At Ugarit, then, as elsewhere in the ancient Near East, one of the important roles of the earthly king was judicial.

There is, as is well known, evidence that Ugaritic *ṭpṭ*/Hebrew *špṭ* could have a rather more general sense than the specific 'dispense justice'. It is noteworthy that, in the Ugaritic texts, *ṭpṭ* is considered a suitable parallel term to *mlk* 'king' and *zbl* 'prince'. The divine name and epithet *ṭpṭ nhr* 'judge Nahar/River' invariably parallel *zbl ym* 'prince Yam/Sea',[2] while *ṭpṭn* 'our judge' is found parallel to *mlkn* 'our king'.[3]

W. H. Schmidt[4] makes special mention of the following lines:

lysʿ [àlt] ṭ[btk]	Indeed he will pull up the support of your seat;
[ly]hpk [ksà] mlkk	indeed he will overturn the throne of your kingdom;
lyṭbr ḫṭ mṭpṭk	indeed he will break the sceptre of your rule.[5]

As indicated in the above translation, *mṭpṭk* here seems to require some such rendering as 'rule' or 'dominion', rather than 'justice'. This passage is reminiscent of a statement in the Phoenician Aḥiram inscription, dating from about 1000 BCE:

thtsp ḥtr mšpth thtpk ksʾ mlkh   ... let his judicial staff be broken, let
                                           his royal throne be upset.[6]

Also noteworthy is a reference to *mlk nhr* 'king Nahar/River'[7] which may
be an alternative term to the more frequent *ṭpṭ nhr*.

That the root *špṭ* can have this wider significance in Hebrew is suggested
by the fact that the major 'judges' who preceded the establishment of the
monarchy in Israel were charismatic deliverers who ruled sections of the
people for a time, and who, with the possible exception of Deborah,[8] do
not seem to have administered justice in the narrower sense. In the fourth
part of his study on the Israelite Judges, W. Richter[9] considered the task of
the 'judge', and the use of the term *špṭ* and its equivalents in the OT, in
Ugaritic, in the Mari texts, and in Phoenician, and concluded that the
function of the judges is not military and not only juristic, but to rule: his
task is government and legal justice. Schmidt[10] suggests that in Pss 96:13
and 98:9 the root is to be rendered 'rule'. M. Dahood[11] offers the
rendering 'govern' in the above verses; in Ps 2:10 *mĕlākîm* 'kings' is
paralleled by the phrase *šōpĕtê ʾāreṣ*, which Dahood[12] translates 'rulers of
the earth' (as does RSV), and follows E. A. Speiser[13] when he comments on
the verse that, 'The basic sense of *špṭ* is "to exercise authority" in various
matters.' The Köhler–Baumgartner *Lexicon*[14] gives the sense 'master,
ruler' as number 8 under the heading *špṭ*.

From Mari, A. Malamat[15] notes references to the *šāpiṭum*, the counterpart of the Hebrew *šōpēṭ* of the Book of Judges, both of whom, he feels,
were not simply judges, but actually leaders of prominent rank, originat-
ing in the tribal order. It is also noteworthy that in Carthage, the
Phoenician colony in north Africa, the rulers were called *suffetes*, which
Köhler–Baumgartner gives as a Latin development from the root *špṭ*.[16]

All this implies that concern for justice and the upholding of rightness
was believed to be integral to the idea of ruling. However, despite the fact
that *špṭ/ṭpṭ* may, at times, have the general sense 'rule', it is also used more
specifically of one of the primary roles of the ruler, i.e. that of maintaining
justice. A. R. Johnson[17] gives a concise statement of the position in Israel.

> ... if the nation is to prosper, the king must act as the embodiment of
> 'righteousness' (*ṣĕdāqâ, ṣedeq*). That is to say, it is first and foremost his
> concern to see that the behaviour of society at large is thoroughly
> 'righteous' (*ṣaddîq*) and that, to this end, the sanctions of the group,
> particularly the nation's laws, are uniformly observed throughout the
> different strata of society; for it is only in this way, when the individual is
> restrained from doing 'what is right in his own eyes', that the well-being
> (*šālôm*) of the nation, in fact its life or vitality (*ḥayyîm*), can be assured.
> Thus the king is the supreme 'ruler' or 'judge' (*šōpēṭ*), to whom one may go
> in any matter of dispute for a final 'ruling' or 'judgement' (*mišpāṭ*) which,
> ideally at least, will be an act of 'justice' (*mišpāṭ*).

Thus the king was the supreme dispenser of justice in the land, and the
psalmist was able to pray:

> Give the king thy justice, O God,
>   and thy righteousness to the royal son!

> May he judge thy people with righteousness,
>   and thy poor with justice! ...
> May he defend the cause of the poor of the people,
>   give deliverance to the needy,
>   and crush the oppressor.
>
> (Ps 72:1, 2, 4)[18]

The above verses make it clear that one of the king's primary tasks as upholder of justice was to see that the poor and needy were not oppressed; the other classes specially singled out in this way were the widows and the orphans.[19] F. C. Fensham has described this care for the widow, orphan and poor as a 'common policy in the Ancient Near East'.[20] He feels that such people had to be protected, as they had no legal supporters.

A similar concern is expressed in the epilogue of the Code of Hammurabi.

> In order that the strong might not oppress the weak, that justice might be dealt the orphan (and) the widow ... I wrote my precious words on my stela.[21]

According to the text of the Code of Hammurabi it was Marduk who ordered Hammurabi to 'set forth justice', although the picture on the Louvre stela shows the god Shamash commissioning the king, and Shamash is mentioned in the epilogue; it appears that Marduk had taken over some of Shamash's attributes as god of justice.[22]

That this 'common policy' was carried out in Ugarit is clear from Yassib's words when he criticises his father Keret for his inability to perform his kingly functions:

... *ltdn*	... you cannot judge
dn àlmnt lttpt	the cause of the widow, cannot try
tpt qsr npš ltdy	the case of the wretched, cannot put down
tšm 'l dl lpnk	those who despoil the child of the poor,
ltšlḥm ytm bᶜd	cannot drive out those who plunder the orphan
kslk àlmnt	before your face, the widow behind your back.[23]

It is also noteworthy that Dan(i)el sat in the gate[24] and

... *ydn*	... he judged
dn àlmnt ytpt tpt ytm	the cause of the widow, tried the case of the orphan.[25]

The close verbal similarity between these passages and the OT references already noted suggests that it is no longer necessary to look so far afield as Babylon for a close parallel to this aspect of royal responsibility.

The importance of a knowledge of the law by the Israelite king is stressed in Deut 17:18–20, where it is stated that a monarch must make for himself a copy of the law, and study it continually to ensure that he keeps its statutes. J. R. Porter[26] has argued that the Deuteronomy passage suggests that each new king is to 'promulgate the Law afresh as another

Moses' on his accession, and he noted that 2 Kgs 23:2 describes Josiah as reading out the law publicly himself. He thus felt that it would be to go too far to suggest that the king of Israel never promulgated a law-code. G. Widengren[27] has suggested that Moses, the law-giver *par excellence*, was the ideal model of the Israelite ruler. Widengren's rather speculative views on the Israelite monarch have been questioned by E. I. J. Rosenthal.[28] Noting the importance of the Torah for the king, he argued that the royal responsibility did not include expounding the law; the king's duty was to *read* the law. But is it advisable to draw too much distinction between 'reading' and 'expounding'? There would presumably be some didactic purpose in Josiah's reading of the law, although it could be argued that this was a special case as it was a recently discovered law-book which was being read. However, in Deut 17:18ff. the king's reading of the law seems to be primarily for his own edification. These verses make it clear that the reading was to be followed by implementation, for the king must not only *know* the law, he must *keep* it; it is only by knowing and keeping the God-given law that he can ensure justice in the realm. The question of whether the Israelite king could himself promulgate law has more recently been considered by K. W. Whitelam in his detailed study of the king's judicial authority.[29] He suggests that it is likely that the king would have the power to legislate in new situations with which the pentateuchal law could not cope; the relative silence of the OT on this could perhaps be attributed to a necessity to maintain the impression that all law emanated from God and could not be changed. But whether or not this aspect of his argument is correct, he has demonstrated clearly that the OT presents an ideal picture of the king as judge.

Like the earthly king, the divine ruler is often seen in the role of 'judge'. It was noted above that references to gods as judges often form parallel phrases to statements that they are rulers; however, this does not necessarily imply that such references are merely used to achieve parallelism, without carrying the more specific meaning. It seems more likely that it is because 'judging' was such a basic and primary aspect of 'ruling' that the terms 'king' and 'judge' could be virtually synonymous. Thus, when Anat and Athirat say:

mlkn àlỉyn b'l tptn	Our king is the victor Baal, our judge,
ỉn d'lnh	there is none over him.[30]

both titles are apposite; not only has Baal shown through his victory over Yam, the personification of the waters which could threaten chaos, that he is worthy to rule, but he has also established order and thus ensured that the various components of the cosmos are in a *right* relationship with one another. Baal is thus the champion of order and 'right'-ness, and fully deserves the title *tpt*. It is noteworthy that from Ugarit we have the theophoric names *tptb'l* and *b'lmtpt*,[31] while Phoenician and Punic names include *b'lšpt* and *šptb'l*;[32] however, the element *t/špt* does not appear to be found with the name of any deity other than Baal in Ugaritic and Phoenician/Punic personal names.

The Ugaritic theophoric names *ṣdqìl* and *ìlṣdq*[33] suggest that El was believed to be concerned with 'right'-ness. There is some evidence to suggest that the assembly of the gods over which El presided may sometimes have acted as a judicial gathering. The assembly is called the *'dt ìlm* 'congregation/assembly of the gods'[34] and the *pḫr bn ìlm* 'host/assembly of the sons of El/the gods'.[35] In the Ugaritic version of the pantheon of Ugarit (line 28) mention is made of the *pḫr ìlm*; the parallel in the Akkadian version is *dpu-ḫur ilâni*[M].[36] We also, and perhaps significantly, find mention of the *pḫr m'd*.[37] This last term may imply that this could be a judicial assembly.

When Yam sends messengers to demand that Baal be handed over to him, the message is sent to El while he is with the *pḫr m'd*. G. R. Driver,[38] followed by J. C. L. Gibson,[39] translates the phrase 'full convocation', though both add in a footnote that the literal meaning is 'the assembly' or 'totality of the appointed meeting'. R. J. Clifford[40] notes that *m'd* occurs only in this phrase and is presumably derived from the root *y'd* 'appoint, decide', as is *'dt*, hence the second of the literal renderings given above. But this etymology might support a suggestion that this was a decision-making assembly. It must be admitted that the primary purpose of this particular gathering appears to have been for a meal. But it is noteworthy that the demand for Baal is made to the *ìlm*, where the reference may well be to the gods, rather than El, and that Anat and Athtarat are to assist in the handing over. Perhaps there is some justification for suggesting that the decision as to whether to hand Baal over was not in the hands of El alone. There may also be a suggestion that the decision as to whether Baal might have a house like the other gods was not taken by El alone, but by the assembly of the gods.[41]

However, with one possible exception, we do not seem to find El called *tpt* 'judge'. The possible exception is the enigmatic reference to *ìl tpt* in text RS 24.252 line 3[42] – enigmatic because it is difficult to be certain to whom the words refer. The opening lines of the text, with our rendering of C. Virolleaud's translation,[43] are as follows:

[àph]n yšt rpù mlk 'lm	Then he drinks, *Rpu*, the king of the world,
wyšt [ìl(?)] gṯr wyqr	and he drinks, the god strong and majestic.
ìl yṯb b'ṯtrt	(The god) El is seated beside Athtarat,
ìl tpt b hd r'y[44] dyšr wyẓmr	the Judge god (*le dieu Juge*), beside Hadad, the shepherd who sings and plays
bknr	on the lyre . . .

In his comments on the passage,[45] Virolleaud asks whether *ìl tpt* refers to El who is *Rpu*, but notes that in any case this 'judge-god' (*dieu-juge*) is seated beside Hadad (i.e. Baal).

Some of those who have considered this text do feel that the phrase *ìl tpt* refers to El. S. B. Parker[46] feels that *il* here is most likely the proper name of the god El, while F. M. Cross renders the beginning of the third line 'El sits as judge with Haddu his shepherd'.[47] However, the passage is differently understood by others. B. Margulis[48] has suggested that *hdrʿy* and *ʿttrt* may, in this passage, be place-names and that therefore *Rpu* is being described as 'the god dwelling in Ashtaroth, the god ruling (judging) in Edrei'.[49] A. F. Rainey[50] described this as 'the one really interesting proposal made by Margulis', and felt that Virolleaud's interpretation of *ytb b-* as 'is seated beside' is extremely dubious. J. C. de Moor[51] translates the third line of the text 'the god who is judging with Haddu, the Shepherd who sings and plays . . .', taking this to be a description of the god Rpu. A similar view has recently been accepted by G. C. Heider,[52] who takes *il* to be 'the general term for deity'. It is not possible here to consider the many problems of the interpretation of this text; suffice it to say that it is far from clear that it contains a reference to El as *tpṭ*.

In the Ugaritic texts it is the god Yam/Nahar who is, above all, given the title *tpṭ*. It has already been noted that *tpṭ nhr* invariably parallels *zbl ym*, so it must now be asked whether the title is used here merely with its general sense (the specific meaning being only implicit), or whether Yam/Nahar was actually regarded as a judge. A. Jirku renders the phrase *tpṭ nhr* as 'Richter des Stromes', though he does note that 'das Wort schofet hier so viel wie "Fürst, Regent" bedeutet'.[53] W. F. Albright[54] noted that Virolleaud rendered the phrase 'the *suffete* of the river', but rejected this because he felt that *suffetes* reflect an advanced stage of Phoenician magistracy. He therefore suggested the rendering 'the judge, River', and felt that the name might reflect an ancient custom of trial by ordeal in a river. Support for this might perhaps be found in a personal name from Mari, *I-ti ᵈNaruᵐ*, which F. Thureau-Dangin translated 'Le dieu Fleuve sait'.[55]

The second paragraph of the Law-Code of Hammurabi contains the following provisions:

> If a seignior brought a charge of sorcery against a(nother) seignior, but has not proved it, the one against whom the charge of sorcery was brought, upon going to the river, shall throw himself into the river, and if the river has then overpowered him, his accuser shall take over his estate; if the river has shown that seignior to be innocent and he has accordingly come forth safe, the one who brought the charge of sorcery against him shall be put to death, while the one who threw himself into the river shall take over the estate of his accuser.

The above is the translation of T. J. Meek,[56] who notes that the word for 'river' has the determinative of deity, 'indicating that the river . . . as judge in the case was regarded as god'. Meek felt the reference to be to the river Euphrates. G. R. Driver and J. C. Miles, in their commentary on this paragraph,[57] take the reference to be to 'the river-god' or 'the holy river'; although they do not identify the river-god/holy river, they do note other Mesopotamian evidence for a river ordeal, and (in a footnote) mention the Ugaritic *tpṭ nhr*.

While it is clear that trial by ordeal in a river was practised in

Mesopotamia, there seems to be no proof that such a practice was carried on in Ugarit, or that Yam/Nahar ever acted as a judge in the specific sense. The title *ṭpṭ nhr* has been thought to reflect the notion of a trial of the souls of the departed. Thus G. R. Driver claims:

> The Ugar. *ṭpṭ nhr* 'judge river' is a title which reflects the myth that the trial of the souls of the dead before admission to the nether-world takes place on the bank of the world-encircling river or ocean.[58]

J. C. de Moor[59] has found possible support for such a judgement on the bank of the river of death in a reference in text RS 24.293 lines 9–10.[60] W. Schmidt[61] saw significance in the fact that the title *ṭpṭ nhr* occurs only in those texts which describe Yam's attempt to seize the predominance over the gods for himself; Yam is endeavouring to gain the dominion through his rebellion, and it is for this reason that he is called *ṭpṭ nhr*; however, it is Baal who is victorious and becomes *ṭpṭ*. It may, then, be significant that the title 'judge' figures prominently in the account of the struggle for dominance between claimants to kingship – the struggle whose outcome provided the guarantee of cosmic order.

Before turning from the notion of Ugaritic gods as judges, M. C. Astour's suggestion[62] should be noted, that text RS 24.271,[63] a list of divine names, includes the names of some deities connected with justice. In line 14 he sees a pair of names *ṣdq mšr*, which he takes to be personifications of 'righteousness' and 'justice'; he likens these to the Babylonian Kettu and Mēšaru, personified as sons of Shamash, the god of justice. In *Ugaritica* v, the transliteration divides the consonants *ṣdqm šr*; however, the transcription implies that there is no word-divider in the line and that the letters are evenly spaced. Line 15 contains a reference to *ḥnbn il d[n(?)]*;[64] Astour associates the first word with Arabic *haniba*, and renders the phrase 'The Compassionate One, god of judgement', seeing the reference to be to another deity connected with justice.

The theme of the divine king as judge is common in Hebrew thought. The downfall of Yahweh's enemies was seen as a just punishment; hence we find the notion of a Day on which Yahweh would bring judgement upon them:

> At the set time which I appoint
> I will judge with equity . . .
> . . . it is God who executes judgement
> putting down one and lifting up another.
>
> (Ps 75:3,8 MT)[65]

Here we are probably to see the concept of the eschatological 'Day of Yahweh', on which all the enemies of God will be brought to justice,[66] a type of concept which is lacking in Ugaritic thought. But Yahweh's judgeship is not only on a cosmic scale, for he too is concerned with that 'common policy' of the ancient Near East, i.e. care for those who have no legal supporters:

> Father of the fatherless and protector of widows
> is God in his holy habitation.
>
> (Ps 68:6 MT)

L. Bronner[67] has argued that the incident of Naboth's vineyard[68] is intended to show the stark difference between Elijah's God and Jezebel's god. 'It showed that while Baalism went hand in hand with injustice and crime, the religion of the God of Israel was the bulwark of righteousness and justice.' Whether this particular inference is, in fact, justified is debatable, but it can certainly be accepted that in the cycle of stories about Elijah and Elisha polemic against Baalism is to be expected. It is necessary, however, to stress that such polemic was against Baalism as practised. Since certain of the attributes of Baal were taken over by Yahwists to describe the nature and activity of their God, the attributes themselves can hardly have been thought offensive. The offence no doubt lay in the ascription of the attributes to another god, who was demonstrably (cf. the mt Carmel incident[69]) unworthy of the claims made on his behalf. Thus a belief that 'God' had powers to bestow fertility on the earth would not, in itself, be objectionable, unless 'God' was held to be any but Yahweh. The story of Naboth's vineyard is only indirectly a piece of polemic against Baal in that the practices of his devotees bring Baalism and hence Baal into disrepute.

An aspect worthy of particular stress is the fact that the motif of judgement recurs frequently in the Psalms which speak of Yahweh's enthronement. In Psalm 93, statements that Yahweh reigns, and that his power over the seas has been established, are followed by the words:

> Thy decrees are very sure;
>   holiness befits thy house,
> O Lord, for evermore.
>
> (Ps 93:5)

A. R. Johnson[70] suggested that it is Yahweh's supremacy over the sea which proves that he has the power to fulfil his covenant promises, and that in Psalm 95 we see the other side of the picture, viz. Israel's corresponding responsibilities and obligations. Again in Psalm 96 we read that Yahweh's establishment of 'order' is the basis of his role as judge:

> Say among the nations, 'The Lord reigns!
>   Yea the world is established, it shall never be moved;
>   he will judge the peoples with equity.'
>
> (Ps 96:10)[71]

Not dissimilar is the suggestion in Psalm 97 that demonstrations of Yahweh's powers in the realm of nature are guarantees of his justice:

> Clouds and thick darkness are round about him;
>   righteousness and justice are the foundation of his throne ...
> Zion hears and is glad,
>   and the daughters of Judah rejoice,
>   because of thy judgements, O God ...
> The Lord loves those who hate evil;
>   he preserves the lives of his saints;
>   he delivers them from the hand of the wicked.
>
> (Ps 97:2, 8, 10)[72]

In Psalm 98 Johnson noted that the themes of victory, covenant loyalty, and justice are again to be found, while in Psalm 99 a statement that Yahweh is the 'Mighty King, lover of justice'[73] is followed by some instances of great characters of Israel's history who remained faithful to the covenant obligations.

A. Weiser[74] in his commentary on the Psalter, argued that the concept of Yahweh's judgement has its source in the *Heilsgeschichte*, and in the giving of the law:

> The idea of judgement constitutes not only ideologically, but also from the point of view of the cultus the link connecting history and law, these two focal points of the covenant tradition around which the thought of a number of psalms revolves. . . . the entire redemptive work of Yahweh as re-enacted in the cult is frequently summed up by the psalms under the aspect of the idea of his judgement, and termed his 'righteousness'.[75]

C. J. Labuschagne[76] felt that the dominating characteristic which gave rise to Yahweh's incomparability was his miraculous intervention in history as a redeeming God; this characteristic includes many qualities, such as those of mighty warrior, holy and terrible, of a God who works wonders, and not least of a God of justice who cares for the wronged, the oppressed and the weak. Thus an appeal to Yahweh for justice on the part of an individual is based on the interpretation of Yahweh's activity in history as an intervention for the sake of justice.

Against the view of Weiser, J. Gray[77] suggested that while in the Pentateuch judgement seems to be of local significance, this is very different from the cosmic judgement which is seen in the ideology of kingship in the Psalter and the prophetic books. But it is necessary to be wary of assuming that, in passages where the theme of the divine King is present, cosmic justice is divorced from individual justice. Ps 103:6 states:

> The LORD works vindication
> and justice for all who are oppressed.

While in verse 19 the psalmist says:

> The LORD has established his throne in the heavens,
> and his kingdom rules over all.

Thus, in the same Psalm, we find reference to cosmic kingship and to individual justice – justice for all being justice for each and every one. Rather similarly, in Psalm 145, the following statements are made:

> I will extol thee, my God and King,
> and bless thy name for ever and ever . . .
> They [i.e. men] shall pour forth the fame of thy abundant goodness,
> and shall sing aloud of thy righteousness . . .
> The LORD upholds all who are falling,
> and raises up all who are bowed down.

(PS 145:1, 7, 14)

It may thus be concluded that the theme of Yahweh's care for justice for the individual was by no means out of place in the kingship ideology, and was perhaps as integral as the cosmic theme of judgement of the whole world.

In the divine realm, then, it has been noted that Yahweh's establishment of order in the universe and his concern for justice and order in society are closely linked, not least in contexts which present Yahweh as king. In the Ugaritic texts, the contest between Baal and Yam/Nahar is a contest about kingship and Baal's demonstration of his supremacy over the forces of chaos, and it is in the context of this contest that the title *tpt* appears prominently; it may be that as a result of this victory Baal was worthy to be called *mlkn* 'our king' and *tptn* 'our judge'. Although the Babylonian material is really beyond the scope of this essay, it is noteworthy that it is Marduk who has demonstrated his supremacy over the gods by his victory over the personification of the waters, of whom Hammurabi says: 'When Marduk commissioned me to guide the people aright, to direct the land, I established law and justice in the language of the land, thereby promoting the welfare of the people.'[78]

In the cases of Marduk and Yahweh, it is possible to point to evidence of concern for justice in society; but there is no clear evidence that Baal's control over chaos led to any ethical implications. Since Baal is *tptn* 'our judge' this could be simply a matter of silence, but it is dangerous to assume that just because certain elements are common to two or more cultures, all elements must be common. Nevertheless, there does seem to be some relationship between macrocosm and microcosm – right order in society parallels order in the cosmos. Since presumably the notion of god as 'king' is derived from the earthly concept of monarchy, at least in origin, the fact that the king is ultimately responsible for order in society would imply that any god worthy to be called king must be capable of sustaining order. Thus justice can be seen as an integral aspect of the very order of things – order in nature and order in society go hand in hand.

2
LAW IN OLD ISRAEL: LAWS CONCERNING ADULTERY

ARNOLD A. ANDERSON

We hope that this brief study of the above topic will raise some questions which, in some way or other, may make a small contribution to the discussion on law in Old Israel. This means that we shall focus our attention mainly upon the evidence from the pre-exilic period. It is intended to deal with our subject by trying to assess several recent articles on this and related topics, especially those by Henry McKeating[1] and Anthony Phillips. [2] These two scholars represent differing views on the subject and the main difference between them concerns, primarily, the *sanctions* against adultery and their implications.

In a sense, the OT law itself is fairly clear on this point. Thus Deut 22:22 states, 'If a man is found lying with the wife of another man, both of them shall die, the man who lay with the woman, and also the woman; so you shall purge the evil from Israel.' The same sanctions are also prescribed in Lev 20:10 (which belongs to the so-called Holiness Code: Lev 17–26); here we read, 'If a man commits adultery with the wife of his neighbour, both the adulterer and the adulteress shall be put to death.' The essential element in these two laws is the status of the woman, namely, she is a married woman, and it seems that this would also include betrothed girls.[3] The marital status of the man is, apparently, not relevant in such cases while the 'neighbour' is, obviously, any Israelite. There is little doubt that adultery in these laws refers to acts where the guilty parties have been caught *in flagrante delicto*.[4] It seems that cases of suspected but unwitnessed adultery would usually involve a trial by ordeal, as in Num 5:11–31, unless the judgement could be reached on a more rational basis. This procedure appears to be relevant only to the wife who was believed to be guilty.

In Lev 18:20 adultery is described as a defilement, and it is listed in a series of sexual offences. The punishment for the crimes in this list is expressed in the following words, 'For whoever shall do any of these abominations, the persons that do them shall be cut off from among their people' (18:29). It is usually thought that this particular type of punishment refers to the exclusion from the cultic community and not to capital punishment while others have argued that the reference is to a threat of direct punitive act by God. It is not impossible that the 'cutting off' may have denoted different concepts at different times.

It is of some interest that the oldest OT collection of laws, the Book of Covenant (Exod 20:22–23:19), does not make any explicit legal provision for adultery but this does not, of course, mean that such laws did not exist at that point in time. Similarly, the list of the ancient curses or strong prohibitions in Deut 27 does not mention adultery[5] but not all scholars would accept its early dating;[6] moreover, its significance is far from certain.

Much of Phillips' argument depends upon his interpretation of the nature and function of the decalogue. The essence of his thesis is that 'the Decalogue in an original short form given at Sinai constituted pre-exilic Israel's criminal law'.[7] In his opinion crimes always required a mandatory death penalty to be carried out by the community; 'failure to comply with the requirements of the Decalogue brought direct divine punishment on the community'.[8] Phillips also adds that neither the amphictyonic hypothesis nor the supposed link between Hittite treaties and the decalogue, is vital to his argument, although he would assert that the tribes had common religious traditions which found, in a way, their expression in the decalogue. It is his contention that 'it was the Decalogue which both created Israel as a distinct community . . . and secured her survival from the earliest days of the settlement until exile in Babylon'.[9]

However, a great deal of Phillips' argument, although plausible in itself, rests on limited evidence. Furthermore, there may well have existed a similar series of laws long before the decalogue, and in any case we do not know what laws were to be found in the so-called original decalogue. It is equally uncertain that 'the penalty for breach of every commandment was death, the exaction of which was mandatory'.[10]

We propose to test, as far as it is possible, the assertions of Phillips by examining the relevant non-legal material with reference to adultery. At this point it may well be fitting to summarise the opposing arguments on our topic.

Phillips makes it clear that in his view adultery in the OT is not merely a wrongful act against the husband but above all is regarded as an absolute wrong or sin against God, and therefore the death penalty is mandatory, while neglect of this law would bring about divine sanctions. In other words, adultery is treated as a very serious crime and not as a civil offence. Hence the imposition of the punishment is the concern of the community as a whole, and the wronged husband could not pardon the guilty party nor take private revenge nor simply settle for damages or some sort of financial compensation.[11] Herein Phillips sees the distinctive principle of Israel's law of adultery, and he remarks that in contrast nowhere does the 'non-Israelite law make the exaction of the death penalty for adultery mandatory'.[12] He also notes that 'the criminal law governing murder and adultery in Israel was unique in the ancient Near East. Both demanded community, not private, action leading to the execution of the murderer and the adulterer, and after the Deuteronomic reform of the adulteress as well.'[13]

For McKeating 'the law constitutes a forceful statement of what is desirable'[14] and in the light of his exegesis of the relevant non-legal OT evidence, he concludes that 'the sanctions of law against adultery really were, in Israel, employed as a last resort, rarely brought into play ... for the majority of Israelites adultery was basically a private matter ... to be countered by the unofficial action of offended husbands'.[15] Thus, on the one hand, he accepts the view that 'the Old Testament defines adultery as a sacral crime, an offence against God, and therefore to be punished by the whole community'.[16] On the other hand, he asserts that the same OT shows that not infrequently Israelites did not implement the sanctions. Consequently, the OT law on adultery remained 'largely a matter of religious theory rather than practical law'.[17] Perhaps, it is not only a question as to what extent was the law disobeyed but also as to how it 'worked' or functioned in early Israel.

So the basic difference between Phillips and McKeating is that for the former adultery before Deuteronomy brought with it mandatory capital punishment *for the man only* while the latter regards the death penalty as the maximum which more often than not was replaced by some alternative sanction.[18] The practical difference between the two positions is further narrowed by Phillips' view that 'originally a woman was not subject to Israel's criminal law, only becoming so as a result of the Deuteronomic reform whereby women were made equal members of the covenant community with men'.[19] Therefore, in the pre-deuteronomic period only the adulterer was liable to the mandatory capital punishment while the husband would take the appropriate steps against his wife under the provisions of the family law, namely, he could forgive her or, more likely, divorce her. McKeating regards this suggestion as interesting but reserves his judgement.[20]

All in all, we are inclined to agree with McKeating's line of argument and we are not convinced of the main thesis of Phillips for the following reasons:

(1) Although he may be right in claiming that women became equal members of the covenant community at the time of Deuteronomy, we doubt that 'women were not liable under the criminal law of adultery before D and H'.[21] He also refers, e.g., to the stories about Sarah and Rebekah, and concludes that no punishment is envisaged for them in their particular cases. This is true but unfortunately these stories create far more problems than they solve, and it is doubtful that they can serve as evidence

for our purposes; even the supposed adultery belongs to a category of its own. In the light of all the slender evidence, it is more likely that whether or not women were *full* members of the covenant community, they must have been subject to Israel's criminal law or any law for that matter, as far as it was relevant to them. Moreover, it does not necessarily follow that only *capital* punishment was used in all criminal cases. There are some clear exceptions; e.g. a murder was usually punished by death but not in the case of Absalom! Perhaps, we should also mention David's disposal of Uriah, and Joab's killing of Abner and Amasa.

(2) Although most OT laws are formally addressed to men, this may be largely a grammatical feature rather than having any legal or theological implication. Much importance has been attached to Lev 20:10 where, it is argued, the original reference may have been only to the adulterer; later it came to be applied also to the adulteress. The argument is based on the fact that the prescribed punishment is expressed by means of the masculine singular verbal form although the subject (in the present form of the text) is plural, i.e. 'both the adulterer and the adulteress'. However, it is very likely that this final phrase is a later addition and that the penalty clause is a set legal expression. Phillips suggests that 'it may have been thought that any wife who committed adultery did so involuntarily, being forced by the man'.[22] But if so, the woman was not punished because she was not considered guilty and not because she was not liable to the criminal law. It seems possible that the woman's case may have depended on her part in the affair: was it a voluntary or involuntary act? This type of distinction was observed in the case of Deuteronomy (Deut 22:23–7), and the same principle was applied to the law in Exod 21:12–14, which recognises the difference between murder and manslaughter. Of course, one could argue about the antiquity of these provisions.

Furthermore, during the pre-exilic period the wife involved in adultery could be humiliated and/or divorced, as in Jer 3:8 and Hos 2:3 (MT 4), and this, too, must have been regarded as a form of punishment, especially if the divorced wife or her guardian lost the *mōhar* or the marriage payment. All this seems to imply that women also were subject to Israel's criminal law before Deuteronomy.

(3) Perhaps, one could also appeal to the somewhat questionable analogy in Exod 21:28–32 where the goring ox is stoned for killing a person. Obviously, the ox is not a member of the covenant community but he is, nevertheless, stoned. Thus it appears that since killing had taken place, the deed had to be dealt with in the appropriate manner. It is very difficult to believe that a woman would escape the punishment had she committed murder. It may not be irrelevant to note that Jezebel and Athaliah were probably put to death not simply for political reasons but also for their murderous acts.

Thus there is not sufficient evidence, if any, to assert that before Deuteronomy women were not liable to Israel's criminal law even though no woman was actually executed for adultery. An exceptional situation is found in Genesis 38 where Tamar was nearly put to death for harlotry, which may be equivalent, in this context, to adultery. However, we do not intend to make any real use of it because, theoretically at least, it precedes Israel's criminal law as defined by Phillips, and it may reflect a different legal tradition, as is perhaps suggested by the unusual proposed punishment, namely burning, and by the fact that the sentence was imposed, and later rescinded, by her father-in-law. Furthermore, Tamar was thought to have transgressed the rules of *levirate* marriage, but this would not make any real difference, since the status of the 'waiting widow' may have been similar to that of a betrothed girl.

Finally, we shall consider briefly the pertinent OT evidence from the non-legal sources about the possible legal consequences of adultery. We have already expressed our doubts about the relevance of the Sarah and Rebekah stories,[23] since among other things, it is not certain how far they represent historical episodes, if at all. Moreover, here the supposed 'adulteress' appears to be far less guilty than the husband!

The narrative of Potiphar's wife and Joseph stresses one apposite point, namely, that adultery was regarded as a sin against God,[24] but this need not be a reflection of the patriarchal understanding of adultery, and it may be a much later concept.

For our purposes far more relevant are the stories in 2 Samuel. First, there is the affair between Abner and Rizpah,[25] but it is difficult to evaluate this account. It would be an instance of adultery only if Rizpah, Saul's concubine, had become the wife or concubine of Ishbosheth, assuming that an involvement with another man's concubine constituted adultery. According to Lev 19:20ff. sexual relationship with a slave girl, even a betrothed one, was not considered to be adultery in the strict sense.

Equally difficult is the understanding of the relationship between David and Michal. From David's point of view Michal was still his wife, although during his absence she had been married to another man, Paltiel.[26] If David was right in his claim, then both Michal and Paltiel had committed adultery but it is more likely that due to specific circumstances, such as exile, the particular law or laws could be 'neutralised'.[27] Hence neither Michal nor her second husband was charged with adultery.

The most obvious case is David's extra-marital relationship with Bathsheba. From the present narrative it is clear that David was guilty as charged but so was also Bathsheba for, theoretically at least, she could have objected and cried for help.[28] Perhaps, it is significant that, although David's role in the misdeed is condemned, no legal judgement or censure is pronounced against Bathsheba, at least not explicitly. However, her condemnation may be implicit in the death of her child. David, of course, was threatened with divine sanctions,[29] but this section may well be a much later addition; even the interpretation of the death of the child might have been a sort of prophecy after the event.

From this whole episode there emerge two important points which are particularly relevant to our discussion:

(1) David showed little consideration for the so-called Israel's criminal code, and none at all for the implicit divine sanctions.

(2) No legal action was taken against David or even envisaged.

The second point could be explained, at least partially, by the assumption that as king he may have been above the *human legal processes*, simply because there was no higher court which could judge the king. It is, perhaps, for this reason that the usual sanctions were not applicable to him. However, at least theoretically, even the king was not above the *law*, because ultimately he was believed to be subject to the divine judgement.[30] Moreover, as Yahweh's anointed one he could not be put to death by any legal procedure although he could be removed like Saul, or punished by Yahweh himself; we infer this from 2 Sam 1:14 in particular.

The real problem is created by the first point. If the supposed divine sanctions were as important as many have claimed, it is odd that David's actions were in no way influenced by this theological deterrent, at least in the present portrayal of the king. Having committed one crime, adultery, he was more afraid (?) of any steps Uriah might take than by any thought of Yahweh. Consequently, he proceeded to cover his crime by ordering the murder of Uriah. One may forget divine sanctions in a crime of passion but to disregard them in a carefully premeditated crime may imply that the above deterrent had little practical influence upon David. The latter's determined attempts to deceive Uriah and his eventual 'disposal' of the unfortunate husband, may suggest that it was the *husband* rather than the *community* who brought any charges against the adulterer and adulteress.[31] Subsequently it was the prophet Nathan who accused David, but it is a question whether the whole relevant narrative is an interpretation of events, after the death of Bathsheba's child. Furthermore, although Yahweh is, so to say, a free agent, it is surprising that David's crime could be forgiven, following his repentance, even though the child died.

Therefore one is justified in asking whether this supposed criminal law with its mandatory punishments, further safeguarded by divine sanctions, was known and implemented at this point in time, in that particular form. Could it be that the decalogue or its equivalent was addressed to the nation and not to the judiciary, telling them how they should live? Failure to live up to the standard would be dealt with in the existing legal structure. Thus it is possible that in the early period the *husband* could, perhaps, take the appropriate action in a case of adultery even if the punishment might have involved the death penalty, just as the kinsman could act in a similar manner in the event of murder. Judah's judgement on Tamar in Gen 38:24 may belong to this category. However, it does not follow that capital punishment must have been the only legal option; it may well be that the husband could exercise his right of discretion within the limits acceptable to the community. This is probably reflected in Prov 6:32–5, although the passage is exegetically problematic. It seems to suggest that adultery is a dangerous pastime; although compensation is possible, one should not 'bank' on a jealous and outraged husband. One may get away with 'wounds and dishonour' (verse 33) but it would be foolish to predict the husband's reaction. B. S. Jackson[31] has remarked that the husband's non-acceptance of the alternative punishment 'is the result of human jealousy, not of any legal prohibition'. Similarly, McKeating[32] understands Prov 6:27–35 as showing that the husband *may* demand the death penalty for the adulterer but that he was not obliged to do so. 'The penalty is evidently largely a matter of his discretion, and he can in principle be bought off.' However, Phillips[33] objects that the compensation envisaged is to be regarded as an illegal payment or hush-money and that therefore verse 35 really points to the *mandatory* penalty, not to a *legal* option available to the wronged husband. But even if this were so, the implication is that the alluded practice must have been sufficiently widespread for it to appear in the Wisdom literature. The possibility of alternative sanctions seems to be suggested also in Prov 6:33, where it is stated that 'Wounds and dishonour will he get, and disgrace will not be wiped away.' Here, too, Phillips sees an illegal cover-up but he acknowledges the possible widespread use of this 'improper' alternative. He notes that 'since the husband could in any event divorce his wife at will under the family law and need give no reason, the criminal law was always liable to be treated with contempt if the bribe offered to the husband was sufficiently attractive, especially because the prosecution normally rested on him'. But if so, the belief in divine sanctions must have been rather ineffective as a deterrent, at least for practical purposes.

We find also a few relevant passages in the prophetical literature, e.g. in Hosea 2 and Jer 3:6–14; unfortunately, they raise too many exegetical problems. However, we may note two points in particular which may have some bearing upon our discussion:

(1) The adulteress could be divorced, as in Jer 3:8.

(2) The adulterous wife could, apparently, return to her husband if she gave up her unfaithfulness, as in Jer 3:10, 12f.

The first point creates no difficulties, since it would be one of the husband's options, while the second could be taken to imply that the husband (in this case Yahweh) had indeed several options, and that the choice depended upon the response of the repentant wife.

Finally, we may draw certain tentative conclusions. It seems that in the light of our brief survey there are some grounds for questioning Phillips' view that the decalogue was ancient Israel's criminal law, and that women were not subject to the criminal law before the time of Deuteronomy. As regards the sanctions against adultery, it appears that wives were not executed for marital unfaithfulness in the pre-exilic period, otherwise adultery as a theological metaphor would, in its finality, exclude the very possibility of repentance. The subsequent severity of Deut 22:22 may have been balanced by the possible distinction between a voluntary and involuntary act on the part of the woman.

For the adulterer the *maximum* penalty was death, and this would make an allowance for the murderous rage of the jealous husband, but it probably was not mandatory. The scanty evidence may suggest, if our interpretation is right, that there may have existed other punitive measures alongside capital punishment. Whether or not these alternatives were accepted legal options, they must have been widespread practices.

3

'A PERPETUAL STATUTE THROUGHOUT YOUR GENERATIONS'

ROGER TOMES

Most branches of Judaism in the intertestamental period agreed on the perpetual validity and unchangeable character of the law. When ben Sirach identified wisdom with the law in the early second century BCE, he made her say:

> From eternity, in the beginning, he created me,
> and for eternity I shall not cease to exist.
>
> (Sir 24:9)

Philo, writing in Alexandria early in the first century CE, contrasts the Jewish law with the ever-changing legislation of other nations:

> The provisions of this law alone, stable, unmoved, unshaken, as it were stamped with the seal of nature itself, remain in fixity from the day they were written until now, and for the future we expect them to abide through all time as immortal, so long as the sun and the moon and the whole heaven and the world exist.[1]

In the apocalyptic tradition, the Epistle of Enoch (*1 Enoch* 91–108) issues a warning to those who 'alter the words of truth' and 'distort the eternal law' (*1 Enoch* 99:2; cf. Dan 7:25). Jewish Christianity insists that 'till heaven and earth pass away, not an iota, not a dot, will pass from the law until all is accomplished' (Matt 5:18).

There are indications, however, that the idea of perpetual validity could be attached not only to the law as a whole but also to particular laws within it. Tobit, for example, claims to have 'walked in the ways of truth and righteousness all my life' and to have 'performed many acts of charity to my brethren and countrymen' (Tob 1:3), but it is only when he comes to his pilgrimages to Jerusalem for the feasts that he mentions that this duty 'is ordained for all Israel by an everlasting decree' (1:6). Even more strikingly, the *Book of Jubilees* specifies a number of laws which were 'given to the children of Israel as an eternal law for their generations' or are 'written in the heavenly tablets'; sometimes it adds: 'There is no limit of days for this law.'[2]

The laws selected for such emphasis must of course represent those features of Judaism which the author of *Jubilees*, a Palestinian Jew of the second century BCE, believed to be most important, at a time when loyalty to tradition was under strain because of pressures from outside and desire for change among Jews themselves. It is not surprising that he should want to stress that the laws he deals with are not culturally conditioned institutions or taboos which have had their day, but permanent ordinances for the life of Israel, whatever the circumstances. But how did he come to choose these laws in particular as having perpetual validity?

It is not a sufficient answer to say that he found the laws in question in scripture. *Jubilees* pays scant regard to the strict context in which the laws appear. Institutions and laws which according to scripture were given through Moses at Sinai are introduced earlier in association with events in the lives of the patriarchs. It is true that in this way the author solves a critical problem, in that the Genesis narratives presuppose such institutions as tithing and such taboos as those against incest and intermarriage, but in assuming that these laws were actually revealed to and observed by the patriarchs he diminishes the stature of the law as a corpus delivered on one historical occasion. It becomes a mere record of what is written in the heavenly tablets, much of which is no longer a secret by the time the law is given at Sinai. This attitude to the scriptural text is further emphasised by the fact that the tablets given to Moses are mentioned only incidentally in the closing words of the book (50:13).

Nevertheless the author of *Jubilees* almost certainly derived this idea of the permanent validity of particular laws from scripture. In the Priestly Code the word ʿôlām is used 46 times with a noun in the construct state to denote the permanent, unalterable validity of a particular law or institution:[3] ʾăḥuzzâ 'possession',[4] běrît 'covenant',[5] gěʾullâ 'right of redemption',[6] dōrôt 'generations',[7] kěhunnâ 'priesthood',[8] and most frequently ḥōq, usually 'due'[9] and ḥuqqâ, usually 'ordinance'.[10] Those affected are frequently more closely defined.[11] The formula most commonly used is: 'A perpetual statute throughout your generations' (ḥuqqat ʿôlām lě-dōrōtêkem).[12]

Although the laws and institutions which the Priestly Code declares permanently valid by means of these expressions do not coincide exactly with those which the *Book of Jubilees* singles out, there is sufficient overlapping of content – circumcision, sabbath, the prohibition of blood, observance of Passover, Weeks and Booths – and sufficient similarity in terminology to make it almost certain that the Priestly Code is *Jubilees'* source for the idea that particular laws and institutions are in force for ever. In view of this evidence of its subsequent influence, this element in P's style perhaps deserves closer attention than it has generally received.

Our task therefore is to explore the significance of this stress on the permanent validity of particular laws and institutions; to test the findings to see whether they are consistent with generally accepted views of the date and purpose of the Priestly Code; and then to see whether they help towards a fuller picture of the post-exilic period and the part the Priestly Code played in it.

Why should a writer want to stress the permanent validity of a particular law or institution? One suggestion is that he intends to draw attention to an especially important principle or duty. Thus G. J. Wenham says: 'The statement "This is a permanent rule for your descendants" is used a number of times in Leviticus to underline particularly important religious principles';[13] and again, it is 'quite commonly used to underline the importance of carrying out a particular religious duty'.[14] It is unlikely that this is a sufficient explanation. There are other ways of emphasising that a law is important. Breach of it may be designated a capital crime;[15] a curse may be invoked on the person who disregards it;[16] appeal may be made to the previous experience of those addressed[17] or to Yahweh's feelings about the matter;[18] hearers may be reminded of the necessity that Yahweh's people should be holy[19] or simply of the fact that Yahweh has issued the commands.[20] In the Priestly Code itself, the importance of the sabbath is emphasised by declaring non-observance of it a capital crime.[21] For various offences a person may be 'cut off' from Israel (whether this means death or excommunication).[22] The importance of various times, places, persons and things is signalled by declaring them 'holy' or 'most holy'.[23] The laws and institutions singled out as important in these ways do not coincide in more than a few instances with those which are said to have permanent validity (circumcision, sabbath, Passover, consuming fat and blood, undergoing ritual purification) and therefore importance is hardly likely to be the sole explanation of the latter. It would mean for example that in the Holiness Code, which the priestly writers incorporated in their own work, they thought the command to celebrate the Feast of Weeks (Lev 23:15–21) was more important than the command to love one's neighbour as oneself (Lev 19:18). The reason for the use of the 'perpetual statute' terminology must be more specific.

Another suggestion sometimes made is that the formula indicates an attempt to establish an innovation. Gerhard Liedke says that the use of *ḥōq* or *ḥuqqâ* in itself implies the establishment of a new state of affairs.[24] J. R. Porter says that in Lev 7:34, which claims 'the breast that is waved and the thigh that is offered' as portions of the sacrifice which go to the priests, the passage is 'an attempt to authenticate an innovation' on the ground that 'there is no mention of the special treatment of the breast and the right hind leg in the shared offering ritual of ch 3'.[25] Again, Porter regards Lev 16:29 as an attempt to integrate the Day of Atonement into the festival calendar.[26] P. J. Budd, commenting on Num 25:12f., which promises the priesthood in perpetuity to the descendants of Phinehas, says:

'Phinehas represented a Levitical group which had just been appointed to the priesthood.'[27] We shall return to the exegesis of these passages, but for the moment we must question the inherent plausibility of the explanation. It is a strange argument to use for an innovation that it was established as a permanent institution in the remote past. On the one hand, it is difficult to think who would be taken in by it; on the other, it is distasteful to think of the Priestly writers trying to pass off an innovation as an ancient custom.

When an undoubted innovation is being introduced, as in Deuteronomy, quite different arguments are used. As in the Priestly Code, the origin of Israel's institutions is traced back to the time of Moses, but innovations are clearly marked by being contrasted with a previous state of affairs. The law of one sanctuary is introduced thus: 'You shall not do according to all that we are doing here this day, every man doing whatever is right in his own eyes' (Deut 12:8). Practices at variance with the new law are expressly ruled out: 'Take heed that you do not offer your burnt offerings at every place that you see' (12:13); 'You may not eat within your towns the tithe of your grain or of your wine or of your oil, of the firstlings of your herd or of your flock, or any of your votive offerings which you vow, or your freewill offerings, or the offering that you present' (12:17); 'You may not eat the passover sacrifice within any of your towns which the LORD your God gives you' (16:5). Necessary concessions are made: 'However, you may slaughter and eat flesh within any of your towns' (12:15; cf. 20ff.); 'If the way is too long for you, so that you are not able to bring the tithe . . . then you shall turn it into money' (14:24–6); 'If a Levite comes from any of your towns . . . then he may minister in the name of the LORD his God, like all his fellow-Levites' (18:6–8). Essential continuities are stressed: 'Only you shall not eat the blood; you shall pour it out upon the earth like water' (12:16; cf. 23f.). It is clear that one group of legislators at least realised that innovations cannot be established by passing them off as ancient custom.

We shall see that where the authors of the Priestly Code are most likely to be trying to bring in something new, as in the definition of the duties of the Levites and their relationship to the priests (Num 3f.), nothing is said about this being 'a perpetual ordinance'.

It is probable that whenever the formula 'a perpetual statute throughout your generations' or a variant is used, it is because the rule or institution in question, far from being an innovation, is a long-established custom which for some reason has come under threat. The use of the term ḥuqqâ or ḥōq may be significant in a way rather different from that which Liedke suggests. Richard Hentschke, in his painstaking study of the use of these terms in the OT, and hence of most instances of the formulas we are discussing, draws attention to the fact that in Numbers 19 there is a lack of any other motivation than the appeal to permanent validity and adds that this is true of most of the cultic regulations in what must be regarded as secondary P material.[28] He does not develop the point, but the implication seems to be that a ḥuqqâ or a ḥōq was a law or an institution for which it was difficult to invoke any warrant other than that of ancient custom. It is more than a custom in the sense of what is done (for which the proper term would be *mišpāt*; e.g. 1 Sam 2:13); it is something which people feel ought to be done, and yet the original reason has been long forgotten.

However, it takes more than the absence of any other motive to make one declare that a particular law or institution is 'a perpetual statute throughout your generations'. A situation has arisen which makes it necessary to reassert its validity. It is the knowledge that it already has a long history which causes its validity to be reasserted in this particular form. It is necessary therefore to review the passages which contain the formula in the attempt to show, first, that the law or institution was well established at the time of its inclusion in the Priestly Code, and, secondly, that there was an occasion when its validity needed to be reasserted.

At this point something must be said about the composition, date and purpose of the Priestly Code. It is generally held that the following elements in it must be distinguished:

(1) A narrative from the creation either to the death of Moses[29] or to the settlement in Canaan.[30] This may have been a work independent of the earlier pentateuchal sources J and E, or it may have incorporated them.[31] It excludes most of the legal material in P, except that which is an integral part of the narrative. It is often referred to as P[g] (=the Priestly *Grundschrift*). It was probably compiled during the exile as a programme for the expected return.

(2) Legal material older than P[g] which had been incorporated in it either at the time of composition or later. This consists chiefly of the *tôrôt* on sacrifice (Leviticus 1–7) and on the clean and the unclean (Leviticus 11–15)[32] and of the Holiness Code (Leviticus 17–26).[33] This material may well be pre-exilic.

(3) Legal material which has not only been added later to P[g] but originated after it. This is to be found in some additions to Exodus 25–31; 35–40 but chiefly in Numbers. This probably reflects situations in the life of the post-exilic community in Judea.

(4) Revisions of any of the above before or at the time of the completion of the Pentateuch.

While P material can be confidently distinguished from the other pentateuchal sources, it is not always possible to say whether a particular passage belongs to P[g] or to the secondary P material, or where the early material in a section ends and the later revision begins. Nevertheless such an analysis has to be attempted, however tentatively, to account for stylistic differences (e.g. impersonal accounts of ritual and instructions conveyed by direct address[34]), afterthoughts (e.g. the rules for late celebration of Passover: Num 9:1–14) and contradictions (e.g. the age limits for Levite service: Num 4:3; 8:23–6).[35]

The passages which contain the 'perpetual statute' formula, or something closely akin to it, are found in the basic Priestly narrative and the secondary material, i.e. later laws and revisions to earlier laws, but not in the older material which has been incorporated in P. They therefore reflect the concerns of the exilic and post-exilic Jewish communities.

A. THE PRIESTLY NARRATIVE

(1) GEN 17:8; 48:4 POSSESSION OF THE LAND. The Priestly narrative reasserts the title of the descendants of Abraham and Jacob to the land of Canaan as 'an everlasting possession' (*'ăḥuzzat 'ôlām*). It was known to the exiles that their entitlement to share in this inheritance had been challenged not only by the Babylonians but also by those who had been left behind in Judah. Ezekiel reports that 'the inhabitants of these waste places in the land of Israel keep saying, "Abraham was only one man, yet he got possession of the land; but we are many; the land is surely given us to possess"' (Ezek 33:24). Second Isaiah encouraged the exiles to continue to think of themselves as the descendants of Abraham:

> Look to Abraham your father
>   and to Sarah who bore you;
> for when he was but one I called him,
>   and I blessed him and made him many.

(Isa 51:2)

A passage in Third Isaiah suggests that there may have been some dispute after the return as to which element in the Jewish community were the true descendants of Abraham and the true Israel.[36] One group, possibly those who had been left in Judah, seems to be complaining of being disowned by the other group:

> Thou art our Father,
>   though Abraham does not know us
>   and Israel does not acknowledge us.

(Isa 63:16)

It is at least plausible that the Priestly narrator should want to express the exiles' conviction that they still have a title to the land by reason of their descent from Abraham.

(2) GEN 17:9–14, 22–7: CIRCUMCISION. Circumcision is reaffirmed as the sign of the everlasting covenant between God and the descendants of Abraham. Circumcision was undoubtedly a practice of long standing in Israel: why should it be under threat? There would seem to be a double danger. One was that a certain amount of intermarriage must have taken place in exile. Children born of such marriages could be incorporated into Israel, as the sons of Joseph's marriage to the daughter of an Egyptian priest had been earlier (Gen 48:5f. P), but only on condition that they were circumcised. The other was that immediately before the exile the Deuteronomists had been preaching the need for 'circumcision of the heart': 'Circumcise therefore the foreskin of your heart, and be no longer stubborn' (Deut 10:16); 'The LORD your God will circumcise your heart and the heart of your offspring, so that you will love the LORD your God with all your heart and all your soul, that you may live' (Deut 30:6). Jeremiah also had urged the people of Judah and Jerusalem

Circumcise yourselves to the LORD,
remove the foreskin of your hearts

(Jer 4:4)

It was possible to be circumcised physically but uncircumcised spiritually
(Jer 9:25f.). The exiles might easily have drawn the conclusion that
circumcision of the heart alone was necessary, and stopped practising
circumcision of the flesh. That is probably why the Priestly narrator is at
such pains to stress that the circumcision he is talking about is physical
circumcision:

> You shall be circumcised in the flesh of your foreskins. . . . So shall my
> covenant be in your flesh an everlasting covenant. Any uncircumcised male
> who is not circumcised in the flesh of his foreskin shall be cut off from my
> people.
>
> (Gen 17:11, 13f.; cf. 23–5)

(3) EXOD 12:1–20: PASSOVER AND UNLEAVENED BREAD. The next
institution which the Priestly narrator is anxious to emphasise is Passover.
While this was no doubt an ancient institution, it does not seem to have
been the most popular of the Israelite festivals. Neither the Book of the
Covenant nor the Ritual Decalogue include it among the three compulsory
festivals (Exod 23:14–17; 34:18, 22f.), though the latter mentions it in
passing (Exod 34:25). After the settlement it may have seemed to have less
to do with an Israelite's daily life than the agricultural festivals. If the
Chronicler is to be believed, Hezekiah found a lax attitude to Passover
prevailing in Jerusalem and derisive rejection of it in the northern part of
the country (2 Chr 30:1–12). The deuteronomistic historian says of
Josiah's Passover that 'no such passover had been kept since the days of the
judges who judged Israel, or during all the days of the kings of Israel or of
the kings of Judah' (2 Kgs 23:22). Thus it was no foregone conclusion that
Passover would be reinstated after the return from exile. Fast days had
replaced feast days in Jerusalem: it needed a prophetic oracle from
Zechariah to assure the Jews that the situation had improved enough for a
return to the celebration of 'seasons of joy and gladness, and cheerful
feasts' (Zech 7:1ff.; 8:18f.). It is true that Ezekiel included Passover as one
of the two feasts he envisages being restored (Ezek 45: 21–5), but others
could have argued that commemoration of the exodus was no longer
appropriate. One of the prose additions to Jeremiah seems to have been
moving in that direction:

> the days are coming, says the LORD, when it shall no longer be said, 'As the
> LORD lives who brought up the people of Israel out of the land of Egypt,'
> but 'As the LORD lives who brought up the people of Israel out of the north
> country and out of all the countries where he had driven them.'
>
> (Jer 16:14f.=23:7f.)

The need not to take the reinstitution of Passover for granted can hardly be
denied. It may well have been the advocacy of the Priestly narrator that
ensured that the returned exiles and those who had 'separated themselves
from the pollutions of the peoples of the land' did celebrate the Passover
after the dedication of the rebuilt temple (Ezra 6:19–22).

(4) EXOD 29:1–9: THE RIGHT TO EXERCISE PRIESTHOOD. Those who claimed to be descendants of Aaron were no newcomers to the exercise of priesthood in Jerusalem. They claimed descent from Aaron through Eleazar, Phinehas and Zadok, and had been exercising the priestly office when the exile began (1 Chr 6:1–15). Deuteronomy, however, had upheld the right of Levites who could no longer function at country sanctuaries to share in priestly duties in Jerusalem (Deut 18:6–8). This encroachment on the exclusive rights of the Jerusalem priesthood had been resisted at the time of Josiah's reforms (2 Kgs 23:9), and the exclusion of the Levites had been rationalised by Ezekiel as due to their disloyalty to Yahweh in contrast to the Zadokites' faithfulness (Ezek. 44:9ff.). The Priestly narrator accepts the need for high standards, as the story of Nadab and Abihu shows (Leviticus 10): they carried out priestly duties in a way Yahweh had not commanded, and were rejected, although they were sons of Aaron. Fear that standards would be lowered was probably one ingredient in the narrator's resistance, expressed in the story of Korah's rebellion, to the inclusion of the Levites in the priesthood (Num 16:7b–11), let alone to the dangerous idea that 'all the congregation are holy, every one of them' (Num 16:3). Third Isaiah provides independent evidence that this idea was current at the time of the restoration, when he says to the citizens of Jerusalem

> Aliens shall stand and feed your flocks,
>   foreigners shall be your ploughmen and vinedressers,
> but you shall be called the priests of the LORD,
>   men shall speak of you as the ministers of our God.

(Isa 61:5f.)

The need to reassert the perpetual and exclusive priesthood of the Aaronic priests is clear.

So far it has been argued that the main Priestly narrative was concerned to reassert the permanent validity of certain institutions during the exile and at the time of the return. The secondary Priestly material may be expected to reflect later situations in the post-exilic period.

B. THE SECONDARY PRIESTLY MATERIAL

(1) FEATURES OF THE TABERNACLE CULTUS. Some of the institutions declared to be permanently valid are rituals, and the furniture and materials associated with them, in the tabernacle and therefore also in the temple: the daily burnt offering (Exod 29:38–42), the incense altar (Exod 30:1–10), the sanctuary lamp (Exod 27:20f.; Lev 24:1–3), the shewbread (Lev 24:5–9) and the anointing oil (Exod 30:22–33). None of these were innovations in the post-exilic period. The daily burnt offering was made in the time of Ahaz (2 Kgs 16:15) and included in Ezekiel's programme (Ezek 46:13–15): the only uncertainty is whether a second burnt offering in the evening had been introduced before the exile. Incense was offered in worship in pre-exilic times (Jer 6:20; Isa 43:23) and 'the golden altar' of 1 Kgs 6:22; 7:48 was probably an incense altar. Solomon's temple con-

tained lampstands (1 Kgs 7:49) and a table for the shewbread (1 Kgs 7:48; cf. 1 Sam 21:7 (EVV 6)). Priests certainly used anointing-oil (1 Kgs 1:39). Why should the importance of these need to be reasserted? Because it was not at all clear in the post-exilic community whose responsibility it was to provide for the regular cultus. Under the monarchy the king probably accepted it as his duty to do this out of taxation. Ezekiel certainly hoped that there would be a 'prince' to provide the offerings for the daily sacrifice and regular cultic occasions (Ezek 45:16f.; 46:13–15). The early Persian monarchs did provide for the maintenance of the cultus to some extent (Ezra 1:4; 6:8–10; cf. 7:14–20) but this could not be relied upon. In Nehemiah's time it was necessary for the people of Jerusalem to agree to the one-third of a shekel tax to provide for 'the service of the house of God' (Neh 10:33 (EVV 32)). Hence the need to emphasise those elements in the cultus which were permanently required.

(2) THE CULTIC CALENDAR.   The major festivals constitute the next group of institutions whose permanence is reasserted: Unleavened Bread (Exod 12:17), firstfruits (Lev 23:9–14; cf. Num 15:17–21), the Feast of Weeks (Lev 23:15–21), the Feast of Booths (Lev 23:39–43) and the Day of Atonement (Lev 16:29–34; 23:26–32). In Ezra's time 'the heads of fathers' houses, the priests and the Levites' learned, apparently for the first time, how they should be celebrating the feast of the seventh month (Neh 8:13ff.). The passage in question must have been Lev 23:39–43, from the Holiness Code. It is possible that it was in Ezra's time that the Holiness Code was added to the Priestly Code and that the formula 'It is a statute for ever throughout your generations' (Lev 23:21, 31, 41), which is generally regarded as not an original part of the Holiness Code, was inserted at this time.

The only occasion in the cultic calendar said to be governed by a perpetual statute which may not have been an ancient one is the Day of Atonement, which is not clearly attested for pre-exilic times. Ezekiel proposes an atonement ritual on the first day of the first month, to be repeated on the seventh day of the same month, a week before Passover (Ezek 45:18–20). He obviously did not know of any such ritual on the tenth day of the seventh month (Lev 23:27; cf. 16:29; Num 29:7). But in Jerusalem a fast during the seventh month had been instituted during the exile (Zech 7:5; 8:19). This is usually connected with the murder of Gedaliah (2 Kgs 25:25; Jer 41:1–3), but may it not have been intended to replace the feast of the seventh month (1 Kgs 8:2)? It may be that this fast alone continued to be observed after the restoration, alongside the revived Feast of Booths (Ezra 3:4), and became the Day of Atonement. A fast was held in the seventh month in the time of Ezra, though on the twenty-fourth rather than on the tenth (Neh 9:1). The same language, 'afflicting one's soul' ('innâ 'et-hannepeš) is used both of the fast day (Isa 58:3, 5) and of the Day of Atonement (Lev 16:29, 31; 23:27). Thus we may conclude that by the time of Ezra the Day of Atonement was long established in the seventh month. The fact that the observance of the day included the scapegoat ritual may have convinced the Priestly editor that its origins went back far earlier than the exile. But we must also assume that the coming to light of the Holiness Code led to a rediscovery and revival of the traditional way of observing the day, which may have been eroded to some extent under criticism like that of Third Isaiah (Isaiah 58).

(3) THE SABBATH. To some extent the main Priestly narrative had emphasised the importance of the sabbath (Gen 2:1–3; Exod 16) but without in so many words asserting its permanent validity. The mention of the sabbath in the decalogue (Exod 20:8–11; Deut 5:12–15) testifies to its antiquity. But there is evidence that, both before the exile and after, it was difficult to get people to observe the sabbath strictly. The trend before the exile is attested in the prose addition to Jeremiah (Jer 17:19–27) and in Ezekiel (Ezek 20:13, 21, 24; 22:8; 23:38). The trend immediately after the exile is attested in Third Isaiah (Isa 56:2; 58:13f.). Laxity in observance of the sabbath is still a problem in Nehemiah's time (Neh 13:15–22; 10:32 (EVV 31)). It is not surprising that the Priestly writers should stress in a variety of ways the continuing importance of the sabbath (Exod 31:12–17; 35:1–3; Num 15:32–6).

(4) SACRIFICE. The taboo against eating meat with the blood in it is no innovation (Lev 3:17; cf. 1 Sam 14:32–4). It needed to be reasserted, however, because it had been disregarded by those who had remained in Judah during the exile (Ezek 33:25). It was particularly difficult to enforce now that secular slaughter was permitted (Deut 12:16, 23–5; Lev 17:10–14). This may account for the attempt to restore the practice of confining slaughter to sacrifice at the sanctuary (Lev 17:1–9). The attempt may have been made before the exile in the Holiness Code in its original form, but it was reasserted as a 'perpetual statute' when the Holiness Code was incorporated in the Priestly material. It was not an innovation: the practice of secular slaughter, which created the temptation to flirt with non-Yahwistic cults (such as those described by Third Isaiah in Isa 56:3–10; 65:3f.; 66:17?), as well as the temptation to ignore the blood taboo, was the dangerous departure from the traditional norm.

(5) RITUAL PURITY. The ritual purity of those who come into contact with holy things was a concern of Ezekiel (Ezek 22:8). He hoped that the Zadokite priests would 'teach my people the difference between the holy and the common, and show them how to distinguish between the unclean and the clean' (Ezek 44:23). The rules had long existed, but they were not well known, as Haggai's somewhat elementary question to the priests shows (Hag 2:10–13). Malachi later was dissatisfied with the teaching the priests gave (Mal 2:1–9). It is not surprising that the rules for ritual purification needed to be re-emphasised well on in the post-exilic period (Num 19:1–10, 20–2).

(6) THE RIGHT TO EXERCISE PRIESTHOOD. In Num 25:10–13 Phinehas is

promised 'the covenant of a perpetual priesthood'. There can be no question here of Phinehas representing 'a Levitical group which had just been appointed to the priesthood'.[37] The Aaronic or Zadokite priests traced their ancestry back to Aaron through Phinehas and his father Eleazar (1 Chr 6:1–15, 49–53). However, there was another priestly family which traced its ancestry back to Aaron through Eleazar's brother Ithamar. They may have claimed some connection with the Elide priesthood at Shiloh (1 Chr 24:1–6). At the time of Ezra these were probably the main priestly families (Ezra 8:2). It is clear from 1 Chr 24:1–6 that a generation later, when Chronicles was compiled, the Zadokite family predominated, providing sixteen courses of priests to Ithamar's eight. The passage in Numbers 25 may be a defence of this predominance.

(7) PRIESTLY DISCIPLINE AND DUES.   It is understandable that some of the 'perpetual statutes' should be concerned with priestly discipline: dress (Exod 28:40–3), purification (Exod 30:17–21; cf. Lev 22:1–9), anointing sacrifices (Lev 6:12–16 (EVV 19–23)), abstinence while on duty (Lev 10:8f.) and disqualification of the blemished (Lev 21:16–24). Malachi, as we have seen, was concerned about a decline in standards. He also provides evidence that assuring the priests of their income could be a problem (Mal 3:8–10). Hence there are a number of passages which deal with the priests' share of the offerings and other dues (Exod 29:26–8; Lev 6:7–11 (EVV 14–18); 7:28–36; 10:14f.; Num 18:8–19). This income depended very much on the conscientiousness with which people paid their tithes and on the scale of their voluntary offerings. It is doubtful whether the priests made larger and larger claims. The fact that they claim the breast and the right thigh from peace offerings in Lev 7:28–36, while there is no mention of this in the *tôrâ* about peace offerings in Leviticus 3,[38] does not mean that the claim was a new one. The two passages may refer to the same state of affairs from different points of view: ch. 3 says what parts of a peace offering must be burnt on the altar, and says nothing about what is to be done with the rest of the sacrifice; while ch. 7 deals principally with the priests' share in the sacrifice. We know that the priests had been accustomed to a share in animal sacrifices from much earlier times (1 Sam 2:13; Deut 18:3). If they do represent a change in the nature of the priestly dues, it may be that ch. 3 represents the later position. The priests had come to rely less on a share in the lay person's sacrifice, and more on tithes, firstlings and firstfruits. Ezekiel mentions 'the cereal offering, the sin offering and the guilt offering, and every devoted thing' (Ezek 44:29) without mentioning the peace offerings. Malachi mentions only the tithe (Mal 3:8–10). In the period of Ezra and Nehemiah the main income of the priests is clearly firstfruits, firstlings and tithes (Neh 10:33–40 (EVV 32–9)).

(8) LEVITES.   The determination of the status and duties of the Levites in Numbers 3–4 is probably to be assigned to the main Priestly narrative, at least in essentials.[39] Since the proposals are new, there is no appeal to 'a

perpetual statute'. But by the time of Ezra and Nehemiah, the status and dues of the Levites could be regarded as settled by tradition, and therefore the formula is used once of them, in what must be one of the latest passages to deal with their affairs (Num 18:21–4). It seems to be applied both to the nature of their service and to their entitlement to the tithes (from which they present a tithe of the tithe, or a 'second tithe', to the priests (Num 18:25–32)). The need to assert the permanent nature of the arrangements is underlined by Nehemiah's appointment of officials to oversee the tithe and its distribution, to stem the tide of defection by Levites to secular life (Neh 13:10–14).

(9) ONE LAW FOR NATIVE AND STRANGER. The final area to which the 'perpetual statute' formula was applied was that of the common law for the native Israelite and for the stranger (Num 15:15f.). Again, the principle was an ancient one (Exod 20:10; 23:12), but it needed to be reasserted in a community which was far more mixed ethnically after the exile than it had been before. Second Isaiah's promise to Jerusalem that 'there shall no more come into you the uncircumcised and the unclean' (Isa 52:1) had not been fulfilled, and indeed other voices welcomed the fact that the temple was becoming 'a house of prayer for all peoples' (Isa 56:7). But it was clearly much more difficult to keep Jews loyal to their traditional duties if other people could live by different laws, and hence there had to be one law for native Israelite and for stranger (Exod 12:48f.; Num 9:14; 15:14–16, 29f.). Hence Nehemiah imposed the observance of the sabbath on Judaean and Tyrian traders alike (Neh 13:15–22).

The occurrences of the 'perpetual statute' formula and kindred expressions have now, with very minor exceptions,[40] all been discussed. It is not automatically applied to all the provisions of the Priestly Code. We need therefore to consider briefly why it is not attached to other provisions.

It is not attached to the structure and contents of the tabernacle, apart from those features which had their counterpart in the temple: the incense altar, the shewbread and the sanctuary lamp. It is not attached to the description of the ark (Exod 25:10–22; 37:1–9): this probably reflects the knowledge that the ark had disappeared and would not be replaced in the second temple (cf. Jer 3:16). This means that the description of the tabernacle is not an attempt to depict the ideal sanctuary: it is an honest report of traditions about the actual tabernacle which preceded Solomon's temple.[41] The Priestly writers do not expect the tabernacle to be restored or the temple to reproduce it exactly. That is why they take care to point out by means of the formula which of the time-honoured features are still essential.

The formula is not attached to the *tôrôt* on sacrifice in Leviticus 1–5 (apart from the taboo on consuming fat and blood in 3:17). This means that the directions for the various sacrifices were traditional but unchallenged. It is only when the priestly dues and duties come into question in Leviticus 6–7 that it is necessary to assert their continuing validity. The formula is also missing from the *tôrôt* on clean and unclean animals and clean and unclean states in Leviticus 11–15. Again, this is traditional material, as the appearance of the *tôrâ* on clean and unclean animals in Deuteronomy 14 shows. It is unlikely, however, that its validity had been challenged. The food laws, for example, were not an issue during the exile; although Ezra and Nehemiah found the Jewish community slack about many things, they are silent about any neglect of the food laws; the contrast with the Hellenistic period, when the food laws were almost the central issue for Jews in the dispersion and later in Palestine itself, is most marked.

Leviticus 19, with its strong emphasis on justice and compassion for the neighbour, the poor and the stranger, does not contain the formula because it does not need it. On the one hand, the laws are presented as illustrations of the way in which Israel is to imitate the holiness of Yahweh (Lev 19:2). On the other, there is a strong underlying appeal to the universal conscience which recognises instinctively what kind of conduct is just and humane.

In the chapter on the sabbatical year and the jubilee year (Leviticus 25) the notion of perpetuity is attached only to the rights of, and restrictions on, Levites (Lev 25:31, 34). This is probably because the provisions, especially for the jubilee year, are new. They represent an attempt to work out afresh a principle which had become increasingly difficult to apply as the economy had changed from being predominantly agricultural (Exod 23:10f.) to being much more diversified, with many people engaged in commerce (Deut 15:1–11). Human resistance to the law was moreover very strong: 'What shall we eat in the seventh year, if we may not sow or gather in our crop?' said the farmers (Lev 25:20); 'The seventh year, the year of release, is near', said those who were approached for a loan (Deut 15:9). Reassertion of traditional practice would not work in this area.

We have tried to show that the formula 'a perpetual statute throughout your generations' is more than a rhetorical flourish,[42] and that it is not distributed at random through the Priestly material. It is used to draw attention to long-established practices whose continuing relevance has been challenged, but which the Priestly writers consider essential to the life of the Jewish community. The distribution of the formula allows us to determine with some assurance when the Priestly writers are expressing their commitment to the value of traditional practices and when they are trying to work out an old principle in a new way. Comparison with what we know of the exilic and post-exilic periods from other sources enables us to create, again with a fair degree of confidence, the points at which the Priestly writers felt the need to reassert the tradition. Study of the main Priestly narrative from this point of view tends to confirm that it was compiled during the exile and was intended to guide the process of restoration after the return. Study of the secondary Priestly material shows that most of the debates it presupposes were taking place in the time of Ezra and Nehemiah. Therefore it is likely that there was a major expansion of the Priestly Code at that time: the major collections of *tôrôt* (Leviticus

1–7; 11–15) and the Holiness Code (Leviticus 17–26) were probably incorporated then, and the newer material in Numbers was added.

We began by noting the influence of the formula 'a perpetual statute throughout your generations' on the *Book of Jubilees*. The writer of that book was appealing to fellow-Jews to be loyal to the institutions of Judaism, on the ground that they were committed to them in perpetuity, whether other motives could be adduced or not. It is possible that Jews also appealed to this principle in their dealings with the foreign powers to which they were subject. Legislators might appeal to fellow-Jews to keep the Feast of Booths, for example, on the ground that dwelling in booths was a vivid reminder of the wilderness period in their history, but such an argument would hardly weigh with the Persian government. As far as the authorities were concerned what had to be defended was the right of the Jews to live according to their 'ancestral laws' (*hoi patrioi nomoi*). The work of Ezra and Nehemiah testifies to the willingness of the Persian kings to permit this. It is entirely understandable that after the conquests of Alexander the Great the continuation of this degree of autonomy was the chief concern of the Jews.[43] It is conceivable that the term 'ancestral laws' is our formula in Greek dress.

4

THE TEMPLE SCROLL: A LAW UNTO ITSELF?

GEORGE J. BROOKE

INTRODUCTION   Certain sections of the Temple Scroll have been widely discussed and debated, but there has been little consideration as yet of the significance of the Temple Scroll as a whole for the understanding of the status and function of the Pentateuch in the late second-temple period. The purpose of this study is to discuss the Scroll as a whole and to suggest that its significance should not be narrowly restricted to Qumran studies. To this end we shall consider in turn the overall structure and content of the Scroll, its relationship to some other approximately contemporaneous literature, and some of its other characteristics.

The Temple Scroll from the eleventh cave (11QT) is written on 19 sheets of parchment which preserve 67 columns of text.[1] Most scholars would agree with Yadin that the script of both scribes who worked on 11QT may be classified as 'Herodian', suggesting a date for the scroll at the turn of the era. But if Yadin is correct in his identification of fragments from the fourth cave as from the Temple Scroll,[2] then for palaeographic reasons alone there is a strong case that the Temple Scroll was, for the most part at least, composed in the late second century BCE, or even earlier. Yadin also supposes that some parts of the Scroll may be written against either John Hyrcanus or Alexander Jannaeus, and so he assigns the scroll's composition to approximately the same time.[3] This date corresponds to the Qumran site's archaeological period IA, the first period of occupation, in the second half of the second century BCE. Yet Yadin underlines in the English edition of his work that 'it is entirely possible that certain sections of the scroll were composed previously, and that some of the traditions embedded in it originated in an earlier period'.[4]

Yadin has argued consistently that the scroll belongs happily within the spectrum of the Qumran Community as we know it from other sources. More precisely he has proposed that the scroll is to be identified with the 'Book of Hagu' or 'Hagi' (CD 10:4–6; 13:2–3; 14:6–8; 1QSa 1:6–8) which is probably the same as the 'sealed book of the Law' (CD 5:2) and 'the Law' (4QPss[a] 4:8) which, according to the Commentary on the Psalms, was one of the reasons for the persecution of the Teacher of Righteousness; all these may also be identified with 'the Book of the Second Law' referred to in a broken context in 4Q Catena[a] 1–4:14. The final step in the proposal is the identification of the author: 'It therefore seems to me possible, perhaps even probable, that our Temple Scroll was composed by none other than the founder of the sect, whose name was Zadok'[5] and who is more frequently called the Teacher of Righteousness. Much in all this seems at least to be possible, except perhaps at the points where Yadin associates his interpretation unquestioningly with an assumed critical orthodoxy about the history and make-up of the Qumran Community.

THE OVERALL STRUCTURE AND CONTENT OF THE SCROLL   A look at the overall content of the Temple Scroll may be an appropriate starting-point for a realignment of some of Yadin's proposals. The scroll's beginning is missing but it is unlikely that much preceded what is preserved from the eleventh cave. What remains starts with several significant explicit allusions to Exodus 34, the renewal of the covenant, which is supplemented with some phrases from Deuteronomy 7. With many differences from the MT the content then runs through the Pentateuch to the start of Deuteronomy 23, perhaps including reference to Deut 27:22 in 11QT 66:14 as a parallel to the incest material in Leviticus 18 and 20 which is being used to supplement the base text of Deut 23:1 (Heb.). Yadin suggests that the missing top of column 67 may have contained some writing, but what is preserved of column 67 is blank, allowing us to infer either that the scroll is as yet incomplete or that the matters in Deuteronomy 23–34 are not material of concern for the scroll's author. Given that the scroll is clearly written as the words of the Lord addressed to Moses, a case could be made for Deuteronomy 32–4 and even 27–31 as incompatible with the revelation contained in 11QT, since Moses is the obvious speaker in those chapters of Deuteronomy. Furthermore, some of the material in Deuteronomy 23–31 is placed elsewhere in the scroll: for example, Deut 23:26 is placed in the discussion of the firstfruits in 11QT 18–19; Deuteronomy 26, also on firstfruits, is one of the influences behind 11QT 18:10–19:9; Deut 23:11–12, on ritual purification, is alluded to in 11QT 45:7–10; Deut 23:13–15, on latrines, lies behind 11QT 46:13–16, etc.[6] It is quite likely then that the scroll did indeed end with material on incest and sexual taboos; after all, together with riches and profanation of the temple, sexual abuses were counted as one of the three nets of Belial (CD 4:15–18).

The description of the overall contents of the Temple Scroll in these terms allows us to see that it may correspond to the second law which Moses was given at Sinai after the first had been broken because of Israel's idolatry. Notably in Exodus 34 there are cultic expansions, so that what was written on the second set of tablets does not necessarily correspond with what was written on the first set; there is more than adequate justification for the author to give his (correct) layout of the temple building/tabernacle, since the plan of Exodus 25–31 has been abrogated.[7] This association of the Temple Scroll with the law given in Exodus 34 may explain the designation 'the Second Law' and thereby justify Yadin's identification of the scroll with 'the Second Law' mentioned in 4Q Catena[a]. But it should also be mentioned that just as the scroll ends with Deut 23:1 and yet includes material from the later chapters of Deuteronomy, so, although the scroll starts with Exodus 34 and seems to be making a clear statement about the abrogation through Israel's idolatry of the first revelation to Moses, nevertheless it contains some material from the earlier chapters of Exodus: for example, much of Exod 25:18–29 and 30:7–8, 34–5 seems to be represented in the description of the interior furnishings of the temple in the fragmentary 11QT 7–11; Exod 29:38–42 may lie behind the description of the continual burnt offering in 11QT 13; material from Exodus 29, together with other texts, lies behind the description of the sacrifices for the seven days of Ordination in 11QT 15–17; Exod 30:10 may be alluded to in the section on the Day of Atonement in 11QT 27:5, etc.

It may not be too incorrect to suggest that the Temple Scroll is essentially made up from pentateuchal texts from Exodus 34 – Deuteronomy 23:1,[8] texts which have been generally altered so as to be heard as from God himself and which have been exegetically reordered for reasons of classification and supplemented with material from other traditions, especially those concerning priestly and levitical practice (Nehemiah, 1 and 2 Chronicles, Ezekiel) and the figure of David in relation to certain matters (2 Samuel). But this suggestion carries with it the problem concerning the status of the scroll: is it intended to replace the Pentateuch, known in so many exemplars amongst the Qumran scrolls, or is it meant to supplement it in some polemical fashion? Part of the answer to this problem may rest in asking first whether there is any reason to suppose that the author of the Temple Scroll or its tradents had any particular attitude to the material from Genesis, Exodus and Deuteronomy which are nowhere represented – always assuming that these were known in approximately the form that we have them at the time that 11QT was composed (1QapGen suggests as much).

THE RELATIONSHIP OF THE TEMPLE SCROLL TO SOME OTHER CONTEMPORARY WRITINGS   A clue to a probable answer to this question concerning the limits of the content of the Temple Scroll may lie in noticing that the *Book of Jubilees*, as is well known, contains a cultically adjusted version of Genesis 1–Exodus 15, the very chapters of the Pentateuch which are not alluded to in the Temple Scroll itself. *Jubilees* is known in several copies amongst the Qumran scrolls and is almost certainly referred to in the *Damascus Document* (CD 16:2–4). The relationship between *Jubilees* and the Temple Scroll and the possibility that they deliberately complement one another in some way is the subject to which we must turn.

To begin with, although *Jubilees* starts with an allusion to Exod 24:12, the phraseology of *Jub* 1:15, in which God instructs Moses to write a book, corresponds to Exod 34:27, a starting-point similar to that chosen by the author of the Temple Scroll. *Jubilees* purports to be a copy of what the angel of the presence wrote for Moses 'from the first creation until my sanctuary is built in their midst forever and ever' (1:27–8),

> ... and the angel of the presence, who went before the camp of Israel, took the tablets of the division of the years ... from the day of the new creation when the heaven and earth and all of their creatures shall be renewed according to the powers of heaven and according to the whole nature of earth, until the sanctuary of the Lord is created in Jerusalem upon Mount Zion. (1:29)[9]

This descriptive statement of purpose is remarkably similar to the summary statement in 11QT 29:8–10:

> And I will consecrate my [t]emple by my glory, (the temple) on which I will settle my glory, until the day of blessing on which I will create my temple and establish it for myself for all times, according to the covenant which I have made with Jacob at Bethel.[10]

Yadin and others have indeed noted the correspondence of these texts, but apart from observing the parallels, have made little use of the texts to interpret one another.

There are many similarities between *Jubilees* and the Temple Scroll. Most prominent in both works is the cultic interest of the authors, especially in calendric matters: both works reflect a solar year of 364 days, four quarters of 90 days, each with a quarter-day. But there are also numerous items of detail. Yadin has drawn attention to the parallels between the two works concerning the first of Nisan as the start of the new year (*Jub* 7:2–3, Noah's new year; 27:19, Jacob arrives at Bethel on 1 Nisan; 11QT 14:9), concerning the celebration of Passover (*Jub* 49:1, 10–20; 11QT 17:6–9), especially that it should be offered by anybody over 20 (*Jub* 49:17; 11QT 17:8) and should be eaten in the temple courts (*Jub* 49:16–20, 11QT 17:8–9), concerning the celebration of the Feast of Weeks as a feast of firstfruits, a shared interpretation of Exod 34:22 (*Jub* 6:21; 11QT 19:9), concerning the conjunction of the same feast with the bringing of the second tithe (*Jub* 32:10–15; 11QT 43:4–10), and concerning the wood offering (*Jub* 21:13–14; 11QT 23–25:2), as well as in several other less significant cases of overlapping interest.[11] In his major review of Yadin's work Joseph Baumgarten has stressed the Temple Scroll's proximity to the *Book of Jubilees* and pointed to a few further parallels: 11QT 20:4–14 shares with *Jub* 21:7–11 a similar definition of the day ending with sunset, a similar set of peace offerings (as in Lev 3:3–4, 9–10), and both passages conclude with a reminder about salt (Num 18:19); 11QT

60:3–4 and *Jub* 7:36 both allude to Lev 19:23–4 concerning the contribution due in the fourth year.[12]

A further general point of similarity between *Jubilees* and the Temple Scroll lies in their common attitude to Levi. In both works the levitical interest is fostered.[13] Though in *Jub* 31:11–20 Judah receives a blessing alongside, but after, Levi, elsewhere Levi tends to be prominent. The sons of Levi 'will become judges and rulers and leaders for all the seed of the sons of Jacob' (*Jub* 31:15). Levi is the one who is entrusted with a library of books (*Jub* 45:15), with the comment that is possibly autobiographical: 'so that he might preserve them and renew them for his sons until this day'. Most especially in *Jub* 32:3–9 Levi is depicted as fulfilling the role of priest for his father and the clan at Bethel. The connection between Levi and Bethel and the similarity of the passages concerning the sanctuary in *Jub* 1:15–17 and 27–9 and the summary section at the end of the regulations concerning the festivals in 11QT 29 are strong pointers towards the association of *Jubilees* with the Temple Scroll. It is not altogether surprising then to read in the Temple Scroll that the Lord promises to create his sanctuary anew 'according to the covenant which I made with Jacob at Bethel' (11QT 29:10).

In the Temple Scroll's handling of the cultic laws the Levites are given greater prominence than they are in the Pentateuch of the MT. Levitical preferment can be seen in the arrangement of the gates of the middle and outer courts (11QT 39:12-40:14), in the rules for the wood-offering festival (11QT 23–5), in the rules for the distribution of the shoulder at the Feasts of New Wine and New Oil (11QT 21:1, 12), in the explicit mention of the Levites as administrators of justice (11QT 57:13), in the rules for the distribution of the income from tithes (11QT 60:9), etc.[14] Furthermore some of these adjustments in favour of the Levites correspond to the levitical chapters of Ezekiel: for example, the Levites will slaughter the offerings (11QT 22:4; Ezek 44:10).[15] Milgrom sees all this as a protest against the Wicked Priest who, he thinks, may have usurped various levitical privileges which the Temple Scroll's author is demanding back.[16] At the least we have here new information on the struggles amongst cultic personnel at some time in the last two centuries BCE.

The levitical interest, probably influenced by the carriers of the traditions preserved in Ezekiel 43 and 44, is common not only to the Temple Scroll and *Jubilees*, but also can be seen in the *Damascus Document*. Thus Ezek 44:24, with its concern with the levitical attitude to the sabbath may be reflected in the rules concerning the sabbath in 11QT 13:17–14:?, in *Jubilees* 50, and in CD 10:14–11:18. Furthermore in CD 13:3–7 there is a description of how a Levite is to step in and educate the priest should the priest not be learned in the Book of Hagi. In particular, if there is a case of leprosy, the Guardian, whom Vermes for one considers to be a Levite,[17] shall instruct the priest in the exact interpretation of the law; in 11QT 48:17–49:4 there are elaborate instructions regarding skin-diseases. The assertion of the separate identity of the Levites in the *Damascus Document* is well known in the particular version of Ezek 44:15 that is preserved and interpreted in CD 3:21–4:12: whereas the MT reads 'But the Levitical priests, the sons of Zadok, who kept charge of my sanctuary when the people of Israel went astray from me', CD reads 'The Priests, the Levites, and the sons of Zadok who kept charge of my sanctuary when the children of Israel went astray from me.'

The Temple Scroll has much else in common with the *Damascus Document*. The following are some of the more obvious parallels, some already noted by Yadin, between the two documents:[18] 11QT 45:11–12 on sexual purity corresponds with CD 12:1–2, to the extent that these passages share some distinctive phraseology; 11QT 66:15–17, on kinship, matches CD 5:7–11; the seven-year penalty in 11QT 63:14–15 resembles a similar penalty in CD 12:5–6; and the section on the wood offering in 11QT 23–5 might be read in association with the mention of wood in CD 11:18–19, which J. Maier associates in turn with *Jub* 21:12–15.[19] B. Levine has also noted that the section on the monogamy of the king in 11QT 56:12f. is matched with a section in the *Damascus Document* (CD 4:20–5:5) which suggests that this law applies to every individual Israelite: CD 5:2 actually cites Deut 17:17.[20]

It seems clear that the Temple Scroll has many affinities with the *Book of Jubilees* and with the *Damascus Document* and that *Jubilees* and the *Damascus Document* are close to one another; indeed the *Damascus Document* is widely acknowledged to be the work with the earliest explicit reference to *Jubilees* (CD 16:2–4). Given the recent work by J. Murphy-O'Connor and P. R. Davies on the redactional history of the *Damascus Document*,[21] it may no longer be appropriate to see it as a rule for the lay members not resident at Qumran. Rather it may be a rule for the group responsible for such traditions as are preserved in *Jubilees* and the Temple Scroll. Davies concludes that the *Damascus Document* achieved its present form before the foundation of the Qumran Community; it betrays an organised and well-developed community with a clearly expressed ideology. This community did not boycott the temple, but did not believe the temple could be used except under the terms of its own interpretation of the law. It regarded the 364-day calendar as divinely revealed to it in exile, and whilst it had possible affinities with those writing *Jubilees*, surprisingly Davies sees no obvious connections between the two. For Davies both groups are the forebears of the Qumran Community. Though we cannot be sure of this at least we are nearer recognising that the origins of the Qumran Community do not lie with any one homogeneous group of disaffected people. It is more likely that small groups of people of various persuasions found they had enough in common over against what was happening in Jerusalem to make common cause together. With such a scenario it seems possible that *Jubilees*, the Temple Scroll and the *Damascus Document* stand as the self-expression of a group of disaffected Levites who may have been in association with a certain number of priests sympathetic to their cause. These Levites may well have been the heirs of cultic disaffection predating the Maccabean revolt by a century or more, but they were spurred by events after that revolt to present their own polemic. A guess would be that these people found a welcome home amongst those who were responsible for the expansion of the Qumran site at the start of the first century BCE, though the subsequent history of the community there was almost certainly not without its tensions.

To associate the Temple Scroll with the *Damascus Document* and the *Book of Jubilees* in this way is to challenge Yadin's setting for the Temple Scroll within the main lines of the Qumran Community. Yadin has been followed and defended by several scholars,[22] but others have wanted to remove the Temple Scroll from any immediate connection with the Qumran Community as it flourished in the first century BCE.[23] L. H. Schiffman is particularly concerned to distance the Temple Scroll from the *halakah* at Qumran as he sees it legislated and practised in the first century BCE. That there are some things in common with the other Qumran scrolls is sufficient for Yadin to conclude that the Temple Scroll was written by a member of the Qumran Community. From the same evidence Schiffman draws the opposite conclusion and questions 'whether the Temple Scroll originated in and represents the teachings of the group we have come to know as the Dead Sea sect'.[24] In Schiffman's critique of Yadin is yet one further point to supplement the idea that the Temple Scroll originated in a group who were apart from the Essenes at Qumran, but who came to be closely allied with them, perhaps at the turn of the first century BCE; that alliance led to the Temple Scroll being copied again at Qumran, and perhaps to it being particularly influential during the Herodian period for some reason.

FURTHER CHARACTERISTICS OF THE TEMPLE SCROLL   There are several characteristics of the Temple Scroll which have as yet received little attention.

Firstly there is its status as Torah. In his critique of Yadin, Schiffman is keen to assess the Temple Scroll in light of later pharisaic *halakah* and to suggest that its codification lies some way between the Pentateuch itself and that of the Mishnah. Though such a comparison may be helpful for considering the author's compositional techniques, it is based on the assumption that there is a direct line between Torah and Mishnah. This is not the case. The Mishnah stands clearly as a post-canonical document and is careful in its quotation of scripture. The Temple Scroll on the other hand, for all that it may be interpretative, is not *halakah* in a strict formal sense but an alternative Torah; or taken with *Jubilees* it is an alternative Pentateuch. B.-Z. Wacholder's suggestion that the Temple Scroll should be renamed 11Q Torah[25] is good in this respect. Almost consistently the Scroll represents God as speaking in the first person to Moses. It thus in itself suggests its own authoritative status as material direct from God himself. Furthermore, Moses is the one who is addressed and to whom the words are entrusted: his authority as law-giver and teacher is no doubt relied upon too.

Secondly, the overall structure of the Temple Scroll works from the covenant and command to build a temple, from the Holy of Holies outwards through each court and into the city of the sanctuary and beyond. Each physical location has a degree of holiness which attracts various items of law that can be associated with it. As J. Maier comments, the Temple Scroll 'sees everything from the priestly point of view constantly looking from the inside outside'.[26] This composition is priestly in perspective, or perhaps more precisely, in light of what has been said above concerning what the Temple Scroll, *Jubilees* and the *Damascus Document* share, it is thoroughly levitical. It thus stands as if it came from God himself as a direct challenge to any other priestly set of laws.[27]

Something of this priestly interest can be seen in the scroll's implicit hermeneutic, a third characteristic worth brief discussion. For example, it is clear that when all the Pentateuch's material concerning the Day of Atonement is put together, the rules for procedure are far from clear. In columns 25 to 27 the author of the Temple Scroll has tidied up the confusion. He bases his ordering of the materials on the calendric information in Leviticus 23: he opens with quotations from Lev 23:27 and 29 and ends with reference to Lev 23:28 and 30–2 – a neat inclusion. But he clarifies Lev 23:27 and 29 with reference to passages from another calendar, Num 29:8 and 11, verses which contain more explicit information about the animals to be offered and which act in turn as the interpretative key for adjusting Leviticus 16. Leviticus 16 is put in a comprehensible order: firstly the sin offering of one bull, then the ritual for first and second goats, then the whole burnt offerng. Allusions to Leviticus 4 suggest how the ritual of the sin offering should actually proceed, and allusions to Exodus 30[28] provide the details for certain items of furniture and matters of hand-washing as well as probably providing the motif of remembrance (Exod 30:16) which connects the interpretation of Leviticus 16 back with the concluding calendric Lev 23:27 and 29. Furthermore it might not be inappropriate to mention some of the matters from these passages which the author of the Temple Scroll has omitted: there is no mention of the anthropomorphic 'pleasing odour' of Num 29:8, of the precise measures of the cereal offering and its oil mixture (already covered in 11QT 19–20), of the atoning for the holy place (already described in 11QT 13?), and there is no mention of Aaron by name in what survives in 11QT 25–7, even though his name occurs six times in Leviticus 16 and indeed occurs elsewhere in the Temple Scroll.

A fourth and obvious characteristic of the Temple Scroll is its dependence on the books of the Pentateuch in a form not that far away from what is now known in the MT. But here lies the conundrum, because the Temple Scroll has been preserved for us as part of the Qumran library, a library containing many examples of texts from the Pentateuch in a variety of text-types. It seems clear that the scroll is making an implicit claim to be the repository of God's authentic revelation to Moses. But it must be asked whether it is claiming to be the *sole* repository. If we allow some relationship between the author of the Temple Scroll and the Qumran Community, then it seems somewhat unlikely that he viewed his work as a straightforward replacement of a whole variety of pentateuchal texts. Perhaps it is that the relationship between the Temple Scroll and the other versions of these pentateuchal laws is similar to the relationship between Deuteronomy and Exodus found in the Pentateuch itself and between Chronicles and Samuel–Kings: the replacement is deemed by some to be superior but by others can only be properly understood if the earlier materials are also preserved. To view the Temple Scroll by itself is to consider it as a fine example of sectarianism: a document which is a law unto itself but which nevertheless depends upon a particular set of traditions even though it denies their validity. To view the Temple Scroll together with the other pentateuchal texts from Qumran is to recognise that it stands at the very centre of the pre-canonical process in early Judaism: the state of the text is in flux and the Temple Scroll is an authentic priestly attempt to provide an authoritative text of part of the Torah.

CONCLUSIONS   It seems likely that the Temple Scroll is to be associated with the group or groups in the second century BCE who were responsible for *Jubilees* and the earliest forms of the traditions in the *Damascus Document*. These people were probably disaffected cultic personnel. The origin of their disaffection may be traced back into the third century or even earlier, but events in Maccabean times provoked the particular expressions of the proper form of the law that we have in these various documents. Perhaps the circumstances which led to the expansion of the Qumran Community at the end of the reign of John Hyrcanus were also responsible for the traditions of these writings passing into the Qumran library as some of their number became members. No doubt, however much these people had in common with other members of the community, there were also disagreements and changes.

It could be that the Temple Scroll was deemed worth copying at about the turn of the era because it represented the views of a levitically minded group which could have found itself in favour with Herod as he searched for cultically qualified people for his rebuilding of the temple.[29] The Scroll is their attempt to influence that rebuilding programme; its plans, however, were clearly unachievable. Furthermore, however much this group may have found favour with Herod, that did not prevent their criticisms of kingly behaviour in politics, religion and marriage.

Whatever the case it seems that the Temple Scroll demonstrates once again that the members of the Qumran Community cannot all be classified simply as Essenes without further qualification. Neither do those responsible for the Temple Scroll in its earlier and later forms stand merely at the fringes of the Qumran Community or of late second-temple Judaism. They stand rather at the very heart of pre-canonical developments in Judaism. As Torah, the Temple Scroll forces us away from the view that the Massoretic Text really represents what is normative in Judaism before 70 CE. Or again, as Torah, the Temple Scroll cannot be simply classified either on the basis of its form or its content as *halakah*. The Temple Scroll may look like a law unto itself but really for late second-temple Judaism it is a sure witness to the very fluidity which allowed the law to remain alive and relevant in each successive generation.

5

JEWISH LAW IN THE TIME OF JESUS: TOWARDS A CLARIFICATION OF THE PROBLEM

PHILIP S. ALEXANDER

THE ISSUES DEFINED   The problem of 'Jesus and the law' has long been regarded by NT scholars as of central importance for the understanding of the development of early Christianity. It has been argued in a variety of ways that Jesus, whether explicitly or implicitly, took a negative attitude towards the Jewish law of his day, and questioned its continuing validity. In adopting this radical stance he attacked the very foundations of Judaism, and so inaugurated a movement which broke away from (or, according to some, transformed and transcended) Judaism. This view, which was given classic expression by Protestant German scholars before and after the Second World War, has come in for strong criticism in recent years, notably from Ed Sanders. Observing that 'nothing which Jesus said or did which bore on the law led his disciples after his death to disregard it', he concludes: 'We find no criticism of the law which would allow us to speak of his opposing or rejecting it.'[1] As the debate has swung back and forth a fundamental aspect of the subject has remained curiously unexplored: attention has focused on discovering Jesus' attitude; little interest has been shown in defining what is meant by 'the law' in this context. The assumption seems to be that the term 'law' here is self-evident: it is, in effect, the law of Moses, which can be found in the Pentateuch in any Bible. Ed Sanders shares this assumption with his opponents. In his chapter on 'Jesus and the law' in *Jesus and Judaism* he never once defines what law he is talking about. From his passing references to 'the Mosaic dispensation' it appears that, like everyone else, he is thinking primarily of the Pentateuch, but if this is so why should he see the dispute over hand-washing as germane to the discussion, because hand-washing before meals is not directly prescribed in the Pentateuch?

This marked lack of interest in defining the law demands an explanation. At first sight it may appear a simple failure of historical method. It is axiomatic in the scholarly literature that the Torah of Moses is the foundation of Judaism: it is easy to assume that one knows what the Torah is, and in what way it was central to Judaism. But there are probably deeper reasons, related to the aims and methods of NT study (and, perhaps, to its hidden agenda). Much study of the Gospels appears to be dominated by the concern to compare and contrast the teaching of Jesus with Judaism, one coherent body of teaching with another. For some scholars this comparison is undertaken with a view to discovering the uniqueness of Jesus, for others it is aimed at showing that Jesus was not unique, but essentially a conforming Jew of his time. This kind of enquiry will be greatly advanced if Judaism can be defined in a simple, normative way. It will then be possible to lay down a base-line from which to measure Jesus' deviation or lack of it. It is tempting to define the normativeness of Judaism in terms of the centrality of Torah, since that is the one proposition that would appear to be beyond all dispute. To probe too deeply into this proposition might reveal problems and ambiguities which would endanger the whole quest. This desire to find an essentially simple normative, theological definition of Judaism is strikingly illustrated by the work of Käsemann. In his essay on 'The problem of the historical Jesus' (1953), he is prepared to define Judaism as such a tightly constructed system of law that *any* challenge by Jesus to the law, even on apparently minor matters, constitutes a challenge to the system as a whole: Jesus' attitude towards the sabbath and ritual purity 'shatters' the Torah of Moses.[2] Pull out one brick and the whole wall collapses! This approach is deeply ingrained in NT scholarship. If one remonstrates and suggests that Judaism was a much more loosely structured phenomenon, full of inconsistency, tension and even contradiction, one is apt to get an impatient answer which amounts to this: If Judaism in the time of Jesus was *not* a logical system, then it ought to have been. The trouble was that the Jews failed to see the full implications of the Torah of Moses: they had not been properly theologically trained!

The assumption of Christian scholars that they know what the Torah is, and in what way it is central to Judaism, is, paradoxically, unlikely to be challenged by Jewish scholars. There is a curious, and often unnoticed, meeting of minds on this point. Christian scholarship and modern Jewish Orthodoxy basically agree on the substantive definition of Judaism. Of course heated and bitter words have been bandied between the two camps, but it is important to identify correctly the point at issue. The debate is not, in essence, about the nature of Judaism: both accept that law is central to Judaism, Judaism is in some sense a 'legalism'. Where they differ is in their estimate of the value of legalism. To the Jew 'legalism' is something positive, an attempt to work out God's will in the detail of everyday life;

for the Protestant theologian it is something negative, an inferior dispensation to be transcended by the freedom and grace of the gospel.[3]

The purpose of the present essay is to clarify the problem of Jesus and
the law not by analysing Jesus' attitude, but by trying to define Jewish law
in the time of Jesus. Evidence will be brought which suggests that the
nature and content of the law of Moses in the time of Jesus is far from
clear: it certainly cannot be identified *simpliciter* with the Pentateuch. It is
hard to determine what non-biblical traditions it contained. And while the
centrality of the Torah of Moses to Judaism cannot in principle be
questioned, the meaning of that centrality is not self-evident. It was not
necessarily the centrality of a coherent body of doctrine universally
believed. It was more the centrality of a national symbol, which was
acknowledged by all, but which meant different things to different groups.
Individual understandings of the significance of the symbol may have
varied considerably. It is hard to say what would, or would not, have been
an 'acceptable' attitude towards the Torah of Moses. The upshot of the
analysis is that it is difficult, if not impossible, to lay down a base-line from
which to measure Jesus' deviation from, or conformity to, the law. It is
arguable that the whole problem of Jesus and the law, at least as
traditionally stated, is misconceived.

THE LAW-COURTS IN THE TIME OF JESUS   Our analysis will proceed as
concretely as possible. It will not address itself initially to the question of
the role of the law of Moses in Judaism in the time of Jesus. 'Judaism in the
time of Jesus' is essentially an artificial construct which deflects the enquiry
too much in the direction of a theology. Rather we shall consider two
straightforward historical questions: (a) Were there Jewish courts in
Palestine in the time of Jesus, and if so, how did they function and what
was their jurisdiction? (b) What law was administered by those courts?
'The time of Jesus' will be taken in a strict sense, as covering the years
c. 25–40 CE.

For the Jews the fundamental fact of legal life was that Palestine was a
part of the Roman empire. In the last analysis the law of Rome provided
the framework within which all other law functioned.[4] There were
regional differences: Judea was an equestrian province, governed by a
prefect, under overall control of the legate for Syria; Galilee and
Transjordan, on the other hand, fell within the tetrarchy of Herod
Antipas, who ruled these regions as a client king. They were not ruled
directly by Rome.

The Roman prefect and his appointed agents held regular tribunals.
These exercised exclusive jurisdiction in certain areas (e.g. in capital
cases). The governor probably also reserved the right to hear *any* case, or
to intervene in any case. He would not necessarily have administered only
Roman law at his tribunals. According to the circumstances he may have
applied Greek or Jewish law. In practice the Roman governor probably
allowed a considerable degree of autonomy to local courts, whether in the
Greek cities or the Jewish areas. It was, presumably, always open for a

plaintiff to petition for his case to be heard by a Roman court, in preference to the local courts, and there were doubtless problems when the parties in a dispute came from different communities (e.g. a Gentile versus a Jew), but in general the governor did not have the resources to become involved in the detailed administration of justice in the province, and was probably content to leave it to local courts, provided the interests of Rome were not threatened. There was, then, considerable scope for local courts and 'native' law to operate in Roman Judea. A similar situation probably prevailed in Galilee and Transjordan. Though Herod Antipas was a Jewish ruler, it is unlikely that he forced Jewish law on the considerable non-Jewish population of his domains. The Greek cities were probably allowed to run their own courts, and to apply their own traditions of law.

Given the political climate of the period there must have been resentment among the Jews at having Roman law applied to them. Social pressure to maximise the application of Jewish law to Jews would surely have been strong. In later rabbinic law, stress was laid on not submitting cases to Roman tribunals, even where those tribunals administered Jewish law, or came to a decision in keeping with Jewish law: 'Any place wherein you find court sessions in the market-place, even though their laws are like the laws of Israel, you are not permitted to rely on them' (*b. Giṭṭin* 78b). There was plenty of scope for the Jews to exercise their independence. In Jewish law (as indeed in much ancient law) prosecution by the state was not nearly as common as it is today. Many actions which today would be initiated by the state, in ancient times were brought by private individuals. Practical considerations probably dictated this procedure: ancient societies did not have the bureaucratic structure or the policing arrangements of the modern state which make such actions feasible. It was open, therefore, for the plaintiff to decide before which court to bring his action. So by exercising self-discipline the Jews had the possibility of running a largely autonomous Jewish legal system within Roman Palestine.

We have indisputable evidence that a system of Jewish courts operated in Palestine in the time of Jesus. However, many of the details of how these courts were organised remain hopelessly obscure. The problems are well illustrated by the Sanhedrin – the highest Jewish court in the land. The amount of ink spilled on trying to clarify some of the basic aspects of the structure, membership and legal competence of this court bears witness to our ignorance of the practice of Jewish law in Palestine in the time of Jesus.[5] The following is a considered summary of the complex and conflicting evidence. (a) The Sanhedrin was the supreme court, with sole competence for legislating in Jewish law, and for hearing the gravest cases (probably, in principle, all capital cases). It also functioned as the ultimate court of appeal, from the lower courts. (b) The Sanhedrin met in Jerusalem, probably on the Temple Mount. It acted as the city council of Jerusalem, and regulated the running of the temple. (c) The head of the Sanhedrin was the high priest. A significant proportion of its membership was made up of priests, but it contained also lay scribes and men of wealth and family. We do not know how membership of the Sanhedrin was acquired: it is unlikely that it was by any sort of democratic process. Membership was not restricted to Jerusalem families, but embraced families from the countryside as well. (d) The Sanhedrin was a sizable body: there is no good reason to question the rabbinic tradition which puts its number at 70/71. It was not a single-party chamber, but contained factions: it was composed both of Sadduccees and Pharisees. It may have sat in plenary session only rarely, when matters of the gravest import were on the agenda. Everyday business was probably conducted by smaller groups within the body of the Sanhedrin. (e) Besides acting as a law-court, both for legislating and for trying cases, the Sanhedrin along with the High Priest acted as the representative of the Jewish people in dealing with the imperial power, and in other diplomatic matters.

In addition to the high court in Jerusalem there were also local courts. These may have existed at two levels. Most sizable towns would probably have had a court which dealt with very local matters. District courts would have sat in the more important centres to hear more serious cases. Under Roman rule Judea was administratively divided up into eleven toparchies.[6] It is a plausible guess that the district courts would have sat in the chief town of the toparchy. There was, then, a three-tiered system of courts – local, district and national. They obviously constituted a hierarchy – the least power residing with the local courts, the greatest with the national. We can say little as to the detailed competence of these courts, or as to the system of referral which may have existed between them. We know next to nothing about how judges were appointed, or what qualifications were deemed necessary for a judge. After 70 CE the rabbis made strenuous efforts to ensure that only qualified rabbis, duly ordained by the proper authorities, acted as judges, but there is no evidence that they successfully carried this point (at least not before the time of Judah ha-Nasi), or that any system of ordination existed before 70. There were professional lawyers before 70, but it is far from certain that all judges were qualified lawyers. Some doubtless were, but particularly at local level this may not have been the case. In the towns the local grandees may have acted as justices of the peace. One assumes that the Sanhedrin tried to exercise some sort of control over the lower courts, and may have reserved the right to appoint judges. We have no means of telling how effective this control was. The position of Galilee and Transjordan is interesting. Did the authority of the Sanhedrin effectively end at the borders of Herod's territory, or did he allow it some say in the administration of Jewish law within his realm? The latter is likely to be the case. Herod would have had little to fear from the Sanhedrin. He seems to have had considerable influence at Jerusalem, and was probably able to some extent to control the deliberations of the Sanhedrin.

We know little about policing and law enforcement. The high priest had his retainers (as had most men of wealth and position); Herod Antipas had his soldiers. There were temple guards whose business it was to protect the sanctuary from desecration. The Sanhedrin communicated with the rest of the community by means of emissaries (*šĕlîḥîm, apostoloi*) who may, in

Jewish areas, have felt free to apply force. But it is not clear in detail how offenders were apprehended, how punishments (e.g. floggings) were inflicted, or what sanctions a court had against a party prepared to defy its decision. In certain circumstances the Jewish authorities may have been able to call in the Romans. Perhaps in most cases the threat of social ostracism (in the form of *niddûy* or *ḥērem*) would have been sufficient to compel compliance.

THE LAW ADMINISTERED BY THE JEWISH COURTS   There was, then, an established network of Jewish law-courts in Palestine in the time of Jesus, but what law did it administer? Would a judge in court have unrolled a copy of the Pentateuch and reached his decision on the basis of what he found there? Not necessarily. The Torah of Moses, as we now have it in the Pentateuch, can hardly have been, in any simple and direct way, the law applied in the courts. Why not?

First, there is the problem of the form in which the Torah is cast: it is not presented conveniently for everyday legal purposes. It combines with strictly legal material considerable quantities of legally irrelevant *aggadah*. However important that *aggadah* may have been religiously, it would only have been a nuisance to a judge in court. Moreover, the Torah mixes together matters which fell within the jurisdiction of a court and matters which did not. Important rulings on the same subject may be found in different parts of the text, which, when compared, do not always tally. Though, as modern literary analysis has shown, the Pentateuch embodies earlier law-codes, it is not a law-code itself. It lacks the qualities of a good law-code as set out by Maimonides in his preface to the *Mishneh Torah*.[7] There must have been pressure in the second-temple period to codify Jewish law. Concrete evidence that there was is found at Qumran, where attempts were made to codify sabbath law (in the *Damascus Document*), temple law (in the Temple Scroll), and the law of the community (in the Manual of Discipline). It is unlikely that such codifying activity was confined to the Essenes. Unfortunately the other codes, if they were ever produced, are now lost.

Second, the Pentateuch as a body of practical law to be applied in the courts is incomplete. Important areas of law are either not touched upon, or only very sketchily: e.g. laws of contract, marriage and divorce, and inheritance. It is very thin on evidence and procedure. All this is the very stuff of the law, and the courts, if they functioned at all, must have formulated ways of dealing with these matters. The Torah of Moses, if it constituted the law of the community, must have been heavily supplemented. That there was such supplementation is beyond any doubt. The Murabbaʿat texts, for example, attest to certain legal documentary forms current in Palestine in the time of Jesus, as does the *prosbûl* of Hillel. These 'supplements' to the Torah would have come from a variety of sources. One source was presumably the decisions of the courts themselves, which would have created precedent. Another source would have been the custom of the community. Custom (*minhāg*) was recognised by later rabbinic jurisprudence as an important source of law, and there are no grounds for denying that the same would have been true in the time of Jesus. It is possible that there was considerable variation in the detailed application of the law, owing to the force of local custom.

Third, all law in practice requires interpretation. This would have been true of the Pentateuch, even of those parts which are reasonably full and clear. With the passage of time much of this interpretation would have become traditional: lawyers and judges would have generally agreed as to how certain terms and clauses were to be understood. Ancient law tended to be conservative: innovation was not encouraged, at least in the practice of law. There must have been a body of traditional interpretation which stood side by side with the Pentateuch, without which it could not have been applied. This too, like custom and case law, would have supplemented the Torah and created law.

Fourth, not all law found in the Pentateuch was applied through the courts. Some of it was 'civil', some of it 'religious'. This distinction requires clarification because its validity in the case of Jewish law is often denied. It is something of a cliché that Jewish law (like Islamic law, but unlike 'secular' Roman law) is *in toto* religious, since it derives its authority from a God-given text. The theoretical constitution of Israel was theocratic, and did not demarcate between 'church' and 'state', between 'civil' and 'religious'. There is a sense in which this is unquestionably true. The Pentateuch itself does not recognise the distinction. Later rabbinic jurists (though, as will become clear presently, they did make the distinction) treated both aspects of law *equally as halakah*: they applied the same principles to both, and often argued across the division from one aspect to the other. However, the position is not as clear-cut as is often supposed. The definition of Jewish law as *in toto* 'religious' is not without its problems, as Bernard Jackson has rightly stressed.[8] That philosophic issue need not concern us here. For our present purposes it suffices to note that the laws of the Pentateuch fall into two broad classes: (a) those which were, or conceivably could have been, enforced through the courts; and (b) those whose observance was left in the domain of the individual conscience. The two categories correspond roughly to our distinction between 'civil' and 'religious' law (though it must be admitted that some 'religious' laws were enforced through the courts). The actual practice of law introduced an important distinction into the seamless text of the Torah.

An illustration may help to clarify this point. Lev 6:1–7 (MT 5:20–6) states:

> The Lord said to Moses: 'If anyone sins and commits a breach of faith against the Lord by deceiving his neighbour in a matter of a deposit or security, or through robbery, or if he has oppressed his neighbour or has found what was lost and lied about it, swearing falsely – in any of all the things which men do and sin therein, when one has sinned and become guilty, he shall restore what he took by robbery, or what he got by oppression, or the deposit which was committed to him, or the lost thing which he found, or anything about which he has sworn falsely; he shall restore it in full, and shall add a fifth to it, and give it to him to whom it

belongs, on the day of the guilt offering. And he shall bring to the priest his guilt offering to the LORD, a ram without blemish out of the flock, valued by you at the price for a guilt offering; and the priest shall make atonement for him before the LORD, and he shall be forgiven for any of the things which one may do and thereby become guilty.'

Here is a reasonably clear, well-drafted piece of legislation, which describes the restitution a man must make if convicted of fraud. The restitution has both a 'civil' and a 'religious' side: it involves *both* restoring to the cheated man his property (plus a proportion of its value as compensation), *and* the bringing of a sacrifice to God, to atone for having broken God's law. Now there may have been a time in Israel when such cases would have been tried by the priests, and so the civil and religious aspects could have been held closely together, but if such a law were applied in the time of Jesus, in any shape or form, the chances are that the 'civil' and 'religious' aspects would have been *de facto* separated. The courts would have enforced the restitution to the aggrieved party. Restitution to God, however, in the form of a sacrifice in the temple would effectively have been left to the individual's conscience.

It is worth dwelling on this point, because a central issue is involved. As I have already suggested, there is a powerful tendency in NT scholarship to treat the Torah of Moses as an undifferentiated, highly uniform and coherent body of law. In fact the text of the Torah has probably never been treated within the Jewish legal tradition as seamless. If we take the well-documented testimony of rabbinic jurisprudence, we find that rabbinic legalists have introduced many distinctions between the laws, some of which must surely have been recognised in some sense in the time of Jesus. A few of these rabbinic distinctions are of particular interest to us.[9]

(a) The distinction between *mišpāṭ 'ibrî* and *halakah*. The term *mišpāṭ 'ibrî* is used by modern Israeli jurists to cover those areas within the traditional *halakah* which correspond to present-day legal systems. It denotes 'civil' law, and corresponds closely to those aspects of the *halakah* which can be tried by process of law in the courts. The term *mišpāṭ 'ibrî* is of recent coinage, and is objected-to by some traditionalist lawyers, but the distinction it implies must have been recognised at earlier stages of Jewish legal history. It is not far off the traditional rabbinic distinction between *māmônâ* and *'issûrâ*. As I have already suggested the distinction was already functionally present in Jewish law in the second-temple period. It is interesting to note what an academic lawyer like Ze'ev Falk covers when he writes an *Introduction to Jewish Law of the Second Commonwealth*. He deals with: crimes, torts, contracts, property, persons, the family and succession – in other words with *mišpāṭ 'ibrî*. He says nothing about religious law in its strict sense: laws of prayer, of fasting, of festivals, of sacrifice, of temple cult, of ritual purity. Such a restriction is not arbitrary, or imposed from without, because Falk is concentrating on an area of law which would have been differentiated least in practice in the second-temple period.[10]

(b) The distinction between *kārēt* (or *mîtâ bîdē haššāmayîm*), and *mîtâ*

bîdē 'ādām. According to the rabbinic understanding of the Torah certain
transgressions are punishable by 'cutting off' (*kārēt*) or 'death at the hands
of heaven' (*mîtâ bîdē haššāmayîm*). Thirty-six of the transgressions
involved are listed in *m. Keritot* 1:1. The concept involved here is fraught
with legal and philosophical difficulties, but the basic idea is clear: in the
case of certain transgressions of the law regarded as meriting death, the
penalty is not exacted by the courts: this punishment is left to God, who
brings upon the wrongdoer premature death and does not allow him to
live out his allotted span of threescore years and ten. Other transgressions,
however, for which death is equally the penalty are judged by the courts,
and so belong to the category of *mîtâ bîdē 'ādām* – 'death at the hands of
man' (cf. *b. Sanhedrin* 89a).

(c) The distinction between *dînē māmônôt* and *dînē něpāšôt* (cf. *m.
Sanhedrin* 1:1; 1:4). This corresponds to some degree to the distinction
between private and criminal law. Both these categories fall under 'law
enforced by the courts' (i.e. under 'civil' as opposed to 'religious' law), but
there are differences between the two types of case: *dînē māmônôt*, as civil
actions, are brought by the private plaintiff, exercising self-help in the
defence of his rights; in the case of *dînē něpāšôt*, the wrongdoing is deemed
to constitute a public danger, and so the prosecution is brought by the
community or the state. The punishment in *dînē něpāšôt* is death, or
certain other forms of corporal punishment. The two types of case differ as
to gravity – a point emphasised by the fact that, according to rabbinic
opinion, *dînē māmônôt* can be tried by a court of three, whereas *dînē
něpāšôt* require a court of twenty-three.

(d) The distinction between *miṣwôt bēn 'ādām lě-'ādām* and *miṣwôt bēn
'ādām lě-māqôm* (cf. *m. Yoma* 8:9). This is a distinction between commandments which regulate behaviour between man and man, and those
which stipulate how a man should behave towards God. The distinction is
interesting, for in theory all *miṣwôt* are from God, and so ultimately are
'between man and God'. One might expect the distinction to be drawn in
order to emphasise the greater importance of the *miṣwôt bēn 'ādām lě-
māqôm*. This is not necessarily the case. At times the rabbis, with
characteristic acumen, use the distinction to emphasise the greater importance of the *miṣwôt bēn 'ādām lě-'ādām*. God is well able to look after
himself!

(e) Many other distinctions were doubtless drawn. Early modern Jewish
Reformers sharply differentiated the moral and the ritual laws in the
Torah – the former being absolute, the latter of only relative validity.
Despite what some Orthodox Jewish polemicists maintain, such a view is
by no means a modern innovation. Echoes of it can be found in earlier
Jewish sources. Rabbinic jurists sometimes draw a distinction between
legal norms and moral norms, in a way that seems to point up the
limitations of the law: 'If a man caused fire to break out at the hand of a
deaf-mute, an imbecile, or a minor, he is not culpable by the laws of man,
but he is culpable by the laws of heaven' (*m. Baba Qamma* 6:4). Paul in
Rom 2:14–16 expresses a profound distinction between natural and

revealed law – a distinction implicit also in rabbinic speculation on the cosmic Torah.[11] Paul in the same passage seems to presuppose a distinction between the moral and the ritual law, the former ranking higher than the latter. The *Minim* who were attacked by the rabbis for attaching too great importance to the ten commandments also may have made the same sort of distinction between moral and ritual law.[12] When Philo in the *De Decalogo* and the *De Specialibus Legibus* attempts to subsume the various laws under the decalogue he is advocating a rationalist solution to the problem of the *ṭaʿămē hammiṣwôt* which could easily be pushed in the direction of distinguishing the moral bases of the law from the concrete legislation, and perhaps to some extent setting one against the other.

So we could go on, but enough has been said to show that Jewish legalists thought long and hard about the nature of the law, and the result of their deliberations was a series of concepts which had the effect of breaking up the seamless text of the law and introducing important distinctions. The presence of these distinctions opens up the possibility of taking a more nuanced view of the law, of seeing some elements as more important than others. When considering criticism of the law it becomes necessary to ask precisely what aspect of the law is under attack, and how that aspect would have been regarded within the tradition. Particularly interesting is the line of thinking that distinguishes between the moral bases of the law and the actual, concrete legislation. That position could easily become the springboard for a radical critique of the law, the actual legislation being subjected to criticism for failing to embody adequately the norms of the moral law.

There is a *fifth* and *final* argument to be advanced in favour of the view that the Torah of Moses *simpliciter*, even in its civil aspects, would not have been wholly administered and enforced through the courts. It is an argument from historical analogy. In most societies the law as it stands on the statute-book, and the law as it is actually applied, are not precisely coextensive. A number of statutes, though not repealed, are to all intents and purposes held in abeyance and not enforced. There may be different reasons for this state of affairs: obsolescence may be a factor, or the constraint of more powerful law. The same must surely have been the case with the Pentateuch in the time of Jesus. For example, Exod 31:14 (cf. Num 15:32–6) lays down the death penalty for violations of the sabbath. It is surely unlikely that the courts in the time of Jesus tried to enforce that penalty systematically. By the time of Jesus the Torah of Moses in many of its parts was ancient law, which must have suffered some degree of obsolescence. It was also under the constraint of state law, which appears, among other things, to have denied the Jewish courts the *ius gladii*. Ancient Jewish legalists (unlike Islamic legalists with their concept of *naskh*) did not acknowledge a principle of abrogation. At times they came close to it, as when they allowed local custom to override the clear prescriptions of the Torah (see *m. Baba Meṣiʿa* 7:8). In general, however, the laws of Moses were not denied or abrogated. If obsolescent they were either ignored or else radically reinterpreted.

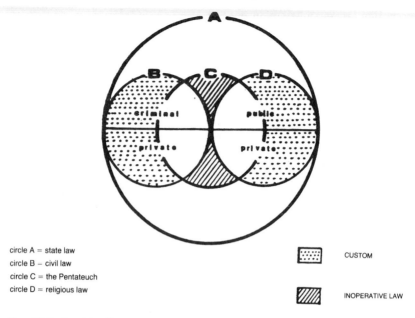

circle A = state law
circle B – civil law
circle C = the Pentateuch
circle D = religious law

☷ CUSTOM

▨ INOPERATIVE LAW

Figure 5.1 The four circles of law

SYNTHESIS: THE FOUR CIRCLES OF THE LAW   We have now introduced all the major elements necessary for a picture of Jewish law in
Palestine in the time of Jesus. Let us now take stock and see if these
elements can be synthesised into a coherent model. This I have attempted
to do in the accompanying diagram. Jewish law can be described in terms
of four interlocking circles. The framework of the law is defined by circle A,
which represents 'state law'. State law may be either Roman law, or the
law of the prince (Herod Antipas, to whom the Romans devolved some of
their power). Circle B represents 'civil law', in the broad sense of law
applied through the courts. This circle may be divided very roughly into
'criminal' and 'private' domains. Circle D is 'religious law' divided, again
roughly, into 'public' (largely concerned with the temple) and 'private'
(concerned with the conduct of personal piety). Both B and D are spheres of
actually applied law. They are made up of an element derived from the
Pentateuch (=the white segments of the circle), and non-pentateuchal
element (=the stippled areas), largely derived from custom. I have already
spoken of custom as a source for the augmentation of the Torah of Moses
in the matter of civil law. It should also be recognised that it was equally a
source for the augmentation of religious law. The fact that religious law
was not, for the most part, enforced through the courts does not mean that
jurists were uninterested in it. A case in point is *m. Keritot* 1:7, which
recounts how Simeon ben Gamaliel gave a ruling which brought about a
reduction in the cost of the sacrificial doves. The circle of the Pentateuch

(circle C) comprises two elements: the white segments represent the parts of the Pentateuch which were actually applied or observed; the hatched areas represent the inoperative parts. The relative proportions of these areas probably varied from time to time. After great national revivals, which seem often to have been marked by a return to the Torah of Moses, one would expect the hatched areas to have shrunk in size. In terms of rabbinic jurisprudence the three circles B C D effectively define the Torah: C *in toto* is *Tôrâ šeb-biktab*; the stippled areas of B D are *Tôrâ šeb-bĕᶜal peh*.

Two problems of the model should be noted. *First*, while circle A circumscribes the other three, and does so in the last analysis because state law constrained the Torah by *force majeure*, it would be possible to justify this subordination *from within* Jewish law. Though rabbinic jurists in principle did not recognise the right of Gentile courts to try Jewish cases, they did give limited recognition to the law of the state. This recognition was embodied in the famous dictum, attributed to the third-century Babylonian scholar Samuel, that 'the law of the state is the law' (*dînâ dĕ-malkûtâ dînâ*). The recognition was limited and did not apply to religious law (*'issûr wĕ-hetter*), but it was an important principle for resolving conflicts between Jewish and state law. Though the principle was never fully justified in rabbinic jurisprudence it would not be hard to do so along the lines that, if the state is essentially just, and in divine providence has been given rule over the Jews, there are no good grounds for not complying with its reasonable demands. These issues must have arisen in the time of Jesus. The way in which Jewish law defined its relationship to state law must have been a major legal problem. The effect of the *dînâ dĕ-malkûtâ dînâ* principle is to build into Jewish law an element of state law. State law and Jewish law form overlapping circles. It is hard to see how this could be represented on our model. A *second* deficiency of the model is that, although circle B denotes civil law administered through the courts, part of that 'civil' law might include matters (e.g. blasphemy or idolatry) which might be thought of as religious.

The model makes the Pentateuch the lynch-pin of the whole system of Jewish law. It is important to clarify what the centrality of the Pentateuch meant in the time of Jesus. The Torah of Moses was the national book of the Jews, a focus of the people's identity. Everyone would in some sense have acknowledged its authority, but different groups and individuals would have spelled out the meaning of that centrality differently. Each would have interpreted the actual words of the Torah in his own way.

There was widespread pride in the law. In writers such as Philo and Josephus this attitude has a clear apologetic setting. It was a definite advantage in the Roman world to be able to represent one's group as 'law-abiding' – the heirs of an ancient and noble constitution. This was one of the things which marked off civilised peoples from the barbarians.[13]

Zeal for the law is also a factor to be taken into account. At times of national crisis and renewal there were attempts to rally round the Torah of Moses, to put it back in the centre of life in a positive way, to enforce *all* its prescriptions. The reforms of Ezra and the Maccabees illustrate this phenomenon. But we do not know how successful in detail these attempts were, or how lasting their effects. Throughout the period there were always those motivated by zeal for the law, who would resort to pressure, even murder, to ensure its observance. There is evidence in Philo, Josephus and the Mishnah for the operation of lynch-law.[14] But the very presence of such zealots testifies eloquently to laxity in the observance of the law.

The centrality of the Pentateuch did not go unchallenged. There is an element of 'sectarianism' to be detected in the period. Works such as *Jubilees* and the Temple Scroll present themselves not as commentaries on the Pentateuch, but as supplements to it, possibly even as replacements for it. These writings appear to claim an inspiration and authority equal to that of the canonic text. They have important implications for our understanding of the process of canonisation in the second-temple period. Such writings were not, of course, universally recognised by Jews in the way in which the Torah of Moses was recognised; if they were not meant to displace the Pentateuch, they created an extended canon which would not have commanded universal assent. We have here incipient sectarianism. There were also potentially radical conclusions to be drawn from the idea current in some circles that the Torah of Moses would in some sense be superseded in the messianic age.[15]

It is not easy to define the centrality of the Pentateuch. Arguably the Pentateuch united Jews not as an agreed body of teaching or law, but as a symbol. To put it boldly there was no universally acknowledged body of laws at the heart of Judaism in the time of Jesus. Any generalisations to which all Jews would have assented would have been at such a level of abstraction as to have very little substantive content. The centrality of the Torah of Moses to Judaism was the centrality of a national flag. All Jews would have emotively rallied to it: each would have interpreted the meaning of the flag in his own way; each group would have had its own definition of what beliefs and practices constituted loyalty to the flag. Attacks on the Torah would have needed to have been of a gross and very sweeping kind to have been regarded as attacks on Judaism, as negations of the law. To put oneself beyond the pale, one would have had to spit on the flag in a very public and conspicuous way.

JESUS AND THE LAW   Has our analysis thrown any light on the problem of 'Jesus and the law'? In one sense the answer must be, No: we seem only to have succeeded in muddying the waters. The problems of discovering what Jesus actually said on legal matters were already well known. We have now added a fresh set of problems related to the definition of the law! Some issues have, however, become a little clearer.

(1) The question of Jesus and the law should take into account Jewish law in all its aspects, not just the Pentateuch. It should, in fact, cover all four of our interlocking circles, including the circle of state law, on the grounds that the relationship of state law to Jewish law is a major issue of *Jewish* law. Ed Sanders rightly remarks that the subject of Jesus and the temple tends to be left out of discussions of Jesus and the law, as though the

temple and its rituals were not governed by law.[16] But many other aspects of Jewish law are also ignored. Jewish law was made up not only of the laws of the Pentateuch, but of a mass of traditions and customs, hallowed by use, some of which, being of considerable antiquity, were actually held to be Mosaic in origin. To discriminate from the outset between the various circles, and to identify the law simply with the Pentateuch, is tendentious.

(2) There is a quantity of material in the Gospels relating to all four circles of law. For example, the story of Jesus and the tribute money (Matt 22:15–22; Mark 12:13–17; Luke 20:20–6) impinges on circle A; Jesus and the temple tax (Matt 17:24–7; cf. Exod 30:11–16; 38:26) touches on circles C and D; the debate on divorce (Matt 19:3–9; Mark 10:2–12; cf. Deut 24:1–4), on circles B and C; the dispute over hand-washing (Matt 15:1–20; Mark 7:1–22) on circle D. I am not convinced that we can, or indeed should, derive from this material a coherent *general* view of the law. It is questionable whether such a view can be extracted even from the antitheses in Matthew 5. And if Jesus did take up a radical position *vis-à-vis* the Torah of Moses, it is open to interpretation what this stance would have entailed. He would hardly have been unique in his time. It is unlikely that his views would have been more radical than those implied by *Jubilees* or the Temple Scroll.

(3) It is important to take a nuanced view of Jewish law in the time of Jesus. In principle the Torah was uniformly divine. In practice all kinds of distinctions were recognised which cut across the seamless fabric of the Torah. All the commandments were not on the same level: like the rabbis, many in the time of Jesus must have distinguished between 'lighter precepts' and 'weightier precepts' (*miṣwôt qallôt* and *miṣwôt ḥămûrôt*) (cf. *m. Ḥullin* 12:5). The implications of denial or abrogation would, therefore, have varied from law to law. The situation would have been further complicated by the fact that there would have been no consensus on what constitutes 'weightier' and 'lighter'. It might be tempting to find a way through the problem along the lines of the rabbinic distinction between *dĕ-'oraytâ* (rules expressly stated in the Pentateuch) and *dĕ-rabbānan* (enactments or decrees of the scholars). It might be argued that while one might sit rather loose to what was *dĕ-rabbānan*, what was *dĕ-'ōraytâ* had to be strictly observed. This approach would once again make Jesus' attitude to the Pentateuch the central issue. But there are problems here too. As rabbinic jurists found, there is no easy way to define what is *dĕ-'ōraytâ* and what is *dĕ-rabbānan*. To which category do interpretations of pentateuchal laws belong? Moreover, the rabbis in general treated their own enactments as having the force of pentateuchal law, and at times even enforced them more rigorously than pentateuchal law. NT scholars tend to accept a narrow, party-political, essentially 'zealot' definition of the law: the Torah of Moses (=the Pentateuch) is absolutely central to Judaism; its laws are eternally valid and none should remain inoperative; to deny or abrogate one is to deny or abrogate the whole. But this is only one of a number of possible Jewish views; to elevate it to the status of

Judaism is a fundamental misjudgement. In modern times it would be equivalent to identifying the Ayatollah Khomeini's views with Islam!

(4) Jewish law in the time of Jesus was a complex phenomenon. Our analysis should have proved that, if it proved nothing else. Whether taken at its broadest, or its narrowest, it is full of inconsistency and even contradiction. It is not a coherent, highly unified body of legislation or doctrine. Given this fact it becomes difficult, if not impossible, to lay down a normative base-line from which to measure Jesus' deviance from, or conformity to, Judaism in general, or the law in particular. The whole problem of Jesus and the law, as traditionally framed, may be misconceived. Realistically we can compare Jesus' views on the law only with those of other Jews of his time. Jesus' views may have annoyed or alarmed powerful people, and so may have led to his prosecution and death, but we should refrain from making the views of those people normative, or of turning them into 'Judaism'. It is one thing to say that Jesus offended the priests in Jerusalem, and was killed for it: that would be a reasonable historical judgement. It is another to say that the handful of legal points on which he may (or may not) have pronounced constitute (implicitly or explicitly) a 'refutation/abrogation' of the Torah of Moses, or lead to a 'transformation' of Judaism: that is a theological assertion beyond all historical proof or disproof.

Part II

The law in the Jesus tradition

6

ALL FOODS CLEAN: THOUGHTS ON JESUS AND THE LAW

BARNABAS LINDARS SSF

A CRUCIAL SAYING   'There is nothing outside a man which by going into him can defile him; but the things which come out of a man are what defile him' (Mark 7:15). This saying has figured very prominently in discussion of Jesus and the law, and my reason for taking it up again is that it makes a focus for a number of crucial issues.[1] In the first place, it is a rare instance in the teaching of Jesus where it can be claimed that Jesus not only sought to radicalise the law by reaching to the heart of it and inculcating its inner spirit, but also appears to have denied the law as such. Leviticus 11 states plainly that to eat the flesh of a long list of unclean creatures causes defilement, and Jesus' words directly contradict this. This raises the question whether he intended to abolish the law, or even to give a new law. Related to this issue is the question why Jesus incurred the opposition of the scribes and Pharisees, which figures so prominently in the Synoptic tradition.

Secondly, the saying of Mark 7:15 has an obvious bearing on the question of the Jewish food laws in general, and this gave rise to a critical issue in the early history of the Church in connection with the admission of Gentiles. It is the subject of a sharp division between Paul and Peter at Antioch according to Gal 2:11–14. It is contended that the trouble would never have arisen if this saying of Jesus had been known to them.[2]

But then, thirdly, it is also claimed that Paul actually refers to this saying in Rom 14:14, when he gives instructions to the Romans on matters of food.[3]

These observations lead, fourthly, to the fundamental question of the

Church and the law. It is clear that the first Christians continued to observe the law. This is strange if Jesus had intended to abrogate it. Were his words not heeded until Paul rescued Christianity from legalism and set it on its true path of a spiritual and universal religion? Or did his closest friends fail to understand his teaching, as Mark indeed so often implies? Or did he on the other hand intend to reinforce the law without any expectation of a wider application of his teaching to the Gentiles? And if so, is not this saying incompatible with such a policy? Finally, what bearing does this saying, if authentic, have upon Christian understanding today?

In what follows I shall argue that the saying should be accepted as authentic, in spite of doubts that have been expressed on this subject recently. It will then be necessary to estimate its bearing on the question of Jesus' attitude to the law. Here I shall side with much modern scholarship in denying that Jesus had any intention of overthrowing it. The opposition of the scribes and Pharisees must be seen in the light of this. I shall then suggest reasons why the saying, though available, did not figure in the controversy over relationships between Jewish and Gentile converts. At this point I will return to the transmission-history of the saying, and this will allow a comment on the possible allusion to it in Rom 14:14. I shall conclude with a brief indication of the wider implications of this study.

THE ORIGINAL FORM   The question of authenticity is always in danger of becoming a circular argument. On general grounds it can be claimed, as has recently been done by Räisänen, that the saying belongs to the controversy about the food laws in the early Church, and therefore it cannot be authentic, because that is the setting in which it arose.[4] Similarly E. P. Sanders, though differing from Räisänen on a number of points, holds that the trouble at Antioch described in Gal 2.11–14 could have been settled once and for all by appeal to this saying, so that it cannot be accepted as genuine.[5] But it is the relationship between the transmission and interpretation of the saying and these controversies which has to be investigated. It needs to be examined first for what it is in itself before this can be established.

The form of the saying is a *māšāl* of the type of antithetic couplet. It thus has a Semitic character, though that in itself does not prove that it was actually composed in Aramaic. Paschen has paid particular attention to the possibility of an Aramaic original.[6] He argues that the commentary on the saying which follows in verses 17–23 includes the whole saying in a form that is likely to be closer to the underlying Aramaic. These verses give an exposition of the saying, in which the two parts of the couplet are treated separately. The Markan redaction can be easily stripped off.[7] When this is done we are left with the pre-Markan composition, consisting of text, 'Whatever goes into a man from outside cannot defile him' (18b), with the exegesis, 'for it enters, not his heart but his stomach, and so passes out into the latrine' (19a), and then the second part of the text, 'What comes out of a man is what defiles a man' (20b), with the exegesis, 'for out of the heart of man come evil thoughts, fornication, theft, murder, adultery, coveting, wickedness, deceit, licentiousness, envy, slander, pride, foolishness' (21–2).

It will be appreciated that this pre-Markan composition is a genuine example of a Christian *midrash* (a term often used loosely and incorrectly by NT scholars), in which a saying from the Jesus tradition is provided with a commentary, as if it were a biblical text. As such, it is not really possible to take the exegesis back to Jesus himself, in spite of the pleas of Stephen Westerholm.[8] In fact, as we shall see, the exegesis is too obvious to be an inseparable part of the saying, which gains from being detached from the exegesis. Westerholm is right, on the other hand, to claim that this is a pregnant saying, and to take this fact as a criterion of probable authenticity.[9]

Paschen reconstructs the text by taking the two parts from verses 18b and 20b, and inserting 'but' from the form in verse 15. Räisänen objects that this makes the foundation text in verse 15 less Semitic than the form which is based upon it, which weakens the case for authenticity. He also points out that Matthew's version of verse 15 is the most Semitic of them all (Matt 15:11).[10] He further finds fault with Paschen (quite rightly in my opinion) in his decision to exclude the verbs 'goes in' and 'comes out' from the original form of the saying on the grounds that they are unnecessary and typical of Mark's tendency to pleonasm,[11] in spite of the fact that they are present in all the forms of the saying as we now have it and are essential to the commentary of verses 19a and 21. This criticism should be accepted.

The other observation, that the derived forms of the saying give a more Semitic impression than verse 15 itself, is however misleading. Matthew's version of verse 15 is a typical Matthean conflation, using the text of verses 18 and 20, which are then subsequently abbreviated.[12] My own attempt to retranslate verse 15 into Aramaic produced a text which I *then* discovered was represented more literally in verses 18b and 20b. This applied to three details: *ouden* ('nothing') requires the negative plus 'all' (cf. 18 *pan . . . ou*); the singular is required for 'the things which come out' (cf. 20, where singular is used); and the verb 'are' (Greek *estin*, following neuter plural) requires representation by the pronoun (cf. 20 *ekeino*).[13] These in fact are the only significant differences between the two forms of the saying. It can thus be concluded that verse 15 is a slightly polished version of the saying, which is best preserved in verses 18b and 20b.

The explanation of this is simple. Mark's source must have contained the whole text of the saying, which was then reproduced in its two parts separately for the sake of the exegesis. This arrangement is comparable to the Qumran commentaries. In making use of this material, Mark has polished the saying, but left it untouched in the commentary. It is notable that *pan . . . ou* is not characteristic of Mark, whereas *ouden* is common.[14] Mark also prefers the plural to the collective singular, and indeed we have another example of this in the summary verse 23, which in my view belongs to Mark's editing.[15] Finally the resumptive use of *ekeino* after *casus pendens* occurs only here in Mark.[16]

We thus have a saying with a very clear Semitic character, and this is one criterion in favour of authenticity. In addition it possesses the criterion of dissimilarity. It is obvious that, at least in its surface meaning, it is dissimilar to normal Jewish teaching.[17] But in so far as ostensibly it is an attack on the Jewish distinction between clean and unclean foods, it does not fit the earliest period of the Aramaic-speaking Church. A Christian parallel has to wait until after the controversy over the admission of Gentiles, which began in the Hellenistic expansion of the Church. At the same time the saying passes the test of coherence, for it is consistent with other sayings of Jesus concerning the law and the *halakah*, as we shall see as we now turn to the interpretation of it.

MARK 7:15 AS LANGUAGE-EVENT   Mark 7:15 is particularly important, because it is a case where Jesus appears to overthrow the law itself. Most of his strictures are directed against pharisaic insistence on customs which had only recently grown up, such as the washing of hands before eating and the washing of the outside of pots before use, which are at issue in the larger context of Mark 7:1–23.[18] It seems to be agreed that these customs, which are not mentioned in the law, had won wide acceptance among devout Jews, as they reduced the risk that food might contract uncleanness through accidental contact with impurity. They were not specifically pharisaic rulings, but they were promoted by the Pharisees in their efforts to promote a high standard of observance of the law. I am assuming that the Pharisees were a lay movement, striving to encourage a priestly style of purity among the common people.[19] This, however, was not at all the way of Jesus. His teaching on purity is directed to the inward purity of the heart, and he appears to regard the rules as a hindrance rather than a help.

On this basis it can be argued that he wished to promote the law, but opposed the multiplication of rules in the oral tradition supported by the Pharisees. Our present saying, however, is concerned with clearly enunciated provisions of the written law itself. Unlike the 'antitheses' of the Sermon on the Mount, it does not confirm the law, while going beyond it to the interior motive. It implicitly denies that the food laws of Leviticus 11 have any relevance for personal holiness before God. It thus belongs with the divorce pericope of Mark 10:2–9, in which Jesus appears to abrogate the law of divorce of Deut 24:1–4.

However, the mere fact that these are the only two sayings of Jesus which show him overthrowing the law should make us cautious. The interpretation of the divorce pericope is nearly always taken in this sense because of its long-standing connection with the prohibition against divorce in the Church, starting with the clear statement of Paul, probably based on it, in 1 Cor 7:10. But if we put aside these considerations and view Mark's story for what it is in itself, it is at once apparent that the case is a trap, and Jesus would have walked straight into it if he had denied the law outright. It is presupposed by his opponents that he teaches a high doctrine of marital fidelity and disapproves of divorce, just like the prophet Malachi before him (cf. Mal 2:15–16). The opponents therefore try to trap him into direct denial of the law by adducing Deut 24:1–4, which presupposes that divorce is permissible in certain circumstances. Jesus places the issue in the more fundamental context of God's intention in the institution of marriage, quoting Gen 1:27 and 2:24 from the law itself. Thus without denying the law he maintains his basic contention that the permission of Deut 24:1–4 morally ought not to be used.[20]

The saying of Mark 7:15 should be interpreted similarly. The clue to a proper assessment of it is the subtlety and ambiguity of it. It has the irony which is such a striking feature of those sayings of Jesus which are most likely to be authentic.[21] Everything depends on the meaning of 'defile' (*koinoō*). All modern commentators reject the view, derived from verse 19, that it refers to uncleanness in a physical sense.[22] In a Jewish setting it would certainly be understood metaphorically in terms of ceremonial uncleanness. It is important to remember that this was not merely a convention, but an ancient taboo, which could operate at a deep level of personal consciousness. Transgresssion of the taboo not only constitutes a formal disqualification for worship, requiring the proper procedure to restore the situation, but also stains the inner conscience, creating a barrier in one's personal relationship with God. Originally this inner barrier of the religious consciousness and the outer expression of it in formal regulations are indivisible. But in an advanced society the two can split apart, creating the familiar contrast between inward and outward religion.[23]

Now in the first part of Mark 7:15 the hearer receives the immediate impression that Jesus is flatly denying the ceremonial law of defilement. It would be likely to cause consternation to promoters of the law, such as the scribes and Pharisees. It would be shocking especially to the genuinely devout, whose religious conscience was tender and who observed the law with real feeling. At the same time it is calculated to arouse a quite unjustified sense of self-satisfaction among the 'sinners', those people who deliberately flouted the law for pragmatic reasons, and with whom Jesus himself was dangerously familiar.[24]

But then the second part of the saying completely changes the terms of reference. If Jesus is not referring here to bodily discharges, he can only mean the sort of evil actions which are listed in the exposition of the saying in verses 21–2. Defilement is now being used to denote the effect of breaking fellowship with God through consenting to evil intentions and allowing them to proceed in evil deeds. The concept of defilement is thus changed. From the point of view of the devout it gives warning that this kind of defilement is the 'real' defilement, so that it points to a revision of the scale of spiritual values. On the other hand the 'sinners' are not let off the hook, because their carelessness with regard to ceremonial purity is not condoned if it is done with evil in the heart, which is the real defilement. Consequently the saying only appears to deny the law of clean and unclean foods. In fact, for the careless it is likely to encourage them to pay greater attention to their spiritual condition, and may well bring about a better attempt at observance of the law, precisely because it is concerned with inner renewal. On the other hand, Jesus is clearly not concerned with the law for its own sake. His interest is purity of heart, and he is prepared to waive the law when occasion demands.

It will be seen that Mark has quite rightly called this saying a 'parable' (*parabolē*).[25] It is more than an aphorism or *chreia*.[26] Like all the best parables, it constitutes a 'language-event', i.e. it effects a change in the hearer's understanding.[27] It does this by the subtle shift in the concept of defilement which takes place in the two halves of the saying. With regard to the law itself it is ambiguous. It appears to deny the validity of the distinction between clean and unclean foods, but by altering the concept of defilement it becomes possible to see the first half entirely in terms of spiritual defilement, therefore leaving the distinction with regard to ceremonial uncleanness intact. Superficially it denies a proposition of the law, but actually it can have the effect of promoting a more deeply religious observance of it. This is because it operates at a deeper level than obedience or disobedience to the written code.

It is not to be supposed that all Jesus' hearers understood this kind of parabolic saying or perceived the real genius of his teaching-method. In this particular example the main thrust is clear enough. But is it intended to weaken the law or even to make a mockery of it? From the point of view of the scribes and Pharisees, trying hard to promote religious observance among the common people, Jesus was making very dangerous statements. It was bad enough that he associated with those whose disregard of many facets of the law was most scandalous. But to teach apparently that the law was wrong was intolerable. If this is what the authorities feared, we can see why the Gospel tradition features attempts to trap Jesus into a definite denial of the law, as in the case of the divorce pericope. This and the various sabbath controversies suggest that the authorities were extremely worried by reports of Jesus' teaching, and did not know what to make of it. The stories naturally show Jesus winning the argument without falling into the trap. It is likely that these traditions owe their currency to the Church's subsequent controversy over the law, and so there is a natural tendency to present them in such a way as to suggest that the law is superseded. But this makes it all the more striking that Jesus is never represented as saying so. The ambiguity in his sayings always remains. The ironical style of his teaching, leaving many hearers guessing, seems to me to be the historic fact that lies behind the accusation that he was 'leading the people astray'. This is referred to in John 7:12 and is known from Jewish sources.[28] Though this does not appear in the trial tradition, it is likely to have been a contributory factor leading to his arrest.[29]

CONTROVERSY AT ANTIOCH   We are now in a position to understand why this saying, and others like it, apparently had no influence on the question of the law in earliest Christianity, and were not appealed to in the beginning of the Judaistic controversy. The first Christians quite rightly did not assume that Jesus had intended to overthrow the law. The opposition of the Pharisees was in their view unjustified. On the contrary, seriously taking to heart the intention of the sayings, they would be likely to obey the law more carefully. At the same time they could exercise a certain freedom in situations where there was a clash between the letter and the spirit of the law. The Jewish–Christian Church, as represented by Matthew at a later date, retained the law, but with a proper regard for Jesus' teaching. Matthew twice quotes Hos 6:6, each time clearly adding it himself to his source: 'For I desire steadfast love and not sacrifice, the knowledge of God, rather than burnt offerings' (cf. Matt 9:13; 12:7). The parallel 'rather than' shows that 'and not' is not exclusive.[30] Matthew thus defends Jesus' apparent departures from the law on grounds which are a legitimate reflection of Jesus' teaching. So also Luke in the early chapters of Acts represents the Jerusalem church as a law-abiding group. Under the leadership of James the Lord's brother it had to take special care not to alienate possible converts in Jerusalem, especially after the affair of the Hellenists (Acts 6–7) and the expansion of the Church in the diaspora and the admission of Gentiles into its fellowship.

In this connection it is significant that, as Haenchen has pointed out,[31] in the story of the conversion of Cornelius, Peter's vision, in which he is invited to eat unclean beasts (Acts 10:10–16), and the complaint of the circumcision party that he had eaten with Gentiles (Acts 11:3) do not lead to the conclusion that the food laws have been abrogated, but that Gentiles may be admitted to Christian fellowship.

These facts must be borne in mind as we return to Gal 2:1–14, where it appears that eating with Gentiles is a critical issue. Westerholm cites evidence that 'Jewish observance of the dietary laws distinguishing clean and unclean foods was widespread and non-sectarian, in the diaspora as well as in Palestine.'[32] He then continues, 'It is clear, moreover, that Gentiles were considered unclean, and it was not only Pharisees and Essenes who refused to associate with them.' It seems to me that the eucharist must have posed a special problem from this point of view, because its religious character would make for observance of purity rules even in situations where there was comparatively free association with Gentiles. Paul in Galatians implies that the Christians at Antioch joined together for a common meal, and this could well have included the eucharist, though he does not say so.[33] Peter, who was visiting the church, had joined in the common meal, but drew back when the circumcision party arrived from Jerusalem and raised objections. Worse still, 'even Barnabas', who had been Paul's colleague on equal terms in setting up the mixed community at Antioch, 'was carried away by their insincerity' (Gal 2:13).

Here again the real issue turns out to be the status of the Gentile converts. Paul points to the inconsistency of Peter. First he was willing, 'though a Jew, to live like a Gentile and not like a Jew', but now he appeared to want to 'compel the Gentiles to live like Jews' (2:14). I take this to mean to be circumcised, and not simply to adopt Jewish customs with regard to food. Thus Peter's withdrawal is not just because of fear of contracting uncleanness from Gentile contact, which previously did not bother him, but because of a more fundamental objection to the existence of a mixed Christian community. The Judaisers wish the Gentile converts to place themselves formally under the conditions of Jewish life, or else to remain a separate community.

This also explains the apparent inconsistency between the demands of these men from James and what had been agreed with James during Paul's visit to Jerusalem, recorded in Gal 2:9. On that occasion the mission of Paul and Barnabas to the Gentiles was fully approved, but James, Peter and John were to continue their mission to the circumcised. Paul and Barnabas, and even Peter himself, thought this did not exclude mixed communities, but the representatives from James evidently thought otherwise. The vacillation of Peter and Barnabas is accounted for if the Jerusalem concordat was not clear enough on the subject, and so was open to both interpretations.[34] We need to remember the great pressure on the Jerusalem church at this time to show itself beyond reproach in fidelity to the law, and the damaging effect of reports from the centres of Christian mission upon the delicate relationship between the Church and the Jerusalem authorities.

If this is a correct estimate of the situation in Antioch, it is easy to see that the kind of freedom allowed by the ambiguity of sayings of Jesus such as Mark 7:15 could not be decisive. Peter observed the spirit of Jesus' teaching, and there is no need to suggest that he did not know it or failed to accept it. But he simply did not perceive it in terms of abrogation of the law, and this was right, because Jesus did not intend it to mean that anyway. The really fundamental threat to the law in the teaching of Jesus was contained in his attitude to the temple and its cultus, and this surfaced in the affair of Stephen and the Hellenists.[35] As this is a large subject in its own right, I will not pursue it here, except to point out that it gave the initial warrant for the inclusion of the Gentiles on the grounds that it was Christ's death that provided atonement for sins rather than the sacrificial system. It is obvious that this really downgrades all the rest of the laws of purity and holiness, so that the tendency to laxity is liable to follow. This is the very thing that James and the Jerusalem church feared after the furore aroused by Stephen. Paul's insistence on the freedom of the Gentile converts from the Jewish law is argued on the basis of the meaning of Christ's death, and thus stems from the central position of the Hellenists and not from ambiguous sayings of Jesus himself.

TRANSMISSION AND INFLUENCE OF MARK 7:15   This takes us back to the transmission of Mark 7:15. Though the commentary in verses 18–22 belongs to a later time, it is safe to assume that it correctly indicates the interpretation which ensured the preservation of the saying. The negative statement of the first part is quickly disposed of, and so the emphasis falls on the second part, with its long list of vices that proceed from the human heart. This was the important thing from Jesus' own point of view, because, as we have seen, it is the second part which provides the criterion for a fresh understanding of defilement in the first part, and so makes the saying a language-event. There is no reason to doubt that this genuinely religious value of the saying was the original reason for its inclusion in an early catechetical collection.

It is not, of course, possible to trace where this happened. But at some stage, most probably in a diaspora situation, the saying was elucidated with the commentary incorporated in Mark 7:18b–19a, 20b–22 before it came to Mark. The exposition shows no awareness of the issue of food laws, and so seems likely to belong to a situation in which this was not relevant, presumably a Gentile church. The list of vices in the second part of the commentary has been shown by Vincent Taylor to approximate more closely to such lists in Paul than in any other part of the NT.[36] The same list appears partially at the start of the description of 'the way of death' in *Didache* 5:1, but that may well be dependent on Matthew's version of our passage (Matt 15:19).[37] That the author was familiar with the passage as a whole is evident from *Didache* 14:2 in connection with the eucharist: 'Let not anyone who has a quarrel with his fellow be included in your assembly, so that your sacrifice may not be defiled.'

For Mark, however, the passage had particular value for his attempt to portray the controversy between Jesus and the scribes and Pharisees. To him, Jesus' ambiguous statements, which were designed to compel attention to the spirit with which the law was to be performed, showed up the hollowness and hypocrisy of pharisaic attitudes. By contrast, Jesus preached a universal religion, not bound by such restrictions. Thus Mark uses this saying with its commentary as the climax of the sequence on pharisaic religion.[38] He underlines the point that, as a result of the saying, the food laws no longer apply by making an addition to his source at verse 19b: 'Making all foods clean'. Here the majority reading of the oldest manuscripts is unquestionably right, according to which 'making clean' is masculine, and therefore Jesus is the subject and the phrase is a parenthesis, as indicated by RSV: '(Thus he declared all foods clean.)'[39] This has been inserted by Mark as his own comment on the logical implication of Jesus' words.[40]

Mark's special interest in clarifying this point is explained by the following pericope of the healing of the Syrophoenician woman's daughter (Mark 7:24–30). By this act Jesus allows this Gentile to partake of 'the children's bread', by which Jewish rules of purity are symbolised.[41] The episode is intended to be a pointer to the Gentile mission of the Church.

It thus seems that Mark at least was aware of the relevance of the saying to the policy of Paul in the Gentile Church. At a later stage we get a further application to the Church's mission in *Thomas* 14, where it seems to suggest that missionaries should not be hampered by scruples about food:

> And if you go into any land and travel in the regions, if they receive you, eat what they set before you. Heal the sick who are among them. For what will go into your mouth will not defile you, but what comes out of your mouth, that is what will defile you.[42]

Can we also see the influence of the saying in Paul? As already mentioned, it is frequently claimed to be the reference of his statement in Rom 14:14 that 'I know and am persuaded in the Lord Jesus that nothing is unclean (*ouden koinon*) of itself; but it is unclean for anyone who thinks it is unclean.' Räisänen refuses to allow dependence on the saying here.[43] He says that the formula 'persuaded in the Lord Jesus' is not an indication of reliance on the Jesus tradition; that where, as in 1 Corinthians 7, Paul explicitly refers to a saying of Jesus (in fact, the divorce saying!) he gives it prominence, whereas here it is an additional consideration; and that the meagre verbal connection (only *ouden koinon*) could equally be claimed for verse 20b, where 'all [foods; cf. 20a] are clean' has the vocabulary of Mark 7:19b, which would then make Paul dependent on words which we have excluded as Mark's own redaction long after Paul was writing. It must also be granted that *ouden koinon* itself relates more closely to Mark's polished version of the saying in Mark 7:15, rather than the more original *pan . . . ou* of verse 18.

These considerations certainly weaken the possibility of direct dependence on the saying as we have it, but should not be taken to imply (as Räisänen does) that it did not exist. Paul's definite appeal to the teaching of Jesus on divorce (1 Cor 7:10) provides no clear verbal links with the sayings in the synoptic tradition. We should reckon with the oral tradition, with its tendency to split into a variety of forms, rather than a fixed verbal formula.[44] Paul's statement in Rom 14:14 reproduces the general tenor of his understanding of Jesus' saying, but significantly without raising the subject of the law. The whole chapter is carefully composed for general application without confining the issue to Jewish law. It is just as much concerned with other scruples over food.[45] It has nothing at all to do with the fundamental argument about the Judaistic controversy which has been the great issue all through Romans 1–11.

This observation reinforces the view expressed above that the saying of Mark 7:15 played no part in the trouble at Antioch recorded in Galatians 2 or in the Judaistic controversy as a whole. It was not seen to be relevant, because it was not understood as an attack on the law. Peter's lax behaviour at Antioch before the arrival of the circumcision party could, of course, be justified from this saying, and must surely have owed much to his intimate knowledge of the practice of Jesus himself. But the reason for his withdrawal from Gentile fellowship was the insistence of the visitors from James that Gentile converts should Judaise properly. This was not covered by the Jesus tradition, because the possibility of Gentile membership was not even raised then. There was no compelling guidance already available, and the issue had to be solved in relation to the new circumstances that had arisen.[46]

Similarly the apostolic decrees of Acts 15:29 show no appeal to the teaching of Jesus.[47] Some minimal regulations are there laid down, which presumably could ease the situation in mixed congregations. It is not assumed that Jesus had said something that would sweep away the food laws once and for all, though that is how Mark saw it when he edited the *midrash* on the saying.

Räisänen explains the failure to appeal to Mark 7:15 by the simple suggestion that the saying did not exist. In his view it was a product of the controversy, and should not be regarded as an authentic item of the Jesus tradition. In this article I have tried to show that this conclusion is both unnecessary and wrong. The sayings of Jesus on the law belong to a situation in which the abolition of the law is not in anyone's mind. Mark 7:15, or rather the original form of it surviving in verses 18b and 20b, is derived from an Aramaic saying which splendidly focuses the real points at issue. Jesus arouses interest by appearing superficially to deny an aspect of the law itself. But the saying is a parable, which so often in the case of Jesus is a language-event. The law-abiding are warned to rethink their concept of defilement. The 'sinners' are warned that they too may be guilty of the real defilement. Whether the law should be maintained or not is not the real issue.

It seems to me that the influence of this saying in earliest Christianity has been wildly exaggerated. Vincent Taylor claims that, 'In laying down the principle that uncleanness comes from within, and not from without, it stated a truth, uncommon in contemporary Judaism, which was destined to free Christianity from legalism.'[48] The work of E. P. Sanders has finally scotched the caricature of Judaism which lies behind these words.[49] Moreover the saying really did nothing to 'free Christianity from legalism'. That was a much more complex story.

What the saying does do, in my opinion, is to illustrate the real genius of Jesus as a religious teacher. I think that we tend to forget that his greatness lay not only in what he said, but in the way he said it. It was his capacity to open up religious understanding and to force his hearers to face basic realities which was the important thing. This was done with a teasing irony which intrigued his hearers and made his words stick in their minds, or at least the gist of what he said. The irony of this particular saying chimes in with the irony that appears in what I regard as the only Son of Man sayings that can claim to be authentic.[50] In both cases we are presented with a Jesus whose power over his audience begins to become explicable, and turns out to be extraordinarily attractive. At the same time the consternation and anxiety which he aroused in the scribes and Pharisees finds a natural explanation. Finally, as Dunn has been especially concerned to point out, the tradition history of the saying shows successive reinterpretations in relation to the issue of Gentile Christianity at a crucial period of the Church's history. Thus the value of this saying is not merely in its substance, which remains valid in any religious context and has lost nothing of its relevance to human life in the present day, but also in its illustrative usefulness in the recovery of the Jesus of history, whose influence broke through the confines of Judaism to create a universal religion.

7

JESUS' DEMONSTRATION IN THE TEMPLE

RICHARD BAUCKHAM

INTRODUCTION   As E. P. Sanders has recently commented, 'It is one of the curiosities of research on the question of Jesus and Judaism that Jesus' sayings and actions with regard to the temple are often separated from his attitude towards the law.'[1] In fact, of course, Jesus' attitude to the temple must be seen as an integral part of the question of his attitude to the law. The so-called 'cleansing of the temple' therefore gains a potentially greater significance than has often been seen in it, and the prominence it gains in Sanders' own reconstruction of Jesus' relation to the Judaism of his day[2] shows how much may hang on the interpretation of this event.

The traditional term 'cleansing of the temple' is doubly misleading. In the first place, it may suggest that Jesus' concern was with the ritual purity of the temple, as in the case of the purifications of the temple by the Maccabees and the Zealots.[3] But, secondly, the term suggests that Jesus actually accomplished a purification of the temple, whereas most recent treatments of the episode recognise that Jesus could have intended only a symbolic action, a kind of prophetic 'demonstration'. As Sanders says, it was 'a gesture intended to make a point rather than to have a concrete result'.[4] What interpreters who take this view are not agreed on is the significance of this 'demonstration'. In particular, since the authenticity of the interpretative sayings in Mark 11:17 and John 2:16 is widely disputed, it is peculiarly difficult to be sure of the meaning of Jesus' actions. Most interpreters assume that Jesus enacted a prophetic protest against, or denunciation of, the activities of the moneychangers and the sellers of sacrificial animals, with perhaps also the implication of announcing judgement on the temple for these abuses. But these interpreters disagree on what it was that Jesus saw as objectionable in these activities. Recently, Sanders, concluding that Jesus could not have seen anything objectionable in them, has understood his action as a symbolic prophecy of the destruction (not judgement) of the temple, prior to its restoration as the eschatological temple.

The present paper attempts a fresh approach to the problem, by using a clue which has gone surprisingly unnoticed in previous discussion: Jesus' view of the temple tax in Matt 17:24–7.

JESUS AND THE TEMPLE TAX (MATT 17:24–7) This paper presupposes a full study of Matt 17:24–7 which I have published elsewhere.[5] In that context I have argued in detail for the authenticity of Matt 17:25–6 as Jesus' comment on the temple tax, and I regard that case for authenticity as strong enough to provide a basis for the argument of the present paper.[6] Unfortunately, that argument for authenticity cannot be repeated here, but a summary of my proposed interpretation of the saying is needed.

Matt 17:24–7 concerns the payment of the temple tax, which was an annual payment of a half-shekel or didrachmon, due from every adult male Jew, to finance sacrificial worship in the temple. Though probably of comparatively recent origin,[7] in current interpretation it was regarded as a tax instituted by Moses (Exod 30:11–16; cf. 38:25–6; 2 Chr 24:5–7). It is important to emphasise that it was regarded as a *tax*, not a voluntary contribution.[8] It was legally required from all adult males, with no allowance for poverty (except that a poor man's tax could be charitably paid by another). The Mishnah's regulations about it may be somewhat idealised, and we do not know how far the powers it grants the tax collectors to distrain the goods of those who could not pay (*m. Šeqalim* 1:3) were actually enforced. But it is likely that the Mishnah accurately preserves the pre-70 *concept* of the tax, as a legal imposition which could in principle be enforced at law. Moreover, it was conceived very directly as a tax levied by and paid to God.[9] The pharisaic ideal was that the tax enabled the people to *participate* in the daily sacrificial worship of the temple by helping to finance it,[10] and doubtless prosperous Jews, like those in the diaspora whose temple-tax contributions are mentioned by Philo and Josephus,[11] readily shared this view. But in first-century Palestine, where the level of taxation seems to have been perceived as burdensome, the temple tax could easily appear, to the ordinary person struggling to make ends meet, just one more financial demand, which aligned the temple theocracy with other forms of oppressive government.

Matt 17:25 is a metaphorical or parabolic saying in which Jesus takes up the common Jewish belief that God is both king and father to his people, a belief which is everywhere presupposed in Jesus' own teaching. He therefore compares God with 'the kings of the earth' (earthly kings, by contrast with the heavenly king, God) who are also fathers to their own families. When earthly kings levy taxation, do they tax their own children or the rest of their subjects? Of course, their own children are exempt from taxation (verse 26). Thus, in the matter of taxation, the father–son relation takes precedence over the king–subject relation. The implication is that this is also true of God in relation to Israel, who are not just his subjects but his *sons*. Theocratic taxation, levied in God's name, is inappropriate in view of God's fatherhood.[12]

Thus Jesus' objection to the temple tax is a radical objection to the very principle of theocratic taxation. He does not argue the point by means of halakic discussion of the scriptural passages regarded as requiring the temple tax, as the Qumran community did in their less radical disagreement with the current interpretation (4Q Ordinances 2:6–7). Rather – consistently with the general trend of Jesus' teaching – he argues from God's relationship to his people as father. God does not lay financial burdens on his people, like the taxes with which 'the kings of the earth' burden their subjects. On the contrary, God is a father who provides for his children's needs.[13]

The objection that Jesus could not have opposed the temple tax unless he 'meant to let the Temple fall into ruin and its services cease'[14] is easily answered. Jesus approved of voluntary giving to the temple, as the story of the widow's offering (Mark 12:41–4) makes clear.[15] Such a distinction between the temple tax and voluntary giving is not a quibble, but corresponds to the felt reality of the tax.

THE DEMONSTRATION IN THE TEMPLE (MARK 11:15–16 PAR)   Our procedure in this section will be to use the clue provided by Matt 17:24–7 to elucidate what is generally regarded as the most historically reliable part of the Gospel traditions of the demonstration in the temple, viz. the four actions of Jesus recounted in Mark 11:15–16: (1) he began to drive out those who were buying and those who were selling; (2) he overturned the tables of the moneychangers; (3) he overturned the chairs of the sellers of doves; (4) he would not allow anyone to carry an object *(skeuos)* through the temple. In view of the widespread doubts about the authenticity of the saying in Mark 11:17, we shall not consider this verse until we have first established the meaning of the actions in themselves. A credible account of Jesus' intention in his demonstration in the temple must either be able to give a coherent account of all four actions, such that they appear consistent parts of a demonstration with a clear overall objective, or else it must at least produce good reasons for rejecting the historicity of any of the four actions and explain how it entered the tradition. Several recent interpretations fail particularly by this criterion of accounting adequately for all four actions.[16]

In my view, John 2:13–15 is dependent not on Mark but on a parallel tradition which can help to corroborate the Markan account.[17] However, the observation that John's version resembles Matthew's redaction of Mark in a tendency to exaggerate Jesus' action (cf. *pantas* in Matt 21:12 and John 2:15) suggests that details attested only in John should be treated with some caution. John or his tradition seems to have interpreted Jesus' first action in Mark's series of four as meaning that Jesus drove out the sellers of sacrificial animals and the moneychangers, and he includes among the salesmen not only sellers of doves but also sellers of sheep and oxen, not mentioned in Mark. Thus, for the purpose of discussion, we may add to the four Markan actions a fifth, purely Johannine, action: he drove out the sellers of sheep and oxen. But since this must be regarded as less securely part of the early tradition, our ability to interpret it consistently with the four Markan actions will be less important to the argument.

We shall consider the five actions in the order most convenient for discussion, beginning with the action to which the use of Matt 17:24–7 as a clue applies most directly:

(1) He overturned the tables of the moneychangers The moneychangers were required in the temple in order to change money into the 'temple shekels' (Exod 30:13) or Tyrian silver tetradrachma in which the temple tax had to be paid. According to the Mishnah (*Šeqalim* 1:3) the tables of the moneychangers were set up in the temple three weeks before Passover (on 25 Adar), and presumably remained there for a week, until 1 Nisan, the date by which payment was supposed to be made (cf. *m. Šeqalim* 3:1–3). During that period not only were individuals paying their tax in the temple, but also large collections of contributions from the diaspora would be coming in, which also had to be changed into temple shekels. The tables of the moneychangers would have been a prominent feature in the temple during that week. There must have been some moneychanging facilities in the temple at other times, to provide for late payment of the tax (cf. *m. Šeqalim* 6:5) and for other business of the temple treasury,[18] but we can reasonably assume that Jesus' action took place at the time when crowds of people waiting to exchange their tax money made this particular aspect of the temple's financial operations one of the most obvious of the activities going on in the temple precincts.[19]

Thus the moneychanging was not a piece of private enterprise going on in the temple court, but a facility organised by the temple treasury. In all probability the moneychangers were priests or Levites on the temple staff.[20] But, in the light of Matt 17:24–7, we can see that it was precisely as the most visible manifestation of the temple's tax-collecting operation that Jesus attacked the tables of the moneychangers. He was not implying that the moneychanging should not be allowed within the sacred precincts, but could properly go on elsewhere.[21] He was not implying that the moneychangers were swindling their customers and making a dishonest profit.[22] Even though the moneychanging involved a small surcharge, which no doubt provided an additional profit for the temple treasury (*m. Šeqalim* 1:6), the moneychanging as such was not the object of Jesus' protest. His was a radical objection to the tax itself, and whereas in Capernaum Jesus had been concerned not to offend the local tax collectors (Matt 17:27), who were no doubt motivated by piety towards the temple and could have understood refusal to pay as a criticism of the sacrificial cult which the tax financed, he now confronted the machinery of tax collecting operated by the temple officials themselves in the temple. His

'demonstration' was therefore aimed directly, and could be seen to be
aimed directly, at those who managed the temple finances in God's name.

(2) He overturned the chairs of the sellers of doves We now need to
ask whether it is possible to understand this action in a way which coheres
with our understanding of Jesus' overturning of the tables of the moneychangers. Of course, the payment of the temple tax and the selling of doves
are connected in the sense that both were financial operations concerned
with the sacrificial worship of the temple. But if, in the case of the tax,
Jesus' objection was not to the sacrificial worship which the tax financed
(*m. Šeqalim* 4:1–2), but to the method of financing it, what could have
been his objection to the selling of doves for sacrifice?

For two reasons it is not without significance that, among the animals
used for sacrifice, the Markan account mentions only doves.[23] In the first
place, it is very probable that the temple treasury had a monopoly in the
sale of doves for sacrifice, whereas this is less likely to have been the case
for cattle, sheep and goats. The requirements that had to be satisfied for a
bird to be fit for sacrifice were so stringent[24] that the rearing[25] and sale of
doves for the temple probably took place entirely under the auspices of the
temple treasurer who was 'over the bird offerings' (*m. Šeqalim* 5:1),[26] and
who alone could certify them fit for sacrificial use. The temple monopoly
could no doubt be justified as the only way of ensuring that ritually
acceptable birds were available to the public, but only because the halakic
requirements in this respect had been so stringently defined. Sanders goes
too far when he asserts that the arrangements for the sale of doves were
actually necessary for carrying out the Mosaic commandments on bird
offerings,[27] especially as the written Torah itself, which insists that cattle,
sheep and goats offered in sacrifice must be unblemished, does not make
the same requirement for birds. It was possible for Jesus to object to the
system of selling doves in the temple without rejecting the sacrificial
provisions of the Mosaic law itself.

Why he should have wished to object to it becomes clear only when we
consider the temple monopoly in the sale of doves in conjunction with a
second aspect of the doves which distinguishes them from the other
sacrificial animals: doves were the sacrifices of the poor (cf. *m. Keritot* 6:8;
Josephus, *Ant.* 3:230). In three cases of obligatory offerings – for the
cleansing of a man (Lev 15:14) or a woman (15:29) who had suffered from
a discharge, and for the cleansing of a Nazirite (Num 6:10) – doves were
the prescribed offering for everybody. But in all other cases they were an
alternative offering for those who could not afford the more expensive
sacrificial animals. This was true of three types of obligatory offerings – for
the purification of women after childbirth (Lev 12:6–8), for the cleansing
of a leper (Lev 14:22), and as guilt offerings (Lev 5:7) – as well as of
voluntary offerings – freewill and votive offerings (cf. Lev 1:14). A poor
person would probably sacrifice an animal other than a dove only very
rarely, but would quite frequently sacrifice doves.

Consequently, if the temple monopoly in the sale of doves operated to keep the price high, it would make the sacrificial system a burden to the poor in the same way that the temple tax did. Jesus would object, as he did to the temple tax, that the God in whose name the temple authorities acted does not burden his people with oppressive financial demands. We shall later consider some general evidence that the temple treasury tended to conduct its affairs as a commercial operation intended to make a profit for the temple. For the moment, we consider an instructive story in the Mishnah:[28]

> Once in Jerusalem a pair of doves cost a golden *denar*. Rabban Simeon b. Gamaliel said: By this Temple! I will not suffer the night to pass by before they cost a [silver] *denar*. He went into the court and taught: If a woman suffered five miscarriages that were not in doubt or five issues that were not in doubt, she need bring but one offering [of a pair of doves], and she may then eat of the animal offerings; and she is not bound to bring the other offerings [four pairs of doves for the other four cases]. And the same day the price of a pair of doves stood at a quarter-*denar* each. (*m. Keritot* 1:7)[29]

The initial price of doves in this story is too high to be credible, but we do not need to accept the literal historicity of the story in order to believe that it reflects conditions and attitudes in the time of Simeon the son of Gamaliel I, a Pharisee known to have been an influential member of the Sanhedrin in the period before the fall of Jerusalem (Josephus, *Vita* 189–96). Simeon's tactic works as follows. The unreasonably high price of doves was possible because of the temple monopoly. Simeon gives a ruling which drastically reduces the number of bird offerings required in certain cases, and so creates a drop in demand for doves. In order to sell their surplus birds for the purpose of freewill offerings, the temple authorities are forced to lower the price. The story shows that the temple treasury was remembered to have set the price of doves at levels which some pharisaic teachers thought too high and sought to reduce. Particularly interesting is the fact that the presumed motive for Simeon's action in the story is similar to the motive we have attributed to Jesus. Simeon must have been concerned that the price was beyond the reach of poor people. In order to bring it within their reach he actually relaxes the law. But this was a relaxation in line with the intention of the law, which provided for bird offerings explicitly in order to enable the poor to afford to sacrifice without unreasonable hardship. Similarly we may attribute to Jesus a desire not to reject the laws on sacrifice but to see their real purpose fulfilled. The special scandal of the temple trade in doves was that the laws specifically intended to make worship possible for the poor were being so applied as to make them a financial burden on the poor.

(3) He prevented people carrying objects through the temple The significance of Mark 11:16 may already have been obscure to Matthew, who omits it, and is not easy to recover today. A link with *m. Berakot* 9:5, which prohibits the use of the sacred precincts as a public thoroughfare (cf. *b. Berakot* 62b; *b. Yebamot* 6b),[30] is unlikely, on our interpretation of the rest of the pericope, since it gives this action no coherence with Jesus' other

actions in the temple. A link with Zech 14:21 has been suggested,[31] but makes little sense: if Jesus thought that the time had come when all vessels in Jerusalem were as holy as the temple vessels, why should he try to keep them out of the temple? Ford's argument that *skeuos* could have been understood to mean 'moneybag' is not linguistically convincing.[32]

A possible explanation is that *skeuos* refers to a vessel or receptacle used to deliver to the temple supplies of the materials used in offerings: flour, oil and wine. The vessels were not being carried from one outer gate of the temple to another, but through the temple from the outer court to the store-chambers in the court of the women (*m. Middot* 2:5). Flour, oil and wine were bought by the temple treasury, which sold them at a profit to people making offerings of them (*m. Seqalim* 4:3; 5:4; cf. 4:8).[33] It seems that, as with the sale of doves, the temple operated a monopoly and fixed the price (*m. Seqalim* 5:4; 4:9). Thus again Jesus was protesting against the way in which the temple treasury had turned the sacrificial system into a profit-making business.

(4) He drove out those buying and those selling   Mark's general reference to those who bought and those who sold in the temple is best understood as a reference to all kinds of commercial transactions in which the temple treasurers and their staff were engaged. Those who were buying could scarcely be worshippers buying materials or animals for sacrifice, whom Jesus would not have driven out. But they could include temple staff buying in supplies for the temple and merchants purchasing valuable items which people had donated to the temple (*m. Seqalim* 5:6).

(5) He drove out those selling sheep and oxen   These are mentioned only in John 2:14–15. Whether John here follows a reliable tradition or an unreliable elaboration of the tradition must remain uncertain. There is little evidence that sheep and oxen were sold in the temple precincts,[34] but it is not improbable. Evidence that the trade was managed by the temple authorities is also sparse (but see *m. Seqalim* 4:7), though they must at least have supervised any such trade in the temple precincts.

Jesus' objections to the way the financial side of the sacrificial system was run, as we have reconstructed them, do not necessarily imply that he thought the temple officials were appropriating the profits for themselves. The point was that the system was being run for the benefit of the temple treasury, so that instead of being a vehicle of the people's worship it was an oppressive financial burden on them. Such a result could be produced by temple officials dedicated to the interests of the temple as they understood them. In the service of such an institution it could easily be thought that serving the temple involved serving the financial interests of the temple treasury.[35] Hence the Mishnah appears to use the principle, 'the Temple has the upper hand', to mean that doubtful cases in financial transactions must always be decided in favour of the temple (*m. Seqalim* 4:8; 5:4). It must be remembered that the temple was a vast economic enterprise, with enormous reserves of money and treasures,[36] employing large numbers of workers,[37] expending huge sums of money on the complex requirements of the cult, and functioning as a bank for the safe deposit of wealth and for loans.[38] The temple treasurers would naturally see their responsibilities for temple income in the areas which roused Jesus' anger as part of this huge commercial operation. Of course, the temple as a commercial and financial institution brought considerable economic benefits to Jerusalem, providing employment and apparently treating its workers well, facilitating commerce and providing Jerusalem with its flourishing tourist trade. Its funds were also used for poor relief (*m. Seqalim* 5:6) and public works (*m. Seqalim* 4:2). But such benefits would be felt only in Jerusalem.[39] People from the provinces, like Jesus, experienced the temple only as taxpayers and worshippers. In any case, the economic benefits would not in Jesus' eyes have offset the distortion of the temple's real purpose as a place of worship.

Jesus' protest was primarily against commercialism rather than corruption. But we should also consider, as adding fuel to the fire, the evidence that the priestly aristocracy who controlled the temple hierarchy were believed to support a conspicuously expensive lifestyle[40] by corruption and violence.[41] The best evidence here is the well-known lament over the evils of the high priestly families:

> Woe unto me because of the house of Baithos [Boethus];
>   woe unto me for their lances [or 'evil-speaking']!
> Woe unto me because of the house of Hanin [=Annas (NT) and Ananus (Josephus)],
>   woe unto me for their whisperings [or 'calumnies']!
> Woe unto me because of the house of Qathros [Kantheras],
>   woe unto me because of their reed pens!
> Woe unto me because of the house of Ishmael b. Phiabi,
>   woe unto me because of their fist!
> For they are high priests and their sons are treasurers
>   and their sons-in-law are temple overseers,
>   and their servants smite the people with sticks.
>
>   (*b. Pesahim* 57a)[42]

That the lament is an authentic tradition from before the fall of Jerusalem is clear. The four families mentioned (of which Kantheras was a branch of the family of Boethus) supplied most of the high priests from the reign of Herod the Great to the fall of Jerusalem,[43] and the lament must intend to refer to the activities of these four families over a period from at least *c*. 6 BCE to at least 60 CE. This is required by the fact that, since the house of Simon Kantheras, son of Boethus, is counted separately, not as part of the house of Boethus, the first line of the lament must refer to the period of ascendancy of the house of Boethus before 6 CE.[44] The other three families did not simply succeed each other in power: all three were influential simultaneously. But they seem to be given in a roughly chronological order, since the period 6–40 CE was especially the period of ascendancy of the high priest Annas and his sons, while Simon Kantheras and his son were high priests in the 40s. The fact that the house of Ishmael son of

Phiabi is placed last may indicate that the lament dates from the time of the second high priest of that name (c. 59–61 CE).[45]

Thus it is not true that the evidence for oppression by the priestly aristocracy refers only to the period after the ministry of Jesus.[46] In this lament the house of Annas, whose control of the temple hierarchy in the time of Jesus is well evidenced by the NT itself (John 18:13; Acts 4:6), are remembered for their 'whisperings' (presumably meaning intrigue),[47] and included with the other families in the accusations of nepotism and violence. In these latter accusations it should be noticed that the temple offices which these families are accused of keeping to themselves are financial.[48] The 'treasurers' (*gizbārîm*) were certainly in charge of the temple finances, including the administration of the temple tax and the temple monopolies in sacrificial materials and doves. The 'overseers' (*'ămarkělîn*) were, in Jeremias' view, in charge of other (non-financial) temple affairs,[49] but the original meaning of the term suggests that they may have been another category of financial official.[50] The implication in the lament is clearly that the priestly aristocracy owed their wealth to their dominance over the fiscal and commercial affairs of the temple. It is not, of course, objective evidence to this effect, but it is at least good evidence of how the high-priestly families were regarded in some circles.

Corroborative evidence for this kind of complaint against the priestly aristocracy is probably to be found in ch. 7 of the *Testament of Moses*, which must date from the earlier part of the first century (after 4 BCE – see 6:8–9[51] – but before 30 CE – see 6:7).[52] Despite the fragmentary character of the text, it is clear that the sinners described in this chapter were priests (7:9–10) who lived like princes (7:8). They are accused of luxurious and gluttonous living financed by ill-gotten wealth. Of course, the charges are stereotyped, but they show how one writer living during the period when the houses of Boethus and Annas controlled the temple regarded them.

The final accusation in the lament ('their servants smite the people with sticks') is strikingly corroborated by Josephus, who relates that during the high-priesthoods of Ishmael II (c. 59–61 CE) and Jesus the son of Damnaeus (c. 62–3 CE), the chief priests[53] sent their slaves to the threshing-floors to collect by force the tithes due to the priests, beating those who refused to hand them over (*Ant.* 20:181, 206–7). Since Josephus comments that as a result some of the poorer priests starved to death (*Ant.* 20:181, 207), and puts the account in the context of the conflict between the priestly aristocracy, on the one hand, and the ordinary priests and the leaders of the people of Jerusalem, on the other hand (*Ant.* 20:180), he clearly means that the chief priests were forcibly appropriating for their own use the tithes which should have gone to the lower clergy. His evidence may well reflect a deterioration from the state of affairs in the time of Jesus, but the evidence of the lament justifies us in supposing that this *kind* of activity was not a wholly novel phenomenon in the early 60s. The role of a slave of the high priest in Jesus' arrest in Gethsemane (Mark 14:47 par) is a minor confirmation of the fact that the chief priests had at their disposal not only the temple police but also armed servants of their

own. If these were sometimes used to enforce the payment of tithes, we can also imagine them being used to enforce the payment of the temple tax.

There does, therefore, seem to be good evidence that the pursuit of the commercial interests of the temple by those who controlled the temple finances was not perceived as purely disinterested. They were not like the fund-raising activities of those who work for respectable modern charities. Rather, the financial interests of the temple were seen to coincide with those of the priestly aristocracy. The profits of the temple as a commercial enterprise would readily be seen, like those of all commercial enterprises in the ancient world, as profits for those who ran the business, and the revenues of the temple's fiscal system would readily be seen, like taxation in general in the ancient world, as benefiting the rulers rather than the ruled. The fact that nominally the commerce was conducted, and the taxation levied, in the name of God himself only increased the scandal. For Jesus it would have meant that at the heart of the religious life of Israel God was being misrepresented and his real relation to his people obscured. Jesus' demonstration in the temple can therefore be understood as a principled religious protest not against some minor abuses of the sacred precincts but against what Jesus must have seen as serious misconduct by the nation's religious leaders.[54]

THE SAYING IN MARK 11:17   Before considering this saying in the light of our interpretation of the four Markan actions of Jesus in the temple, we must deal with the arguments which have been advanced against its authenticity:

(1) The elaborate Markan introduction to the saying (*kai edidasken kai elegen autois*) can tell us nothing about whether Mark found the saying already connected to verses 15b–16 in his source.[55] Mark will have introduced this formula because he wanted to make this scene the introduction to the theme of Jesus' teaching in the temple, which is important to him (cf. 12:35, 38; 14:47). It is hard to believe that the pre-Markan tradition consisted only of verses 15b–16 or merely served as an introduction to Mark 11:28–33.[56]

(2) In John 2:16 a different saying occupies the place of Mark 11:17 in the Markan version. It has sometimes been suggested that John here preserves a more original saying, for which Mark 11:17 has been substituted by Mark or his tradition.[57] But it is more likely that John 2:16 is a redactional paraphrase of the saying in Mark 11:17.

This point will be better appreciated if we first compare Luke's redaction of Mark 11:17 (Luke 19:46). Luke's version of the first half of the saying (*kai estai ho oikos mou oikos proseuchēs*) eliminates the prophecy of the worship of the nations in Jerusalem and substitutes a *commandment* that the temple should be a house of prayer.[58] Not only is Luke here sensitive to the fact that the prophecy, understood as an eschatological prophecy of the pilgrimage of the Gentiles to Jerusalem, had not been fulfilled; but his redaction is also consistent with his exclusion from his work of any reference to an eschatological temple: he omits Mark 14:58;

15:29 from the passion narrative, and in Acts 6:14 allows only a version of this saying which makes no reference to a new temple.

These redactional considerations would apply with equal or greater force to John, who clearly had no place for an eschatological temple (John 4:21) and who carefully reinterprets Jesus' prediction of a new temple (2:19–22). So he suppresses the first half of the saying in Mark 11:17, and paraphrases the second half in a way which he may have thought more appropriate to the context than Mark's 'cave of brigands' (see (5) below). That he thereby eliminates the OT allusions is no problem for this view,[59] since John's interest in the OT is overwhelmingly *christological*. For the non-christological allusions to the OT in Mark 11:17 he substitutes a christological application of scripture in John 2:17.

(3) The fact that the saying quotes one OT text (Isa 56:7) and then alludes to another (Jer 7:11) cannot be held against its authenticity. In the first place, it is far from a *mere* quotation, but a creative juxtaposition of two OT references to the temple to form an accusation against the temple authorities. Secondly, the early Church's interest in adding OT references to the Gospel tradition was very predominantly an interest in Jesus' fulfilment of messianic and eschatological prophecies. But Mark 11:17 is not of this type. More appropriate quotations for the early Church to have introduced would have been Mal 3:1–3 or Zech 14:21, texts often quoted in modern studies of our subject,[60] whose influence is surprisingly absent from the Gospel accounts of Jesus' demonstration in the temple.[61] John 2:17 does in fact supply an appropriate quotation of this kind (Ps 69:9), from a psalm which was widely understood as christological (Matt 27:34, 48; Mark 15:36; Luke 23:36; John 19:29; Acts 1:20). Neither of these arguments proves that the saying in Mark 11:17 could not derive from the early Church,[62] but they considerably reduce the probability of this.

(4) With regard to the first quotation, from Isa 56:7, given in the Septuagint version in Mark 11:17, Harvey,[63] followed by Sanders,[64] objects that the meaning, 'a house of prayer for all the Gentiles', 'could hardly be extracted from the Hebrew version which Jesus would have used'. But this is very misleading. The Septuagint of Isa 56:7 is a quite literal translation of the Hebrew. It is true that, in the context of Isa 56:6–7, the clause quoted in Mark 11:17 most naturally refers to proselytes from all nations, but this is no less true of the Septuagint than of the Hebrew. Taken out of context, it might be understood of Gentiles *per se*, but again this applies equally to the Hebrew and to the Septuagint texts (since *'ammîm*, used in Isa 56:7, is frequently in the OT equivalent to *gôyîm* and is therefore quite correctly translated *ethnē* in Isa 56:7 LXX). That Jesus would have used the Hebrew text therefore makes no difference either to the interpretation of the saying or to its authenticity.

(5) The authenticity of the second half of the saying has been questioned on the grounds that the phrase *spēlaion lēstōn* is inappropriate to the activities described in Mark 11:15–16, since *lēstēs* means not a thief (*kleptēs*), but a brigand, a violent raider or even a guerrilla fighter, and the moneychangers and sellers of doves were not guilty of robbery with

violence.[65] Buchanan therefore proposes that, in view of Josephus' frequent description of the Zealots as *lēstai*, Mark 11:17 should be regarded as an originally separate saying composed after the fall of Jerusalem with reference to the Zealots' occupation of the temple in 68–70 CE.[66] We shall consider the appropriateness of the phrase *spēlaion lēstōn* below, but at this point it is worth noticing that if the phrase is as inappropriate to its Markan context as these scholars allege, it is hardly less difficult to see why Mark or his tradition should have attached it to this context than it is to see why Jesus should have done.[67]

Our next task is to show positively the saying's coherence with Jesus' demonstration in the temple, as interpreted on pp. 74–81 above, and consequently the probable authenticity of the saying.

Mark 11:17 is an antithetical saying which contrasts God's intention for the temple (*gegraptai*) with what the temple authorities (*humeis*) have made of the temple. The fundamental contrast is between the two scriptural descriptions of the temple: *oikos proseuchēs* (Isa 56:7) and *spēlaion lēstōn* (Jer 7:11). There may be some reason to doubt the originality of the phrase *pasin tois ethnesin*, since Matthew and Luke agree in omitting it. But if we accept the two-document hypothesis (as I do), it is not difficult to explain this coincidence in Matthew's and Luke's redaction of Mark. Both or either may have wished to avoid, after 70 CE, the suggestion of an unfulfilled prophecy (cf. pp. 81 above, on Luke). Both or either may have seen that the main point of the saying is in the contrast between *oikos proseuchēs* and *spēlaion lēstōn*, and felt the phrase *pasin tois ethnesin* to be an unnecessary distraction from this main point. If we were to accept the originality of Matthew's version of the saying,[68] rather than Mark's, we should have to suppose both that Matthew and Luke knew a more original text of Mark 11:17 than ours[69] and that the addition of *pasin tois ethnesin* in our text of Mark 11:17 is due to a scribe who, recalling Isa 56:7, completed the quotation. This is by no means impossible, but seems less likely than that our text of Mark 11:17 is original. However, whether or not this is the case, the stress in the first half of the saying is on *oikos proseuchēs*, and so we shall postpone consideration of *pasin tois ethnesin* for the moment.

The contrast is between 'house of prayer' and 'cave of brigands', not between 'house of prayer' and place of sacrifice.[70] Even though the term 'house of prayer' is elsewhere used of the temple only in Isa 56:7 (*bis*), which Jesus quotes, and Isa 60:7 LXX, while *proseuchē* in the sense of 'place of prayer' is used rather of synagogues (Acts 17:1, etc.), there is nothing novel or surprising in the thought of the temple as pre-eminently the place of prayer. It was classically expressed in Solomon's prayer at the dedication of the temple (1 Kgs 8:33–53), which could hardly fail to influence later Jewish thought about the temple (3 Macc 2:10). The temple was a place where Jews went to pray (2 Macc 10:26; Sir 51:14; Luke 2:37; 18:10), but this was not simply a function additional to the temple's role as a place of sacrifice. Isa 56:7 clearly uses the term 'house of prayer' to describe the temple precisely as a place of sacrifice. The sacrifices were regarded as expressions of prayer and were intended to be accompanied by prayer (1 Bar 1:10–14; Josephus, *Ap.* 2:196; cf. Neh 11:17). In particular, the burnt offering of the people (the *tamid*), offered every morning and afternoon and financed by the temple tax, was the occasion for congregational worship and prayer (Sir 50:17–19; Luke 1:10; Acts 3:1; *m. Tamid* 7:3). Even Jews living far away from the temple prayed at the times when the morning and afternoon burnt offerings were presented in the temple (Dan 9:21; Jdt 9:1),[71] so that the temple cult was central to the daily prayer even of Jews outside Jerusalem.

In using the term 'house of prayer', therefore, Jesus was not rejecting or downplaying the sacrificial cult. Rather he was insisting on its purpose: to be the expression of the prayer of those who came to the temple to worship.[72] It was this real purpose of the sacrificial cult which was being frustrated by the temple authorities when they made it a means of financial exaction.[73]

To form the antithesis to 'house of prayer', Jesus skilfully selects a scriptural phrase which describes an abuse of the temple: *spēlaion lēstōn* (*mĕʿārat pārîsîm*). The sense of this phrase in Jer 7:11 is that people guilty of the worst crimes regard the temple as a place of safe refuge. Because of their confidence in the invulnerability of the temple (7:4), they think they can commit crimes with impunity, like brigands who after every raid can resort to the safety of their caves. It should be noted that in Jeremiah's use of the phrase, *pārîsîm* (which, like *lēstōn*, denotes men of *violence*) is as metaphorical as *mĕʿārā* (=*spēlaion*), since the crimes in question include, but are by no means limited to, crimes of violence (7:6, 9). The point is that these criminals regard the temple in the way that a band of brigands regard their cave. Jesus is making the same point about the temple authorities in his day.

At least since the time when David gathered his band of malcontents in the cave of Adullam (1 Sam 22:1–2; 2 Sam 23:13), caves in Palestine had been the resort of people who lived by raiding the countryside, and Herod's campaign against *lēstai* who lived in caves in the mountains (Josephus, *BJ* 1:304–11) shows that Jeremiah's metaphor would still be a meaningful one for Jesus' hearers. But just because Josephus regularly uses the term *lēstai* to describe guerrilla fighters against Rome (so also, probably, John 18:40; Mark 15:27 par), it does not follow that the term necessarily carried this connotation.[74] This usage is derogatory, and its point is that people who regarded their cause as political were seen by their enemies as no better than common brigands. This derogatory usage *presupposes* that *lēstēs* did also mean common brigand (cf. Mark 14:48 par; Luke 10:30; 2 Cor 11:26).

Jesus, of course, has shifted the metaphor somewhat from its significance in Jer 7:11. His point is that the priestly aristocracy, who by virtue of their control of the temple hierarchy occupy positions of privilege and unassailable authority, are abusing these positions as means of plundering the people.[75] They treat the temple, so to speak, as a base from which they go out on marauding raids and to which they return with the loot. We do not need to press the metaphor of *violent* robbery, but it is possible that even this aspect was more literally applicable than previous commentators have noticed. Jesus' hearers might well have thought of the slaves of the chief priests, who 'beat the people with sticks' (*b. Pesaḥîm* 57a).

In Jeremiah the phrase 'cave of brigands' had a certain irony: the people think the temple is a safe refuge, but they are deluded (7:4). In God's judgement on their sins the temple will become as desolate as Shiloh (7:12). The theme of judgement and the destruction of the temple is so prominent in the immediate context of Jer 7:11, that it is hard to believe that Jesus' use of the phrase 'cave of brigands' does not contain a hint of judgement. It will be no more than a hint, but there are two reasons why we may, with caution, detect it. In the first place, that Jesus did, during his final days in Jerusalem, prophesy the destruction of the temple is well authenticated (Mark 13:1–2 par; Mark 14:58 par Matt 26:61 par *Thomas* 71 par John 2:19; cf. Acts 6:14; Mark 15:29 par Matt 27:40). Secondly, Jeremiah was the most natural source of scriptural allusion in any prophecy of judgement on Jerusalem and the temple. Thus, for example, *Pss. Sol.* 8:1–5 seems inspired by Jer 4:11–21; 23:9. Jesus the son of Ananias, in his oracle of judgement on Jerusalem and the temple, echoed the refrain of Jer 7:34; 16:9; 25:10 (Josephus, *BJ* 6. 301). Matt 23:38 (par Luke 13:35) alludes to Jer 12:7; 22:5.

Finally, we must consider the significance of the words *pasin tois ethnesin*. Jesus could very naturally have taken Isa 56:7 as a prophecy of the eschatological temple,[76] but he cannot have thought of the description 'a house of prayer for all nations' as one which could apply only to the eschatological temple in the messianic age. The temple authorities could not be accused of contradicting a divine intention which was meant to be fulfilled only in the eschatological temple. The thought must be rather that what is going to be fully realised in the messianic age – in the pilgrimage of the nations to Zion – has been God's intention for the temple all along. In that case *pasin tois ethnesin* must have had some referent in the present.

It is also a mistake to attach too much importance to the location of Jesus' demonstration in the outer court of the temple,[77] though it is very probable that this is where the activities to which Jesus objected went on.[78] The title 'Court of the Gentiles' is a modern one, and there is no evidence that the outer court was thought of positively as the place where Gentiles could worship, rather than negatively as the limit beyond which Gentiles could not go.

As we have already noticed, the stress in the first half of the saying falls on *oikos proseuchēs*, rather than on *pasin tois ethnesin*, but the latter helps to strengthen the contrast with the second half of the saying. The crowds queueing to pay their temple tax and to purchase offerings would include not only diaspora Jews but also many proselytes – the 'foreigners' to whom Isa 56:6–7 most naturally refers. Proselytes, with the enthusiasm of the convert, would no doubt be as eager as anyone to visit Jerusalem for Passover.[79] Uncircumcised Gentile Godfearers also visited Jerusalem for the feasts,[80] and may well have been among those purchasing doves for freewill offerings. Jesus' saying means that the temple is a house of prayer *for all these people*. The sacrificial cult is not intended for the private benefit of the priestly aristocracy or even for the temple itself as an institution, but, quite the contrary, as a means of worship for *all nations*.

As an antithetical saying Mark 11:17 may be compared with other sayings about the law in the Gospel tradition (Mark 2:27; 3:4; 7:10–12; 7:15). The explicit citation of scripture in the first half of the saying is highly appropriate in a saying which aims to establish God's intention in the law, and may be compared with Mark 2:25–6; 7:10; 10:6–8. Though the authenticity of some of these sayings is frequently doubted, they share a consistent style of teaching about the law which may at least as easily be attributed to Jesus as to the early Church.

It lies beyond the scope of this paper to relate the demonstration in the temple and the saying in Mark 11:17 in detail to their immediate context in Jesus' last visit to Jerusalem, where the triumphal entry and the prophecies of the destruction of the temple would be the most relevant material, or to their wider context in Jesus' whole message and activity. In these contexts Jesus' indictment of the temple authorities for their abuse of the temple and his hint of judgement to come cohere with the sense of eschatological crisis which pervades Jesus' preaching and with his sense of his own eschatological–prophetic or messianic mission to renew Israel. But a discussion of this must be left to another occasion. Here we shall take up only the question of the relation between the demonstration in the temple and the process which led to Jesus' death, because this relation is an important issue in E. P. Sanders' treatment of the demonstration in the temple.

JESUS' DEMONSTRATION IN THE TEMPLE AND HIS DEATH   The interpretation of Jesus' demonstration in the temple which has been argued in this paper differs considerably from that proposed recently by E. P. Sanders.[81] He sees Jesus' action as a symbolic prophecy of the destruction of the temple, whereas in our interpretation Jesus' demonstration was a symbolic denunciation of the activities he attacked. The destruction of the temple was not symbolised,[82] though in the saying with which Jesus interpreted his prophetic action it was implied, as divine judgement on the abuses Jesus denounced.

However, Sanders' interpretation has the merit of being worked into an attempt at historical explanation of the factors which led to Jesus' death.[83] In proposing an alternative view of Jesus' demonstration in the temple, I wish to show that in fact it explains the opposition of the temple authorities, which led to Jesus' death, better than Sanders' interpretation does.

The points at which Sanders' position seems to me to be weak are three:

(1) His understanding of the demonstration permits the historicity of only two of the four Markan actions: the overturning of the tables and the chairs, which can be seen as symbolising destruction.

(2) He understands the demonstration to be a symbol of the destruction

of the temple – *not* as divine judgement on the people of Jerusalem or the temple authorities for their misuse of the temple, but simply as the removal of the old temple in order to make way for the eschatological temple. The point is not really the destruction so much as the *replacement* of the temple. But is this a natural meaning for a symbolic action which *symbolises* only destruction?[84] Verbal prophecies of the destruction of the temple in Jewish literature normally[85] refer to divine *judgement* (e.g. Mic 3:12; Jeremiah 7; 26; *Sib. Or.* 3:265–81; 4:115–18; *Apoc. Abr.* 27; *2 Bar.* 1–8; *4 Bar.* 1–4). Even *1 Enoch* 90:28, if it does describe the destruction of the present temple to make way for an eschatological temple, follows the critical reference to the present temple worship in 89:73. 11 QT 29:8–10 seems to *imply* the removal of an old temple, which is in no way criticised but is conceived as ideal, in order to make way for the eschatological temple, but the removal is *only* implied. Precisely because the destruction of the old temple is not the real point it goes unmentioned. But Jesus' prophetic action symbolises, in Sanders' view, only the destruction of the temple. It is hard to believe that its meaning, in this case, would not be perceived to be divine *judgement*, rather than mere divine removal.

(3) In view of Sanders' understanding of Jesus' demonstration in the temple and Jesus' prophecy of the temple's destruction, it is hard to understand how they could have played the principal role in bringing about Jesus' death, which Sanders attributes to them. He insists that this was not the result of any misunderstanding of Jesus' prophecy about the temple.[86] The significance of Jesus' action and words, as announcing the removal of the present temple so that it could be replaced by the eschatological temple, was clear within the context of contemporary Jewish expectation and was correctly understood by the people and the Jewish leaders. But then why was this 'threat' to the temple so offensive to Jewish reverence for the temple?[87] According to Sanders, Jesus did no more than prophesy as an event of the near future what most Jews[88] believed would happen some day. Indeed, it was their devout *hope*. To say that the present temple must go so that God could build his more glorious, eschatological temple, was no insult to the present temple. Sanders says: 'When the action and the saying [of Jesus against the temple] came to the attention of the Jewish leaders, they surely saw them both as arrogant and wicked.'[89] They may well have seen them as arrogant, especially if Jesus claimed he would be God's agent in the miraculous removal of the temple (Sanders is undecided on this point),[90] but why *wicked*? The parallels with Jeremiah (ch. 26) and Jesus the son of Ananias (Josephus, *BJ* 6:300–9), which Sanders adduces,[91] are not true parallels to the Jewish authorities' action against Jesus, as Sanders understands it. Jeremiah prophesied the destruction of the temple as divine judgement on the sins of Jerusalem, which would leave the city and the sanctuary desolate, not prepare for the immediate arrival of the eschatological Zion. In the case of Jesus the son of Ananias, his prophecy implies the destruction of Jerusalem and the temple as *judgement*, not only by echoing Jeremiah's prophecy, but also by the

repeated use of the term 'voice', which Aune argues was 'a well-known, recognizable idiom which refers to the voice of God pronouncing judgment'.[92]

We must now indicate briefly how, on the interpretation of Jesus' demonstration in the temple offered in this paper, it can be seen to have been a major factor in the process which led to his death. (A fuller account would have to consider in detail its links with other factors, especially the triumphal entry and the prophecies of the destruction of the temple.)

(1) As an attack on the whole of the financial arrangements for the sacrificial system, Jesus' action would undoubtedly have aroused the anger of the chief priests. In itself, this need not have led to his death. Essenes, who criticised the temple hierarchy even more strongly, lived safely in Jerusalem. But Jesus was preaching in the temple courts, and his criticism of the way the chief priests ran the temple would surely have gained a sympathetic hearing, if not with the people of Jerusalem, at least with pilgrims from Galilee and elsewhere. This was an attack which, if not nipped in the bud, might have explosive consequences.

(2) Jesus' demonstration in the temple raised the question of his *authority* to challenge the rulings and actions of the chief priests (cf. Josephus, *Ap.* 2:194).[93] Mark 11:28, which can only refer to the demonstration in the temple, is credible here, and may be corroborated by John 2:18. The demonstration in the temple made clear to the chief priests that Jesus intended to assert the authority he claimed and had already made public in Jerusalem in the triumphal entry, *as a challenge to their own authority*. Evidently they did not perceive an immediate physical threat of insurrection, or they would have had Jesus' disciples arrested along with him. But Jesus' view of his own authority, expressed in his demonstration in the temple, made him a potential troublemaker, especially in the context of the crowds of pilgrims thronging the temple at Passover time, when eschatological hopes ran high. The demonstration in the temple would also be evidence by which they might convince the Roman authorities that Jesus was a danger to civil order.

(3) As Horsley has recently shown,[94] when the sanctity of the temple was infringed by the Roman authorities in this period, the high priests and the priestly aristocracy showed themselves less concerned about the desecration of the temple than about the danger of popular insurrection. This demonstrates that the temple was important to them primarily as their political–economic power base, for the maintenance of which the general political *status quo*, in which they collaborated with the Roman authorities, was essential. In this context, they would have perceived the provocativeness of Jesus' action in the temple not in terms of its offensiveness to Jewish reverence for the temple (as Sanders supposes), but in terms of its challenge to the political–economic *status quo*. In these terms it was peculiarly dangerous, since it was a challenge to their own authority to manage the temple finances, in a context which created a danger of popular insurrection against the whole structure of power in which they and the Roman overlords were partners. Even worse than the spectre of

rebellion against Rome was the spectre of rebellion focused on a challenge to their own power. But this provides a motive for their action against Jesus; it did not supply a legal charge.

(4) It seems that in order to formulate an adequate legal charge against Jesus, the chief priests seized on Jesus' prophecy of the destruction of the temple, which, though only implicit in the demonstration itself, was explicitly pronounced, no doubt, in close connection with, or soon after, the demonstration. By putting the charge in the form of a prediction that Jesus himself would destroy the temple (Mark 14:58; 15:29; cf. Acts 6:14), they made the most of it. The charge in this form could imply that Jesus was actually plotting to destroy the temple. (For such an implication to be credible, Jesus would not have to be supposed to have a private army capable of capturing the temple, since arson was a plausible strategy.) A charge of plotting to destroy the temple had the advantage of being both a serious religious charge in the Sanhedrin, and also representing Jesus to Pilate as a dangerous insurrectionist.[95]

It is perfectly credible that the disciples would learn, by means of leaks and rumours, the initial charge on which Jesus was arrested. *Gos. Pet.* 7:25, which in my view rests on tradition independent of the synoptic Gospels, plausibly represents the disciples in hiding after the crucifixion, fearing arrest for intending to set fire to the temple.

(5) The complexity of the discussion about the trial of Jesus makes it impossible to enter it here, but if the Gospels can be believed on this point, it proved impossible to substantiate the charge of plotting to destroy the temple. The chief priests therefore fell back on the vaguer charge of the messianic pretensions suggested by the triumphal entry and the demonstration in the temple. This charge is intelligible when the alleged claim to messianic status is seen, not in abstraction, but as a claim to have authority to do what Jesus did in his demonstration in the temple.[96]

8

Q, THE LAW AND JUDAISM

CHRISTOPHER TUCKETT

Study of the Q material in the synoptic Gospels has been dominated in recent years by the attempts to apply the techniques of redaction criticism to this material. Many scholars have tried to identify specific features which characterise the theology of the Q material and to try to see where a 'community' which preserved this material might be placed on the first-century map.[1] In studies that have appeared so far, several important themes in Q have been extensively analysed and debated. For example, a lot of attention has been given to eschatology, the Son of Man sayings, ideas about Wisdom, the theme of the rejection of the prophets, and so on. One theme which does not appear to have received very extensive treatment is that of the law in the Q material. This article will therefore attempt to look at the theme of the law in Q and to see if one can make any further deductions about the place of the 'Q community' within first-century Christianity and first-century Judaism.

LUKE 16:16–18 AND PARALLELS   An obvious starting-point for any discussion about the theme of the law in Q is the saying in Matt 5:18 par Luke 16:17.

Matthew	Luke
Truly I say to you, till heaven and earth pass away, not an iota, not a dot will pass from the law until all is accomplished.	It is easier for heaven and earth to pass away, than for one dot of the law to become void.

There is almost universal agreement that this saying stems from Q, though the precise reconstruction of the Q wording is debated. The interpretation of the saying at the levels of both MattR and LukeR[2] has given rise to enormous debate. In so far as there is scholarly agreement about anything in relation to this verse, most would probably agree that the final clause in Matthew's version *heōs an panta genētai* (verse 18d) is due to MattR.[3] Moreover, it seems most plausible that the purpose of this addition by Matthew is to modify the force of the saying which comes to him from his tradition. The tradition says that the law remains in force until 'heaven and earth pass away',[4] and Matthew interprets this temporal clause by his second *heōs* clause in verse 18d. The implication may be that, for Matthew, in some sense 'all is accomplished' (whether in the coming of Jesus or in the death and resurrection of Jesus); thus the conditions of the temporal clause have now been met, and hence in the new age of the Christian Church, one iota or *keraia* of the law might fall, as indeed the following antitheses suggest.[5] Matthew's use of Q is thus to qualify very radically a statement which Matthew himself may have understood as implying that the law would remain valid for at least the whole of the present era.

The meaning of Luke 16:17 at the level of LukeR is much debated. Elsewhere in the Lukan writings, it would seem that the law was not regarded as permanently valid for the Christian, and the issue of whether the Christian should obey the detailed commands of the law does not seem to have been a very pressing one for Luke.[6] Some have argued that the form of the saying in Luke 16:17 should be interpreted along the lines of the formally similar saying in Luke 18:25 ('It is easier for a camel to go through the eye of a needle than for a rich man to enter the kingdom of God'). To say that 'it is easier for x than Y' does not necessarily mean that x is totally impossible, but only that it is something that will happen only with great difficulty.[7]

Nevertheless, it is hard to see such an interpretation of the saying being the correct one at the level of Luke's source. The precise wording of the source here is not absolutely certain, though most would argue that Luke's version is more likely to be original: for example, Luke's use of *eukopōteron* is not easily explicable as LukeR.[8] Some have pointed to the clumsy nature of Matthew's two *heōs* clauses and argued that it cannot be the case that both *heōs* clauses are due to MattR, so that at least one *heōs* clause must have been part of Matthew's source here. Hence either Q contained one such *heōs* clause and thus Luke's *eukopōteron* form of the saying is due to LukeR, or Matthew and Luke had access to different forms of the saying in their traditions.[9] However, Matthew may have wished to modify the force of the Q saying by adding verse 18d, and he prepared for this by changing the form of the 'heaven and earth passing away' clause into a temporal clause in verse 18b. The slight clumsiness may then be due to Matthew's redactional activity modifying the Q saying in two stages. Almost certainly the Q saying is asserting the abiding validity of the law in the present.[10] Thus P. D. Meyer comments aptly: 'Q's saying, in contrast to Matthew's revision, is not concerned with the future possibility of the

Law becoming void but with the present impossibility of its being void.'[11] Such an idea is not really that of either Matthew or Luke and hence we are probably justified in seeing here a particular facet of the theology of at least one part of the Q material.

The probable context of the saying within Q is also revealing. Most would agree that the saying about the law comes from a small sub-section in Q containing at least the verses Luke 16:16–18 with their Matthean parallels.[12] The problem of identifying any common thread running through the whole of the material in Luke 16 at the level of LukeR is well known, and hence many have suggested that Luke has simply repeated a block of sayings which in part comes to him from his tradition. The possibility that these three sayings occurred together in Q is also supported by a consideration of the Matthean contexts of the sayings. Matt 5:17 looks suspiciously like Matthew's rewriting of the saying in Luke 16:16. (Matthew's close parallel to Luke 16:16 comes elsewhere in Matt 11:12f.; however, the relocation can be adequately explained as due to MattR, whereas the converse change is very difficult to explain as due to LukeR.) Matthew also has a parallel to the divorce saying of Luke 16:18 in Matt 5:32. The close proximity of the parallels to Luke 16:16, 17, 18 within Matthew 5, in verses 17, 18, 32, thus adds additional weight to the argument that these three verses belonged together within Q.

Within this slightly wider Q context, the saying in Matt 5:18 par Luke 16:17 gains added force. The preceding saying in Luke 16:16 par Matt 11:12f. raises far more problems than can be dealt with here.

Matthew	Luke
From the days of John the Baptist until now the kingdom of heaven has suffered violence, and men of violence take it by force. For all the prophets and the law prophesied until John.	The law and the prophets were until John; since then the good news of the kingdom of God is preached and every one enters it violently.

It is however almost universally agreed that the more original form of the saying is represented in one half by Luke 16:16a (Matt 11:13 is probably MattR with its inversion of 'law' and 'prophets' and its use of the verb to 'prophesy'). The more original form of the other half of the saying may be represented in Matt 11:12 (Luke 16:16b clearly owes a lot to Luke R: cf. the use of *pas* and *evangelizetai*.[13] The version in Q thus probably said that 'the law and the prophets were until John'. Quite apart from the problem of the relative position of John, the saying states that in some sense at least the era of the law is ended. The following saying in Luke 16:17 par Matt 5:18 clearly has the effect of modifying this considerably, or at least of guarding against one particular interpretation. Whatever Luke 16:16 implies, it must not, according to this interpretation, be taken as suggesting that the law is no longer to be applied. A new era may in one sense have superseded that of the law and the prophets; but the law is still to be obeyed. It looks very much as if the second saying is a reaction against the first.[14] The positioning of Luke 16:17 in Q thus probably represents the redactional activity of at least one stage of the Q tradition, imposing its own interpretation and modification of a saying (Luke 16:16) that in all probability goes back to Jesus.

The saying which follows in Q, Matt 5:32 par Luke 16:18, is again notoriously difficult to interpret.

Matthew	Luke
Everyone who divorces his wife, except on the ground of unchastity, makes her an adulteress; and whoever marries a divorced woman commits adultery.	Everyone who divorces his wife and marries another commits adultery, and he who marries a woman divorced from her husband commits adultery.

The apparent total ban on divorce in this saying is certainly open to very different interpretations. According to some, it represents a radical attack on the written law of Deut 24:1 itself.[15] According to others, no such attack is intended: being stricter than the law requires does not constitute a fundamental attack on the law itself.[16] If this is a radical attack on the law, then one would have to ascribe the verse to a later stage of the Q redaction, modifying again the strict nomism of the preceding saying. On the other hand, the verse could be seen as an example of how the general saying of Luke 16:17 is to be put into practice by the Q community. The law is to be obeyed, and obeyed even more rigorously than by some Jews, with no appeals to any 'let-out' clauses such as the divorce regulations. In favour of this last interpretation, one could appeal to Qumran texts such as the *Damascus Document* and the Temple Scroll which appear to suggest that at least some members of the Qumran sect regarded divorce as wrong, though without in any way making any radical attack on the law itself.[17] If this latter interpretation is adopted, then the three Q verses considered in this section present a reasonably coherent and consistent viewpoint. With the arrival of John and Jesus a new era has dawned, but this is not one where the law loses any of its validity. The demands of the law still apply for the Christian. Such an attitude to the law emerges from other parts of the Q material as we shall see.

TITHING   Q evidently contained a series of sayings against scribes and/or Pharisees. In Matthew 23, all the sayings are directed against the 'scribes and Pharisees', apparently viewed as an undifferentiated group. This stereotyped address is almost certainly due to MattR.[18] In Luke 11, and perhaps also in Q, the sayings are divided into two groups, one set of sayings directed against *pharisaioi*, the other against *nomikoi/grammateis*. In all the woes, there are at times quite marked differences in the wording of the Matthean and Lukan versions, though in general terms the existence, and the general meaning, of the Q version is not in doubt. I start with the saying about tithing in Matt 23:23 par Luke 11:42.

Matthew	Luke
Woe to you, scribes and Pharisees, hypocrites! for you tithe mint and dill and cummin, and have	Woe to you, Pharisees! for you tithe mint and rue and every herb and neglect justice and the love of

neglected the weightier matters of the law, justice and mercy and faith; these you ought to have done, without neglecting the others.	God; these you ought to have done, without neglecting the others.

Some differences between Matthew's and Luke's versions are relatively easy to explain; others are less important in the present discussion. As we have already seen, Matthew's address, 'scribes and Pharisees', is probably MattR,[19] so that the Lukan version is probably more original in having the saying directed against 'Pharisees' alone. Matthew's reference to 'the weightier matters of the law' may also be MattR. The difference between 'justice, mercy and faith' (Matthew) and 'love of God' (Luke) probably need not concern us here.[20] In either case, Jesus is contrasting the tithing practices of the Pharisees with more fundamental principles which evidently should have precedence.

The final phrase of the saying clearly changes the accent. Whether Matthew's *aphienai* or Luke's *pareinai* is more original here again need not concern us at this point. What is important is that the phrase 'without neglecting the others' looks very much like a secondary comment by a later writer seeking to correct any 'misunderstandings' which the rest of the saying might imply. Without the final part, the *logion* could easily be taken as suggesting that tithing is unimportant and to be regarded as an optional extra. The final phrase makes it clear that this is not the case. Tithing must still be undertaken and any appeals to great principles such as justice, etc. must not undermine in any way the actual practice of tithing. Thus many have seen Luke 11:42d as a redactional addition in Q, reasserting the principle of tithing. At the level of this Q redaction, it would appear that the editor wants to insist on the importance of this particular legal practice for the Christian community. It is not the case that for Q, some reassessment of the Jewish law is in mind here, as if the ceremonial law were being made subservient to the ethical law.[21] This may be the case in Q's tradition (i.e. without the final part of the saying). The effect of the Q redaction is to go in the opposite direction and to assert that the ceremonial aspect of the law is on a par with the rest.[22]

What precisely is the practice being commended here in Q? Unfortunately certainty is not possible since Matthew and Luke disagree in their wordings. In Matthew the (scribes and) Pharisees are accused of tithing 'mint, dill and cummin'; in Luke it is 'mint, rue and every herb'. Rules about tithing were of particular concern to the Pharisees, as far as we can tell.[23] The OT decreed that farm and garden produce, especially 'corn, wine and oil' (often mentioned in this context) should be tithed, and we know that later rabbis had lengthy discussions about what was and was not liable to tithing. As in all such instances, we can never be certain whether the decisions recorded in later times applied in first-century Judaism. However, according to the later rabbis, dill and cummin were required to be tithed (*m. Ma'aserot* 4:5; *m. Demai* 2:1). Mint is not mentioned in this context. Rue is explicitly excluded as liable to tithe (*m. Šebiʿit* 9:1), and it is regarded as certain that not 'every herb' was tithed. Thus the Matthean version gives three items which probably were tithed (the position of mint being uncertain); the Lukan version gives at least two items which were not tithed.

Almost without exception, commentators have accepted the Matthean version as more original, because it fits our knowledge of Judaism better.[24] This may be the case, though we cannot be certain. Saying anything about the Pharisees with confidence is notoriously difficult, but it would appear that the Pharisees of the pre-70 era were above all concerned with food laws, tithing and purity laws, and they took enormous care to ensure that the law was kept.[25] Moreover, they were evidently prepared at times to take upon themselves more demands than the law strictly required. *If* the Pharisee's prayer recorded in Luke 18:12 reflects anything at all of pharisaic practice, it suggests that at least some Pharisees paid more in tithes than was strictly necessary. Jeremias suggests that the Pharisee of Luke 18 was paying tithes on his corn, wine and oil to cover the possibility that the person from whom he had bought them had not paid full tithes already.[26] But it could equally well be the case that some Pharisees decided to pay tithes on more things than were strictly required by law. If this is the case, the Lukan version of the saying might make more sense than its parallel in Matthew. Indeed, if the Lukan version is more original, then the force of the saying becomes all the greater: the comment is not just about those who keep the law but about those who voluntarily do more than the law requires.

Perhaps the precise details do not affect the main issue here too much. What is important is that the practice which is implicitly questioned in the opening part of the saying, but reaffirmed with the final (Q-redactional) clause is the practice of *pharisaic* law.[27] The Q community is thus expected to continue the practice of tithing as practised by the Pharisees (though whether this is intended to stay within the current rules, or to go beyond them in works of supererogation, is not quite clear.)

PURITY Apparently very near the saying about tithing in Q is the saying about purity (Matt 23:25f. par Luke 11:39–41).

Matthew	Luke
Woe to you, scribes and Pharisees, hypocrites! for you cleanse the outside of the cup and of the plate but inside they are full of extortion and rapacity. You blind Pharisee! first cleanse the inside of the cup and of the plate, that the outside also may be clean.	Now you Pharisees cleanse the outside of the cup and of the dish but inside you are full of extortion and wickedness. You fools! Did not he who made the outside make the inside also? But give alms for those things which are within and behold, everything is clean for you.

Unfortunately the precise Q wording is probably irrecoverable as both evangelists have worked over the tradition independently.[28] Further it is not clear where (if at all) the saying shifts from being a statement about purification practices to being a metaphor about the moral state of a person. Clearly both Matthew and Luke regard the saying as ultimately metaphorical, referring to people rather than cups. This may well be right at the level of Q too (and indeed of Jesus, if the saying goes back to Jesus). It is however worth noting that the saying does not condemn the practice of purity rites in any way.[29] It is true that there is no explicit affirmation of such rites (as in Luke 11:42d) but the accent lies elsewhere.

It is also worth noting that the saying has force only if the practice referred to in the opening statement, 'you cleanse the outside of the cup', corresponds with current practice of those addressed. J. Neusner has sought to show that such practice can be identified fairly precisely.[30] M. *Kelim* 25:1 states that the outside of the cup and the inside are separate for the purposes of purity considerations. Hence if one part becomes unclean it does not affect the other. Neusner examines the discussion of *m. Berakot* 8:2 in *y. Berakot* 8:2 and concludes that the practice implied in this gospel saying reflects the views of Shammaite Pharisees. Hillelites thought that the inner part of the cup was always decisive: the outer part was always held to be unclean. Thus the outer part had no effect on the inner part. The school of Shammai disagreed, holding that the two parts were independent, and hence one can cleanse the outside of the cup first. The force of the metaphor depends on the practice described, i.e. first cleansing the outside of the cup, being generally accepted by the listeners. Hence the saying would have force primarily for those who are putting Shammaite beliefs into practice. Neusner accepts that the thrust of the gospel saying is at the metaphorical level of people, not utensils, but his analysis makes some striking observations about the *Sitz im Leben* in which such a saying would have force.[31]

SABBATH   Another Q tradition which is relevant for the present discussion is the saying about rescuing someone from a pit on the sabbath (Matt 12:11f. par Luke 14:5).

Matthew	Luke
What man of you, if he has one sheep and it falls into a pit on the sabbath, will not lay hold of it and lift it out? Of how much more value is a man than a sheep!	Which of you having a son or an ox that has fallen into a well will not immediately pull him out on a sabbath day? [For the text, cf. below.]

This is not always regarded as a genuine part of Q,[32] though the substantial agreement between Matthew and Luke here makes it highly likely that a saying of this nature did form part of Q. Once again the precise Q wording is uncertain and the situation is complicated by some doubt about the precise Lukan text at this point. In particular there is textual doubt about who/what has actually fallen into a pit, with various manuscript support for 'son', 'ox', 'ass' or almost any combination of these three. I have examined this tradition elsewhere and so will not repeat the same analysis again.[33] The conclusion of that discussion was that the most primitive form of the saying is one which referred to a 'son' who had fallen into a pit on the sabbath. Matthew's reference to a 'sheep' is probably MattR and the additional references to animals in Luke 14:5 may be due to assimilation to, or influence from, the similar story in Luke 13:15.

Part of the problem raised by the tradition here is to know the precise legal background, and again the limited nature of our knowledge of first-century Judaism becomes a critical factor. However, as far as we can tell, it would not have been regarded as a legitimate breach of the sabbath law to rescue an animal which had fallen into a pit; but it would have been regarded as legitimate to rescue a person in such a situation. The Q saying thus appears to reflect very precisely the interpretation of the sabbath law by contemporary Jews in a way that other strands of the gospel tradition do not. (Mark's Gospel is notorious for having Jesus justify his behaviour in a way that no Jew would accept;[34] so too Matthew's adaptations of the Q tradition fail to satisfy Jewish sensibilities, since no Jew apparently accepted that one could rescue a sheep from a pit on the sabbath.[35])

Matt 12:11f. par Luke 14:5 appears at first sight to be an isolated saying in Q. There is no clear evidence of the context in Q in which the saying occurred. Nevertheless it is clear that the saying must have been part of a wider context. It cannot have existed in isolation. It clearly acts as the first half of an *a minori ad maius* argument; and the argument cannot really have been anything other than an attempt to justify Jesus' working on the sabbath. The point to notice here is that such an argument would have real force in a Jewish context in a way that defences by Jesus in other strands of the gospel tradition do not (cf. above). Jesus is here appealing to an example which the Jews themselves would accept as a legitimate breach of the sabbath law. It may well be that such an appeal would not have convinced Jesus' opponents about the legitimacy of some of the specific actions of Jesus on the sabbath recorded in the Gospels: after all, rescuing a man from a pit was a matter of saving his life and the principle of working to save life on the sabbath was accepted by all; the problem with Jesus' actions on the sabbath as recorded in the Gospels is that they are not actions which necessarily save physical life.[36] We do not have the second half of the argument in Q, and hence we do not know precisely what action of Jesus on the sabbath is here being defended. However, the force of the saying is clear. Jesus is shown as not acting wantonly. If he does break the sabbath law, he does so by appealing to accepted and legally defined exceptions to the law. The Jesus of Q thus operates on the sabbath within the law as defined by later tradition to a far greater extent than the Jesus of Mark or the Jesus of Matthew.

OTHER EVIDENCE FROM Q   Other Q texts may provide some subsidiary evidence to supplement the picture which has emerged so far. In particular, the versions of the double love command in Matt 22:34–40 and Luke 10:25–8 may be relevant here. I have argued elsewhere for the existence of the Q source at this point in the tradition.[37] The extensive agreements between Matthew and Luke against Mark, many of which are hard to explain as redactional, are most easily accounted for by the existence of a version of this story in Q as well as in Mark. The one point worth noting here is that in Q the question about the great commandment is apparently a hostile one (Luke 10:25 *ekpeirazōn* Matt 22:35 *peirazōn*). The question is put by a *nomikos*, which links with the second half of the series of woes in Luke 11 par Matthew 23 where the final three woes are directed against the *nomikoi*. It is of course notoriously difficult to identify precisely the *nomikoi* and the *pharisaioi* in the Gospels, and to see what links if any it is justifiable to draw between either group and the later rabbis. J. Bowker has suggested that there was probably a steady increase in overlap between the two groups during the second-temple period.[38] It would not be unreasonable to see the Q community as also envisaging some connection between the two. It is true that the Q woes distinguish between the two groups, but the fact that the woes (probably) occur together in Q suggests that for Q the two groups are not unrelated. Thus the pericope of the great commandment shows that the Jesus of Q is facing and dealing with some suspicion on the part of scribes/lawyers and/or Pharisees over the question of the law. The detailed reply of Jesus in Q (apart from the actual double love command itself) is probably irrecoverable. Matt 22:40 almost certainly represents MattR of Mark, and Luke's version has been strongly redacted to link up with the following Parable of the Good Samaritan.[39]

Further hostility in relation to scribes and/or Pharisees is also evidenced in the remaining Q woes which we have not considered in detail here. However, it is worth noting that all the remaining woes (with the possible exception of Matt 23:4 par Luke 11:46) concern the behaviour of the Pharisees or lawyers: what is attacked is their love of publicity, their inner 'impurity', their guilt in inflicting violence on the prophets, and so on.[40] Matt 23:4 par Luke 11:46 may be the exception in that the lawyers are criticised for 'loading' people with 'burdens hard to bear'. (Presumably the reference is to the detailed prescriptions of the interpretation of the law.) Yet the real critique is that the lawyers have failed to help other people with their burdens. The burdens themselves are not really questioned in principle.

What picture emerges from the Q texts considered so far? The Q material demanded here appears to exhibit a strongly 'conservative' attitude to the law. It shows a deep concern that the law should be maintained; it is aware that Jesus could be seen as antinomian, and Q appears to represent a strong movement to 'rejudaise' Jesus. Further, there is some strong concern to uphold the pharisaic interpretation of the law. However, coupled with this is an intense awareness of hostility from non-Christian Pharisees and/or non-Christian scribes. Does such a picture have any further implications for where the community which preserved this Q material, and for which its sentiments were presumably congenial, might be placed on a first-century map?

Q AND THE PHARISEES   In a recent article, R. A. Wild has considered the whole question of the phenomenon of the Gospels' accounts of the conflict between Jesus and the Pharisees in the light of recent discussions about the

Pharisees.[41] Drawing heavily on the famous work of J. Neusner on the Pharisees,[42] Wild takes as a starting-point the fact that in the pre-70 era the Pharisees were probably very much of a minority group within Judaism. In contrast to the general picture in the Gospels, where the Pharisees are regularly represented as the leading figures within Judaism, Pharisees were not very numerous and probably not very influential at this period. (Josephus' rather different picture in the *Antiquities* is probably due to his own propagandist efforts to convince the Romans that the Pharisees were the most important party in Judaism, as well as reflecting the *de facto* situation after 70 CE).[43] Further, the prime concern of Pharisees was with food laws, purity laws, tithing and so on. However, the small number of Pharisees within Judaism meant that they could not, and hence probably did not, try to convince the ordinary masses that they should follow them. The ʿam hāʾāreṣ could be dismissed, ignored, pitied, loved, but one presumes not violently attacked. Why then should the new Christian movement have apparently provoked such violent reaction and opposition from the Pharisees? Why did the Pharisees take any notice of the early Christians? Or conversely, why did the Christians (or Jesus) take any notice of the Pharisees? The gospel picture might be simply a reflection of the post-70 era, when all agree that pharisaic Judaism came to the fore and became the dominant force within Judaism. However, the tradition of controversies with Pharisees looks to be too deeply embedded for that.

Wild's suggestion is that, in fact, there were far closer links between the early Christian movement and the pre-70 Pharisees than is usually allowed. Wild examines two Q texts (the sayings on tithing and purity considered above) and the traditions in Mark 7:1–15 and 2:15–17. He argues that the Jesus of all these traditions appears to accept pharisaic interpretations of the law, and hence he concludes with the tentative suggestion that Jesus may have had a lot in common with the pharisaic party.

Wild's argument is persuasive in several ways. The suggestion that Jesus had close links with the Pharisees has been made by many others before,[44] though not quite via this kind of argument which in many respects is convincing. However, his detailed arguments are of varying value and perhaps his case needs some more careful nuancing. His suggestion that the Q texts show Jesus accepting pharisaic rules seems well founded, as indeed I have argued above in examining these sayings. However, the evidence from Mark is less clear-cut. The saying in Mark 7:15, for example, may be more polemical than Wild suggests. At what stage the saying was attached to the hand-washing debate is not clear. Many would argue that the (almost certainly) redactional nature of verse 14 suggests that the connection between verse 15 and what precedes is due to MarkR.[45] In any case it is hard to eliminate completely all elements of polemic from the saying. Wild follows the suggestion of many others that the form of antithetical parallelism in verse 15 should not be taken as an absolute negation of the first half of the saying. 'It is not A but B' should be taken as implying that B is more important than A, but that A is not excluded.[46] Nevertheless, even if the saying originally was not to do with all the food laws of Leviticus,[47] it is still placing concerns about external purity at a lower level than concern for 'inner purity'.[48] There is certainly nothing in Mark 7:15 corresponding to the injunction in Luke 11:42d par. Thus, whilst Wild is justified in pointing to the fact that the debate in Mark 7:1, 2, 5 presupposes that Jesus' disciples are apparently being expected to observe specifically pharisaic mores (in particular here the practice of ritual hand-washing which all agree was not required of all Jews at this period), the Jesus of Mark 7 comes over as rather more opposed to such discipline. The same applies in the case of Mark 2:15–17.

Wild may thus be right in suggesting that originally Jesus' disciples had close links with the pharisaic movement, so that other Pharisees apparently expected the disciples to conform to their own mores. Such a picture emerges from both the Markan and Q material examined. However, it is only in Q that Jesus himself emerges as one who affirms these links positively. In Mark, and perhaps in Mark's tradition, we see Jesus distancing himself from the pharisaic viewpoint. It would thus appear that the community which preserved the Q material also preserved positive links with the pharisaic movement in a way that most other primitive Christian groups about which we have any evidence did not. Further, the possible connection of some of the sayings considered with the views of Shammaite Pharisees would tie in well with Neusner's further theories about the dominant position of Shammaite Pharisaism in the pre-70 era.[49] Certainly Q reflects a strongly conservative Jewish–Christian group within primitive Christianity.[50] The Gentile mission *may* be presumed,[51] but prime interest in references to the Gentile mission in Q is in relation to the judgement which threatens Israel.[52] So too the dominance of the theme of judgement of 'this generation' in Q is well known.[53]

A lot of this would fit together if Q emanated from a Christian community in close touch with Pharisaism, experiencing some hostility or suspicion from non-Christian Pharisees, but also claiming to be a true part of the pharisaic movement. Such a suggestion by no means solves all the problems of the *Sitz im Leben* of Q. Moreover, the legal sayings examined here do not cover the whole compass of Q by any manner of means. Much of the material about non-retaliation, etc. in the great sermon may also suggest other aspects of the Q community's existence.[54] Further, one should beware of assuming that all the Q material is of a unitary nature. Q may have undergone several stages of development.[55] Nevertheless the conclusion of this study is that, at some stage at least, the Q community may have had a close relationship with the small sectarian movement in pre-70 Judaism which we call Pharisaism. No doubt this relationship was a dialectical one in that non-Christian Pharisees were evidently hostile to the Christian group. But the very existence of such hostility may well be evidence that the Christian group was claiming to be a genuine part of the pharisaic movement. If it were not, the group would probably have been ignored by the non-Christian Pharisees. Q may thus provide us with evidence for the existence of a group of Christian Pharisees within early Christianity.[56] As such it should alert us to the great variety within early Christianity and to the complex nature of the relationships between Christianity and Judaism in the formative years of the new Christian movement.

9
CHRIST AND THE LAW IN JOHN 7–10*

GEORGE J. BROOKE

The Fourth Gospel's attitude to, and use of, Jewish scriptures has been the subject of some considerable re-examination over the last four decades, since C. K. Barrett wrote his much-quoted article 'The Old Testament in the Fourth Gospel'.[1] This re-examination has involved the reconsideration of the explicit quotations of the Jewish scriptures in the Gospel[2] as well as the allusions to whole incidents or careers which illuminate the author's understanding of the significance of Jesus, incidents like the manna in the wilderness,[3] careers like those of Moses, Elijah and Elisha.[4] It is now commonplace to read that the use of the Jewish scriptures is very widespread in the Fourth Gospel, but sometimes its use appears veiled to us either because the Jewish or Jewish–Christian audience would have been more attuned to what was said than we can be, or because in the very process of the Gospel's compilation something of what might have been clear in the first draft, so to speak, becomes less obvious as other ideas from the surrounding literary context crowd in. Furthermore there is a deliberate intention in the Fourth Gospel to portray things at at least two levels, though that does not of itself necessarily lead to the concealment of scriptural allusions.[5]

Following the surface of the text for John 7–10 it is possible to see that these chapters fall into two sections, one large, one small, surrounded by editorial remarks that form an inclusion through their several common features. In 7:1–9 Jesus does not want to go about in Judea because the Jews seek to kill him, his brothers suggest that he should show his works to his disciples, his brothers do not believe in him, he remains (*emeinen*) in

Galilee; in 10:40–2 Jesus goes out of Judea to Transjordan and remains (*emeinen*)[6] there, those who come to him remark that John did no sign, many believed in him. The two sections within these editorial remarks are set one at the Feast of Tabernacles (7: 10–10:21) and one at the Feast of Dedication (10:22–39). That the material in 7:10–10:21 belongs together may be demonstrated not just from the logic of the narration itself, which places all the action, even the healing of the blind man on the sabbath (ch. 9), during Tabernacles, but also from certain motifs which belong exclusively to this passage. For example, the theme of schism (*schisma*) is confined to John 7:43; 9:16 and 10:19, each time in association with some christological comment; or again, the notion that Jesus is possessed by a demon is confined in the Fourth Gospel to 7:20; 8:48, 49, 52; 10:20, 21. In fact, from these two examples it could be concluded that 10:19–21 are deliberately composed in order to demonstrate that 9:1–10:18 belong with the Tabernacles chapters that immediately precede it. 9:1–10:18 in themselves have not always been taken as a unit together but the recent work of M. J. J. Menken,[7] quite apart from the rather dangerous use of word- and syllable-counting, offers sufficient evidence of their unity including a demonstration of the double-duty function of 9:40–1 as the conclusion of ch. 9 and the opening of the two monologues of Jesus in 10:1–18.[8] C. H. Dodd had long ago argued a similar case, suggesting also that 10:22–39 are an appendix to what precedes, even though set at a different feast.[9] Perhaps we only need recall that Dedication is associated with Tabernacles in 2 Macc 1:9 to justify taking the two major sections of John 7–10 together.[10]

The proposal of this paper is that, in addition to all the evidence already mentioned, the unity of these four chapters (John 7–10) rests in their treatment of the figure of Christ in relation to the law. More specifically, it seems that at some stage in the history of their composition an interpretation of the ten commandments, the Ten Words, has been combined with the typology of Moses as law-giver in order to argue that Jesus and the law are intricately interdependent. The significance of chs. 7–8 in particular and the blasphemy section in ch. 10 in relation to the Jewish law in its broadest sense has often been noticed; it forms a large part, for example, of the extensive discussion of S. Pancaro, *The Law in the Fourth Gospel*,[11] and so provides a convenient starting point for our discussion.

REFERENCES TO THE DECALOGUE   The first reference to the law in ch. 7 comes at 7:19. Jesus is in the temple defending the authority of his teaching. The dialogue focuses implicitly on whether Jesus has broken the law in such a way as to deserve the death penalty. The issue concerns the sabbath healing of the lame man which has been recounted in ch. 5. Many commentators point to Lev 24:17, part of a possible lection for Tabernacles,[12] to illuminate the meaning of the passage by showing how breach of the sabbath, even for healing,[13] could carry the death penalty, but reference should also be made to the sabbath commandment itself (Exod 20:8, Deut 5:12).[14] Jesus' defence rests not in the healing of

lameness, for having already waited 38 years the lame man could surely
have waited one more day in order to preserve the sabbath. Rather, Jesus
likens his action to circumcision performed on the sabbath. The healing of
the lame man is a gift of wholeness like circumcision, a gift which includes
the receiver within the creative activity of God. Furthermore the reader
should note that the discussion goes beyond whether Jesus has broken the
sabbath or not. In giving wholeness Jesus is working God's work, which in
relation to the sabbath (Gen 2:2) was thought by some Jews to be still
continuing;[15] one cannot but help noticing that in the Exodus tradition the
justification for the sabbath commandment is based on the Genesis
creation account.

The same breadth of purpose is apparent in ch. 9, another sabbath
healing done to enable teaching on who is a sinner, that is, who is a law-
breaker.[16] Again the teaching is the manifestation of the works of God
(9:3). The Pharisees are challenged by the man given sight on every count
but they are unable to see beyond the letter of the commandment: 'This
man is not from God, for he does not keep the sabbath' (9:16). In the MT
and the LXX 'keep the sabbath' reflects the version of the decalogue in
Deuteronomy 5, though the Samaritan Pentateuch appears to assimilate
Exod 20:8 to Deut 5:12, reading šāmôr in its Exodus version. Since such
assimilation between the two forms of the decalogue is common in the
Qumran phylacteries too,[17] it is difficult to be precise about which version
of the decalogue may lie behind John 9:16. In the gospel narrative Jesus'
defence against sabbath-breaking is given by the Pharisees themselves,
who are divided over the issue. The offering of sight to the blind is a feature
of the LXX text of Isa 61:1, another possible reading for Tabernacles.

Another commandment is referred to and used in 8:49, though again
few commentators make anything of it. In a continuing and increasingly
vitriolic dialogue concerning Jesus' origin and descent Jesus answers the
charge that he has a demon by reference to the fifth commandment: 'I have
not a demon, but I honour my Father.' The significance of this allusion
rests firstly in the way in which it enables the theme of the glorification of
the Father to be introduced (8:50); in 2 Pet 1:17 honour and glory are
similarly combined in the allusion to the transfiguration, which tradition is
commonly associated with Tabernacles. Secondly this reference to Exod
20:12 or Deut 5:16 is another example of how the collection of ideas in
John 5 (here 5:23) is replayed with variations in John 7–10, perhaps
reflecting a lively homiletic activity associated with a debate about the
authority of Jesus' followers to heal on the sabbath. Thirdly, beyond Jesus'
outward obedience in his keeping this commandment is the implication
that those descendants of Abraham who challenge Jesus' descent disclose
the falsehood of their own position in their inability to see Jesus in the line
of God's relationship with his people of which the decalogue is a prime
example. The charge against Jesus that he is both a Samaritan and demon-
possessed may be a reference to accusations of idolatry made by Jews
against certain Jewish Christians: this accusation the narrative swiftly
reverses.[18]

A third text which has close verbal similarity to the Septuagint texts of the decalogue is 10:33. Jesus is charged with blasphemy and threatened with stoning because 'you being a man make yourself God (*su anthrōpos ōn poieis seauton theon*)'. This reflects Exod 20:4 or Deut 5:8: 'You shall not make for yourself an idol (*ou poiēseis seautǭ eidōlon*).' As with the fourth and fifth commandments already discussed, John 10:33 has a parallel in John 5, at 5:18.[19] Furthermore, as with the discussion of the sabbath in 7:19–24, Jesus answers the Jewish charge with a reference to the law, though the text is most likely from Ps 82:6 rather than from the Pentateuch.[20] Psalm 82, possibly a psalm in use at Tabernacles,[21] is used to point the discussion away from any particular christological title with which Jesus may be described. As with healing on the sabbath it is the works of God which Jesus does that are significant and are the basic matter for belief. Jesus has been consecrated (10:30:*hagiazō*) by the Father so that he may in turn glorify the Father's name (12:28).[22]

ALLUSIONS TO THE DECALOGUE   The debate about the sabbath in John 7:19–24 which has already been discussed opens with a verse that provides the key to understanding an allusion to another commandment. 'Did not Moses give you the law? Yet none of you keeps the law. Why do you seek to kill me?' (7:19). In part at least, the Jewish breach of the law is not just in any subsequent comment that Jesus makes about practices which over-ride the sabbath commandment, but is about the intention of some to kill him. Intentional killing is murder. At 7:1 the reason stated for Jesus remaining in Galilee is that the Jews 'seek to kill' him; this phrase recurs five times (7:19, 20, 25; 8:37, 40), the verb *apokteinō* occurring alone also at 8:22. The use of *zēteō* with *apokteinō* underlines that the killing is premeditated: indeed the standard translation of that rare but very Johannine-looking word *anthrōpoktonos* (8:44)[23] is 'murderer'.

If in this theme in John 7–8 there is an allusion to the prohibition from murder,[24] it is as well to ask why *phoneuō* (LXX Exod 20:15; Deut 5:18) was not used of the Jews' intention. In the Septuagint *apokteinō* is never used to translate *rāṣaḥ*, the verb used in the commandment, but it is used to translate *nākâ*, *ḥāram* and *hārag*, the only other verbs which are translated by *phoneuō*. Given the thematic interest in the Fourth Gospel in life, particularly as it is available to those who obey or hear the words which Jesus speaks (5:24; 6:63, 68) and as it can be identified with the commandment (*entolē*) of God (12:50), it seems as if in chs. 7 and 8 the author has deliberately chosen to use *apokteinō* to underline not just that the Jews wish to break the commandment and murder Jesus but also that in so doing they betray the life-giving purpose of the commandments, which same purpose is now to be recognised in Jesus too. On one level Jesus' death is murder by the Jews but on another it is the defeat of the murderer, the devil,[25] through whom death was introduced. On this deeper level Jesus remains in control of his own fate and is lifted above the casuistry of who is to blame for his death and how they should be treated. The deliberate avoidance of *phoneuō* takes the reader to the heart of the matter: he or she is involved in life and death, not in deciding between murder and manslaughter. Here is a challenge to the Jew or Jewish Christian: the life-giving function of the law,[26] intended to express the purpose of creation, is being seen in a new light.

In John 7–10 another person who comes to kill is mentioned in 10:10: 'The thief comes only to steal and kill and destroy.' In the parabolic material of the Shepherd and the Door Jesus contrasts himself with the thief (10:1, 8). Quite apart from the fact that the Septuagint translates Exod 20:14 and Deut 5:19 with *kleptō*, the discussion concerning the meaning of that prohibition in *Mekilta* and elsewhere in rabbinic literature[27] may throw significant light on the use of Jesus' teaching. The rabbinic debate concerned whether the prohibition referred to the theft of a person, which was a capital charge, or the theft of property. The majority of rabbis seem to have decided for the former by analogy with the other commandments. The Fourth Gospel seems to have Jesus agree with them: Jesus' opposition to the thief is that he lays down his life for the sheep (10:11, 15, 17). The Gospel then has Jesus explain the problem of the relation of the initiative of God in Jesus' death to the apparent agency of the thief in taking his life: 'No one takes it from me, but I lay it down of my own accord. I have power to lay it down, and I have power to take it again; this charge (*entolē*)[28] I have received from my Father' (10:18).

In the parabolic material in John 10 the Father's commandment functions as a key to understanding how Jesus' death is 'of the law' despite the thief's breach of the eighth commandment. Earlier in John 7–10 the first reference to the Father comes as the climax to the debate concerning Jesus' origin and authority. The Father is a witness alongside Jesus himself (8:18). In the immediate context the charge against Jesus is: 'You are bearing witness to yourself; your testimony is not true' (8:13). As with the sabbath commandment, we should not refer solely to Jewish casuistry to understand the intention of the passage, that is, whether one witness is ever sufficient, or whether the witness of two witnesses can ever be challenged.[29] Rather the reader is to perceive that the 'light of life' (8:12) available in Torah[30] is available in knowing the one who keeps the law of Exod 20:16 and Deut 5:20 in association with the Father himself.

JOHN 8:21–59   This section of the Gospel contains two dialogues. In the first (8:21–30), with the Jews, Jesus discusses both the content and authority of his teaching. In this dialogue both *lalō*, what Jesus does, and *didaskō*, what the Father does, have overtones of *dbr* and *yrh*, words used in the giving of, and instruction in, the law.[31] The second dialogue (8:31–59) is with some Jews who had believed, and is made up of an introductory saying of Jesus concerning the abiding of his word (8:31–2)[32] and three sets of four small speeches. The first and third sets contain in each speech explicit mention of Abraham. In the narrative he functions through his fatherhood of Israel, but he may also be referred to because in tradition he was revered as the first to keep Tabernacles.[33] Furthermore he is noted for his stand against idolatry[34] and his keeping of the commandments.[35]

The central set of four speeches (8:41–51) drops the direct use of Abraham. This set may contain allusions to three of the ten commandments. Firstly in 8:41 the Jews deny that they were born of fornication. Although, as with the commandment concerning murder, our author does not use the precise Greek word for adultery at this point, it seems that that prohibition may lie behind the construction of the dialogue. In any case *porneia* occurs only here in the Fourth Gospel and as such is worthy of further consideration. *Porneia* or its verbal associates is used in the LXX together with, or as a synonym of, *moicheia* and its cognates in two traditions.[36] One is the tradition of the prophets: in Hosea[37] concerning Israel's unfaithfulness, which is fornication and adultery (are John's readers here Jews who have fallen away from belief in Jesus?), in Isa 57:3 as synonyms in an oracle of judgement, in Jeremiah[38] of Judah's playing the harlot adulterously, and in Ezekiel[39] in ch. 16 in an attack on Jerusalem and in ch. 23 in an attack on both Samaria and Jerusalem – a combination many see to lie behind the use of Ezekiel 34 in John 10:1–18.

The second tradition that associates fornication and adultery is that of Wisdom. In Prov 6:23–6[40] there is advice concerning the harlot who may be hired for a loaf of bread and the adulteress who stalks a man's life, all this briefly after a verse reading, 'The commandment (*miṣwâ*) is a lamp and the teaching (*tôrâ*) a light' (6:23). In Sir 23:23 are listed the three counts against the woman who leaves her husband and provides an heir by a stranger: 'First of all, she has disobeyed the law of the Most High, second, she has committed an offence against her husband; and third, she has committed adultery (*moicheia*) through harlotry (*porneia*) and brought forth children by another man.' Together with these details should be set the well-known association of the law and Wisdom (Sir 24:23) which is often cited as illumination of the Christ of the Fourth Gospel.[41] In denying their descent through fornication the Jews are portrayed as apostate, unable to see the significance of the law either in its old form as precepts or in its new form as Wisdom, Jesus, with whom they dare to argue about the fatherhood of God. Perhaps the somewhat veiled allusion to the prohibition from adultery caused someone at a later time who recognised an interpretation of the decalogue in John 7–10 to insert a more obvious passage about adultery (7:53–8:11)!

Jesus proceeds to take the argument further. The Jews' denial of their descent through fornication prompts him to put it positively: 'You are of your father the devil, and your will is to do your father's desires (*epithumias*)' (8:44). Like *porneia* in 8:41, *epithumias* occurs only here in the Fourth Gospel; it is from the same root that is used in the LXX at Exod 20:17 and Deut 5:21: 'You shall not covet.'[42] Since the first object of covetousness in the prohibition in the LXX is 'your neighbour's wife', it is perhaps not surprising to find an allusion to this commandment, the tenth, as the dialogue develops from the subject of adultery.

The third item in this section of the dialogue is a question: 'Are we not right in saying you are a Samaritan and have a demon?' (8:48); Jesus' answer, the fourth component in the dialogue, is: 'I have not a demon but I honour my Father.' This is a more obvious allusion, this time to the fifth commandment which has already been discussed above.

JOHN 10:22–39   It has already been noted that John 10:33 contains an allusion to the second commandment. Close reading of 10:22–39 suggests that it may also be possible to see allusions to the first and third commandments in these verses associated with the Feast of Dedication. In 10:25 Jesus answers the request for plain speaking with: 'I told you and you do not believe. The works that I do in my Father's name, they bear witness to me.' In John 7–10 the phrase 'Father's name' occurs only here; all the other references to the Father's name in the Fourth Gospel link it with Jesus' glorification of the Father in his exaltation, his death.[43] This is what the works prefigure, this is how the Father's name is glorified or hallowed, which is to put positively what is prohibited in the decalogue: 'You shall not take the name of the Lord your God in vain' (Exod 20:7; Deut 5:11).

In John 10:30 at the end of the same speech Jesus comes out with the much discussed phrase, 'I and the Father are one', the only other reference to the Father in this particular speech. Whether this unity be ontological or moral or whatever, here is again a prohibition from the decalogue put positively: 'You shall have no other gods before me' is turned into a statement on the singleness of God. This prohibition is already put positively in the Shema[44] which, of course, with the decalogue belonged in the daily prayer of many Jews in the first century.[45] As the story continues, this reorientation of the Shema and first commandment by Jesus leads to the Jews reaching for stones. When asked why they do so, their response is 'because you, being a man, make yourself God', the close verbal parallel to the second commandment (Exod 20:4; Deut 5:8) already noted. It thus seems to be the case that the first three commandments, those concerning God, are associated with the material concerning the Feast of Dedication, whilst the last seven, those concerning humanity, are connected with the Feast of Tabernacles. The structure of John 7–10 thus represents in reverse the structure of the decalogue itself: this would seem to be deliberate.

FURTHER SUPPORTIVE ARGUMENTS   In addition to the division of the commandments according to the two Feasts in John 7–10 several items from within the Fourth Gospel help justify all these references and allusions to the decalogue. Firstly, five of the commandments may be similarly used in ch. 5,[46] suggesting that this pattern of relating Jesus to the law in general and to the decalogue in particular was not simply a one-off affair at some point in the homiletic development of John 7–10, but was part of a broader reflection on those issues in the polemic or missionary work of the Johannine community. Furthermore the christological element of this reflection is apparent in the Fourth Gospel's use of Moses and material from the book of Exodus: this would make it likely that there might be some reference to the decalogue in the Gospel. The use of particular septuagintal terms associated with the giving of the law indicates this too. The Fourth Gospel's christological use of the major Jewish festivals is widely recognised, so it is possible that texts associated with some form of regular Jewish worship might be put to similar ends; the Shema and the decalogue would be obvious candidates, especially if they were in some cases read together with festival lections at certain times. Indeed the Fourth Gospel's particular use of 'I am' sayings (possibly reflecting the introduction to the commandments: 'I am the LORD your God . . .')[47] and the association of Jesus with Wisdom and hence the law are also general supports for such a possibility. In other words, the use of the decalogue in John 7–10 as proposed in this paper coheres with what is generally recognised of the christology and the use of the Jewish scriptures in the Fourth Gospel.

Alongside these considerations from within the Fourth Gospel should be set various external factors which lend credence to this presentation that at some point John 7–10 is based on, or makes use of, an interpretation of the decalogue. Firstly, while it is notoriously hazardous to suggest anything very strongly on the basis of a possible Palestinian lectionary in use in the first century, nevertheless it is not inappropriate that A. Guilding suggested that Deuteronomy 5 and 6 were part of the sabbath readings that would have been used during the Feast of Tabernacles in the third year of the three-year cycle.[48] Surprisingly she made no use of this in her interpretation of the Feast of Tabernacles in John 7–8; she rested her case for these chapters upon festival lections deducible from later rabbinic sources. But even here it is not insignificant that several passages variously associated with Tabernacles (Leviticus 23–5; Isaiah 61; Psalm 82) have close affinity to some aspects of the decalogue discussed above. The combination of a similar set of lections in 11Q Melchizedek[49] provides a contemporary example of the interpretative treatment of festival passages.[50]

Further external support for the existence of such an interpretation of the decalogue as is proposed here may be found in the likelihood that through the Christian appropriation of the decalogue it was dropped from the daily prayers of many Jews in the first or second centuries. The change in Jewish practice can be seen in that some of the phylacteries of Qumran contain Deuteronomy 5, albeit in a form often assimilated to Exodus 20,[51] whereas the Talmud proscribes it: 'The Decalogue should have been read every day. Why, then does one not read it? Because of the hostility of the *Minim*, lest they say, these only were given to Moses at Sinai' (*p. Berakot* 3c). There is no evidence that at the end of the first century the *Minim* can be identified with a particular group of Jewish Christians, as has been commonly argued,[52] but it is likely that the Jews who at that time deserved this negative description would have been sympathetic to the early Christian emphasis on the decalogue as the summary of the law[53] and would have approved the Jewish–Christian stress on the decalogue as part of the catechesis of new converts.[54] At the least it is significant that there was a diversity within Judaism that only could be challenged through liturgical change.

Alongside this adjustment in the daily prayer of many Jews must be set some remarks concerning the text-type of the decalogue in liturgical use. We have already noted that in some cases it is not easy to determine whether the interpretation of the decalogue in John 7–10 is following Exodus 20 or Deuteronomy 5. The two texts were also evidently assimilated to one another in liturgical use. More generally, G. Reim has pointed out that it is not always easy to decide in the Fourth Gospel's use of Moses typology if the tradition of Deuteronomy or of Exodus is dominant in the writer's mind.[55] However, with the rabbinic determination of the text-type of Exodus and Deuteronomy after the fall of the temple, the differences between the two traditions of the decalogue are stressed and made authoritative, as is reflected in later rabbinic discussions of those differences.[56] The process of fixing the text-type of the Pentateuch acted as a further lever in pushing standardisation and conformity upon synagogue congregations.

The assimilation of Exodus and Deuteronomy is an issue in the Samaritan Pentateuch too. Though there must be caution in seeing Samaritan theology behind many aspects of the Fourth Gospel,[57] nevertheless it is the case that the Samaritan Pentateuch at Exodus 20 contains an elaborate set of texts from Deuteronomy to illuminate the significance of the decalogue for the Samaritans; in fact, in effect the Samaritans renumber their commandments so that mt. Gerizim can be mentioned in the tenth. The most prominent addition for our purposes is the inclusion of Deut 18:18–22, the passage which describes the prophet like Moses who is to come to declare all that the Lord commands him. The prophet will arise from 'their brethren' (cf. John 7:5). These verses are widely supposed to lie behind John 7:40 and may also elucidate why Nicodemus wants the Pharisees to hear (*šmʿ*: Deut 18:15; John 7:51) Jesus himself, even though they insist that no prophet (John 7:52) is to arise from Galilee. Furthermore, the man born blind identifies Jesus as 'prophet' (9:17), whilst the Pharisees with splendid irony insist that they are the disciples of Moses (9:28). The existence of Samaritan Exod 20:21 amongst the proof-texts of 4Q Testimonia and the way in which in the Fourth Gospel Jesus effectively denies the Samaritan tenth commandment (John 4:21) suggest that it is unlikely that the Gospel necessarily represents Samaritan thinking in any pure form. The Samaritan Pentateuch offers at the least a literary parallel to the combination of the decalogue with the prediction of the prophet like Moses who is to arise, the combination that is also present in John 7–10.

SETTING AND PURPOSE   As it has been described here, the interpretation of the decalogue in John 7–10 does not seem sufficiently obvious to have been part of the overall purpose of the final editor of these chapters. Nevertheless sufficient explicit and implicit traces of the whole decalogue are discernible, particularly as its structure may have continued to influence the structure of John 7–10, to allow the suggestion that an interpretation of the decalogue formed part of the life of the developing Johannine community at some time.

Though it is difficult to be too specific about the setting and purpose of this kind of interpretation, two interdependent areas that have occupied scholars extensively in recent years deserve consideration. On the one hand there is the internal development of the Johannine community of believers; on the other that same development needs to be set against the debate with those outside the community, especially the synagogue Jews reflected in John 9:22 and elsewhere in the Gospel. D. Moody Smith has listed a set of interests which suggest to him that the Johannine community either contained or was in debate with 'less orthodox forms of Jewish life and thought than' the pharisaic–rabbinic type alone.[58] Amongst Jewish interests behind the Fourth Gospel, Smith mentions the Qumran Literature, the Odes of Solomon, the concern with and reaction against John the Baptist, the interest in Samaria, the many parallels with the writings of Philo, Jewish mystical and speculative texts from circles with gnosticising tendencies, and contemporary speculation about Wisdom. Smith does not distinguish clearly between which of these elements he sees as reflecting people inside the community and which suggest groups outside; perhaps that is because he is more interested in mentioning what he discerns as the presence of charismatic prophetic activity in the community.

At any rate some focus can be given to elements within the developing community, as has been pursued, perhaps sometimes too vigorously, by R. E. Brown in relation to the entrance of Jews of anti-temple views and their Samaritan converts,[59] and as was suggested more generally for the first stage of the life of the community by J. L. Martyn.[60] Or again some focus can be given to the Jews with whom the developing community enters into debate: alongside their membership of the synagogue (John 9:22; 12:42; 16:2) J. L. Martyn has set the possibility of the part some Jewish court may have played in excommunicating certain Jewish Christians.[61] More particularly, A. Kolenkow has argued that the points at issue between the Johannine community and the Jews were the sabbath healings performed by Jewish Christians.[62] Because of the several Jewish interests that form part of the community–synagogue debate it seems increasingly likely that the synagogue(s) contained a variety of kinds of Jew, some more interested in the interpretation of the law in all its breadth and detail, some more speculative in outlook, concerned more with the overall meaning and purpose of the law.

In relation to the christological interpretation of the decalogue that may belong somewhere in this intangible morass of more-or-less likely scholarly guesswork, a few remarks will show that, as with the final form of the text, there is nothing inherently inconsistent in the proposal of this essay. To begin with, for the developing community the homilies that use the decalogue in chs. 5 and 7–10 could have been used to attract new Jewish converts in and could then have functioned as elementary catechesis.[63] The interpretations show that Jesus did not break the law and neither do his followers when they continue his work, that the law has a christological intent and that Jews who do not recognise that align themselves with the law-breakers in respect of each commandment. At this point the decalogue may also reflect a lively polemic between the Johannine community and the synagogue or the Jewish courts. For the synagogue the Jewish–Christian appropriation of the decalogue may have contributed to its use there being discontinued;[64] for the courts, the Johannine apologists argue vehemently that neither Jesus nor by implication they themselves have broken the law so that the Jewish charges against them, especially of sabbath-breaking and blasphemy, are unfounded. Furthermore, in using the decalogue to exemplify the relationship of Christ to the law and Wisdom there is an appeal on the basis of part of the synagogue's regular or festival use of scripture to that element in the Jewish community more interested in the depths of religious speculation and in the summary of the law[65] than in political dogmatics and the breadth of Jewish legislation.

Once it is acknowledged that the Jews with whom the Johannine community was in debate are not all monochrome, then it is no longer possible to say blandly that John 7–10 is basically anti-Jewish, a group of chapters that shows early Christian invective against the synagogue at its most hostile.[66] Rather the use of Wisdom language may have been part of a 'missionary' appeal to certain members of the Jewish community who were wavering.[67] The appealing use of the decalogue in a manner not totally dissimilar from Philo's creative reordering of the laws in the Pentateuch in line with the Ten Words, might have been sufficient to convert some, once they had admitted that Jesus and his followers had neither broken nor abrogated the law. Those Jews who remained unconvinced were caricatured as blind Pharisees descended from the devil.

The struggles within Judaism after the fall of the temple resulted in the Jewish Christians removing themselves from the synagogue or being thrown out. It could be that when they left they took with them the decalogue whose real christological meaning and purpose they claimed to know.[68] The Jews left behind could only protect themselves from the influence of such claims by no longer saying the decalogue in their prayers; the standardisation of the text contributed to the need to stop saying it, since it became invidious to decide which version should be recited, as textual standardisation led to dissimilation between the two forms of the decalogue.

In sum there is sufficient evidence to suggest beyond mere conjecture that interpretations of the decalogue in part (John 5) and as a whole (John 7–10) formed part of the homiletic life of the developing Johannine community, either as catechesis for internal purposes or as apologetic for external purposes. The decalogue, prominent in Jewish life and liturgy, was taken over by the Johannine community for christological ends to demonstrate that Jesus and his followers were unjustifiably accused of breaking the law and to offer instruction for those who desire Wisdom; they can now find her in the person of the Christ, who is both the law-giving prophet promised by Moses and the very meaning and purpose of the law itself as he gives eternal life to those who believe in him and keep his commandments.

Part III

The law in Paul and the apostolic tradition

10
PAUL AND THE LAW IN RECENT RESEARCH

F. F. BRUCE

W. D. DAVIES   Let 'recent research' be taken, for the present purpose, to mean 'research published during the past twenty-five years', and let me begin with W. D. Davies' article on 'Law in the New Testament' in the third volume of the *Interpreter's Dictionary of the Bible*, published in 1962. One section of this article is devoted to 'Paul and the law'. Here Davies sees clearly that

> ... it was Paul's very zeal for the law of God that had blinded him to the Son of God and led him to persecute his church (Gal. 1:13–14; 3:13; Phil. 3:5–6) – the law had proved a veil to hide Christ (II Cor. 3:14–15). This fact governed his re-examination of the law.[1]

This consideration is of basic importance, and yet it is often given all too little weight in discussions of Paul's attitude to the law. Looking back as a Christian on his earlier career, Paul saw that the law, to which he had been totally devoted, not only failed to protect him against the sinful course of persecuting the Church of God; it was his devotion to the law that actually led him into that sinful course.

Another insight in this article, difficult for many Lutheran theologians to accept, is that Paul sometimes understood Christ in terms of the law, as when he ascribed to Christ attributes which in Judaism were ascribed to the law.

> The influence of the Reformation, because of its emphasis on the gospel as justification by faith, makes it difficult for us to do justice to this aspect of Paul's thought. ... His criticism of the law is a consequence of his faith in Christ, not its center.[2]

A fuller exposition of the theme ('Paul and the law') was published by Davies in an American law journal in 1978;[5] an abridged version of that paper was contributed to the *Festschrift* for C. K. Barrett (1982).[4] Here he draws attention to pitfalls to be avoided in the study of Paul's treatment of the law. Paul's wrestling with the relation between law and gospel cannot be appreciated when his arguments are detached from their Jewish background and read by Gentiles who are for the most part untouched by Judaism. Nor can his treatment of law be understood when it is divorced from the total messianic situation in which Paul believed himself to be standing. It was in this situation that Paul accepted believing Gentiles as members of the people of God without observance of the law – something which was in any case a scandal to his fellow-Jews, but something unintelligible except in relation to that revelation of Jesus Christ which he received on the Damascus road. Davies sees Paul adopting an interpretation of sacred history attested here and there in rabbinical tradition, in which the age of the Messiah is to follow and supersede the age of Torah.[5] If Messiah has come, as Paul believed him to have come in the person of Jesus, then the age of law has ended; if, as some of his judaising opponents maintained, the validity of the law continues in full force, then the messianic age has not yet dawned: Jesus therefore is not the Messiah – and that is why Paul invoked on those whose premises led to this conclusion the stern anathema of Gal 1:8f. For Paul, the transition from the old age to the new marked a radical break: 'but now we are discharged from the law, dead to that which held us captive, so that we serve not under the old written code but in the new life of the Spirit' (Rome 7:6).

Davies recognises that Paul's treatment of law in Galatians differs from that in Romans. The 'almost unrelievedly pejorative' treatment in Galatians may be due to its being 'Paul's first serious attempt at dealing with the law', or to its reflecting 'an untempered, polemic reaction to Jewish Christians who had been as extreme as he himself had been'. His more balanced treatment in Romans could have been due to the failure of his arguments in Galatians to win back his converts to the cause of gospel liberty – we do not know. But in Romans 'he presents a more positive treatment of the Law even while he still strikes against it'.[6]

Paul transforms the demands of the law by placing them in the light of Christ. The believer is raised with Christ to newness of life and is called to live out his resurrection daily; he looks to Jesus as an object of imitation, and the reproduction of the Christ-likeness in his life is the work of the indwelling Spirit. But in addition to this 'vertical' dimension there is the 'horizontal' dimension – the communal life of believers in Christ, and their responsibility to the wider society of the world.[7]

C. E. B. CRANFIELD   In 1964 C. E. B. Cranfield published an important study of 'St. Paul and the law',[8] in which seven basic points were made. For Paul, (1) the law is God's law, (2) the law makes sin manifest as sin – that is, disobedience to God, (3) the law, by being law, actually enhances sin, (4) it makes people sin more, (5) especially in that it establishes the possibility of legalism, (6) it pronounces God's condemnation and curse, but (7) its ultimate goal and inner meaning are found not in the condemnation of sinners, but in Jesus Christ. The text for this final point is, of course, Rom. 10:4: 'Christ is the *telos* of the law for righteousness to every believer', which Cranfield takes to mean: 'Christ is the goal of the law, and this means that righteousness is available to every one who believes.'

Cranfield maintains that Paul drew a distinction in his own mind between law *per se* and legalism. Law *per se* is good; legalism is bad. But Paul had no convenient Greek term to express the idea of legalism; therefore he used the phrase 'the works of the law', *(ta) erga (tou) nomou*, for this purpose. But when the sense of his argument had been established by the use of this phrase, then he might use the simple *nomos* in the following context in the sense of *erga nomou*. Thus, in Gal 2:16 the phrase *erga nomou* is used emphatically three times over – it is not by these, it is insistently repeated, that one is justified before God. Therefore, when Paul says, later in the same paragraph, 'If righteousness is through law, then Christ died in vain' (Gal 2:21), one naturally takes *dia nomou* in the sense of the threefold *ex ergōn nomou* of verse 16.

For Cranfield, law in its proper sense is God's law (as, of course, it was for Paul). It may be misused and perverted, as indeed is inevitable when it operates on the human will with its sinful propensities – Paul speaks of the *adunaton* of the law, its being weakened by reason of 'flesh' – but in the new gospel order, *'the giving of the Spirit is the establishment of the law'.*[9] That is to say, the Spirit enables the will of God to be accomplished in the lives of those whom he indwells: as Paul puts it, 'the *dikaiōma*, the sum-total of the law's righteous requirements, is fulfilled in those who lead their lives not *kata sarka* but *kata pneuma*' (Rom 8:4).

C. F. D. MOULE   In his discussion of 'Obligation in the ethic of Paul' (1967),[10] C. F. D. Moule refers to Cranfield's point that Paul knew no distinctive term for legalism, and observes that Paul equally had no distinctive word or phrase for various other aspects of law; hence he stresses the necessity of deducing from the context the special nuance that Paul had in mind. Moule distinguishes in particular what he calls the 'revelatory' and the 'legalistic' senses of *nomos*. The important question, he says, is 'whether a man is trying to justify himself by keeping the law, or whether he allows law to be a medium through which God reveals himself'.[11]

By means of this distinction Moule is able to give a satisfactory answer to the question whether, in Paul's view, Christ has abrogated the law or not. As for Christ's being the *telos* of the law (Rom 10:4), Paul (says Moule)

> ... saw Christ as the *fulfilment* of law, when law means God's revelation of himself and of his character and purpose, but as the *condemnation* and *termination* of any attempt to use law to justify oneself. And it is this latter use of law [he says] which may conveniently be called (for short) 'legalism'.[12]

When C. K. Barrett, in his commentary on Romans, says that 'law means the upward striving of human religion and morality, and therefore colours all human activity with sin',[13] it is Moule's second sense of 'law' – its 'legalistic' sense – that is presumably intended.

It is the use of law by human beings, their attitude to it, that makes the difference, according to Moule. Those who were accepting circumcision in the Galatian churches were treating the law, or certain elements in it, as an insurance policy: lest faith in Christ should prove insufficient for salvation, 'they must add the safeguard of Judaism'.[14] If that is your attitude, says Paul, then, 'having adopted the law as a "safeguard", you must abide by it in a spirit of meticulous literalism'. Paul does not urge the abolition of law as an antidote to the Galatian error; 'what needs to be abolished is the arrogantly human use of the law for the purposes of human "safety"'[15] – this is the legalism that Paul attacks. The intention to claim God's favour by establishing one's own righteousness is not only futile, but sinful, 'because it implies an uncreaturely refusal to accept men's need of God and dependence on him'.[16]

The obligation to do the will of God, to live a life of love, is none the less binding for those who are no longer 'under law'; it is by living 'under grace' that one is at last in a position to fulfil this obligation. Moule goes on to argue that Paul's position was in line with that of Jesus: both Jesus and Paul attacked legalism, both affirmed law, both taught that moral decisions have to be taken in a situational way, not by applying an automatic rule but by viewing the situation in the light of the kingdom of God, 'in the light of the new strength of love'.[17]

E. P. SANDERS   A new chapter in the study of Paul's attitude to the law was opened with the appearance in 1977 of E. P. Sanders' *Paul and Palestinian Judaism* – the most important work in the field since the publication of the first edition of W. D. Davies's *Paul and Rabbinic Judaism* in 1948.

The first, and major, part of Sanders' book deals with Palestinian Judaism. It was designed largely to correct the unsatisfactory view of Jewish religion which has dominated much NT scholarship, and to a considerable extent it has succeeded. We are not likely to see a repetition nowadays of Schürer's description of 'life under the law'. The Jew of NT times did indeed live 'under the law', but at the same time he lived within the covenant. Within the covenant the pardoning mercy of God was assured to those who were truly repentant, and, so long as the temple stood, the sacrificial system and in particular the great sin offering of the Day of Atonement made provision for all breaches of the law except those that were committed in a spirit of deliberate defiance. To sum up Jewish existence under the law and within the covenant Sanders uses the expression 'covenantal nomism',[18] which has now become part of our theological vocabulary.

The second part of his book, devoted to Paul, is about one-third of the length of the first part. In Paul he finds a completely different pattern of religion from that which he finds in Palestinian Judaism, a pattern which cannot be accounted for in terms of any form of Judaism to which Paul might have been attached before his conversion. Paul's pessimistic picture of the plight of humanity (both Jewish and Gentile) is unlikely to have been taken over from his Jewish past; it is suggested, therefore, that he reconstructed it on the basis of his soteriology – that the solution, in fact, preceded the problem.[19]

Sanders rightly insists that Paul's call to evangelise the Gentiles was an essential element in his conversion experience, and was a powerful factor in the dethronement of the law in his thinking. If salvation was for Gentiles, as Gentiles, it could not be by the law, but if the Gentiles' salvation was apart from the law, then the Jews' salvation must also be apart from the law, since it was one and the same God who was 'rich in mercy' towards Jews and Gentiles alike. But an even more powerful factor in the dethronement of the law for Paul, which Sanders, like several other writers on the subject, does not adequately emphasise, was Paul's sudden realisation (mentioned above) that the law had let him down: if it had not actually led him into his career as a persecutor, it had done nothing to guard him against it.

Over against the covenantal nomism of Palestinian Judaism, the pattern of Paul's religion reveals itself, according to Sanders, as 'participationist eschatology',[20] and the main theme of his theology is found in his 'participationist' language rather than in righteousness by faith. While 'righteousness' in Judaism keeps members of the covenant community within it, in Paul's usage 'righteousness' puts people into the community of the saved, makes them members of it; it is a transfer term, not a maintenance term.

What Sanders says about 'participationism' is quite reminiscent of Morna Hooker's exposition of the theme 'interchange'.[21] She examines his covenantal nomism in her contribution to C. K. Barrett's *Festschrift* (1982).[22] After reading the first part of *Paul and Palestinian Judaism*, she says, many will have felt that Paul was thoroughly Jewish after all – Jewish according to Sanders' pattern of Palestinian Judaism – and she expresses surprise that in the second part his pattern of Paul's religion is so different from what it is commonly supposed to have been. She argues that Sanders is mistaken in setting Pauline 'participationism' in such opposition to Jewish covenantal nomism. If, to retain Sanders' distinction between 'transfer' terms and 'maintenance' terms, between 'getting in' and 'staying in', one were to ask Paul how a man or woman is saved, he would reply in terms of participating in Christ; if he were then asked how those who are now 'in Christ' are expected to behave, he would reply (as he does in Gal 6:2), in terms of fulfilling 'the law of Christ'. By partaking of Christ, one enters into the blessings of the new covenant; within that covenant one is responsible for rendering the 'obedience of faith' – not by painstaking working-to-rule but by responding to the initiative of the indwelling Spirit, who reproduces the Christ-likeness from within. Thus while, for Paul, salvation and justification are wholly by grace, judgement is uniformly according to works. So Paul's religion could be spoken of as a pattern of covenantal nomism, though the covenant is not what he regarded as the temporary, and now obsolete, sinaitic covenant but the better covenant, established with Abraham and ratified by the sacrifice of the cross, and the *nomos* is no longer the law of Moses but the law of Christ. Yet the content of the law of Christ is not so different from that of Moses' law: it can be itemised in a series of commandments of the decalogue, which are summed up in the one comprehensive commandment: 'You shall love your neighbour as yourself' (Gal 5:14; Rom 13:8–10).

Similarly C. K. Barrett in his recent study of Galatians finds that Paul's account of the history of salvation seems 'to tally in some remarkable ways (though not in every way) with the covenantal nomism of E. P. Sanders'.[23] Paul insists that God, in grace, established his covenant with Abraham long before the law was given through Moses. Covenant forms the background or context of law, and this suggests to Paul the only valid answer to the question: In this covenantal nomism, is the *nomos* principle so powerful that it neutralises the covenant principle, so that law supersedes grace and works supersede faith?[24] The answer is 'Of course not.' Sanders may say that Judaism never suggested that law did supersede grace, or that works superseded faith, but Paul must be allowed to know more than we can about the teaching of the agitators in the churches of Galatia, and about its practical implications.

Another critique of Sanders' position has come from R. H. Gundry.[25] Gundry sides with Sanders against those who have criticised his treatment of Palestinian Judaism, but takes issue with his treatment of Paul. In particular, he argues that Paul makes no great point of the distinction between getting in and staying in. People get in by faith and stay in by faith (Rom 11:20): neither for getting in nor for staying in is there any other way. The 'obedience of faith' implies obedience as an element in the initial act of faith as well as in the ongoing life of faith.

Gundry's critique has been able to take account of Sanders' later volume, *Paul, the Law and the Jewish People* (1983), in which he has amplified, strengthened and in some respects corrected his treatment of Paul in the earlier volume. But even here he does not seem to engage at a deep enough level with Paul's personal reassessment of the way to get right with God. The dispute in Galatians is not simply, as he says, 'about whether or not one had to be Jewish'.[26] Paul's appeal in Gal 3:2–5 to the Galatian believers' experience of the power of the Spirit in their lives suggests a concern with more basic religious issues than the necessity or not of maintaining the Jew/Gentile distinction.

The Jew/Gentile distinction, indeed, is temporary, but the way of faith, hope and love, by which men and women both come to God and walk with God, is never to be superseded. Even in Galatians the Jew/Gentile distinction is abolished in Christ (Gal 3:28); in Romans Paul's universalism reaches its climax in his insight that God's purpose in bringing in a verdict of disobedience against all, both Jews and Gentiles, was 'that he might have mercy on them all' (Rom 11:32).

When Sanders says that, for Paul, the real defect in Judaism was that it was not Christianity,[27] one can agree with what he means. Once Paul recognised that the Christ had come in the person of Jesus, it followed that the course of salvation history had moved on a further stage.[28] The age of law, which (as he now realised) had never been intended to be more than a parenthesis, had reached its goal and been superseded; and with the fulfilment of the promise to Abraham the reign of grace had been inaugurated. The promise to Abraham was fulfilled through the death and resurrection of Christ – through God's vindication of one who had been condemned by the law and died under its curse. So much the worse for the law!

A system which failed to reckon with the new thing that God had done in Christ was out of gear with the saving purpose of God: Judaism, in other words, had its inadequacy shown up by the fact that it was not Christianity – though that is an awkward and opaque way of putting it.

A similar consideration will account for Paul's ignoring the provision made for Jews within the covenant to have their sins atoned for by sacrifice. For Paul, the shift involved in the Christ-event meant that, whatever had been true before, there was henceforth no atoning sin offering apart from the sacrifice of Christ, who had been 'delivered up' for his people's offences (Rom 4:25).

H. HÜBNER   Hans Hübner's monograph *Das Gesetz bei Paulus* was published in 1978; an English translation, *Law in Paul's Thought*, appeared in 1984. The outstanding feature of this work is its separate treatment of Galatians and Romans. The relevant passages in each of the two letters are analysed exegetically, but no attempt is made to construct a synthesis of the two.[29] Writers who undertake to produce a study of Paul's understanding of the law, drawing indiscriminately on the two letters, tend inevitably to minimise or overlook the differences between them. Hübner quotes one recent writer who argues against the natural and contextual sense of Gal 3: 19b (as represented, e.g., by the RSV rendering) on the ground that to take it in this sense is 'to ignore some of the insights of the Roman letter, ever the best commentary on Galatians'.[30]

Paul's attitude to law, Hübner insists, is much more negative and critical in Galatians than in Romans. Thus, in touching on the angelic administration of the law in Gal 3:19b, Paul regards the angels as hostile, indeed demonic: their intention was to make the law the means of bringing human beings to perdition. But the over-ruling wisdom of God is seen in his taking up the angels' hostility, together with the consequent multiplication of transgressions and even the demonic power of sin itself, and forcing them to be the instruments of his own saving purpose. In the corresponding passage in Rom 5:20f., on the other hand, hostile angels do not appear: the law is God's temporary ordinance. It was not *intended* to multiply the sinful deeds of individual sinners (although, since sin was already in the world, the introduction of law had the inevitable result of increasing the sum total of sinful deeds); God's intention was rather that the increase of sin in world history which followed the introduction of the law might subserve his higher purpose of sovereign grace.[31]

The 'whole law' (*ho pas nomos*) which is fulfilled in the commandment of love to one's neighbour (Gal 5:14) is plainly, says Hübner, not identical with the 'whole law' (*holon ton nomon*) which a man who accepts circumcision is obliged to keep (Gal 5:3). The 'whole law' of Gal 5:3 is the entire law of Moses, the aggregate of its individual precepts; the 'whole law' of Gal 5:14 is the whole law for the Christian, the sum of Christian duty.[32] But this antithesis disappears in Rom 13:8–10, where the 'law' which is summed up in the commandment of love to one's neighbour comprises individual precepts of the decalogue. The polemic against the Torah which is so characteristic of Galatians has been replaced in Romans by something else – by what Hübner calls a 'reduction' of the Torah.[33] (He agrees, however, that in Romans 14 we find not reduction but abrogation of those Mosaic precepts which are cultically based.)

Other matters of interest in Hübner's exposition are his treatment of the 'establishment' of the law by the gospel (Rom 3:31) and the significance which he sees in the absence from Galatians of the concept of the 'righteousness of God' which is basic to the argument of Romans.

Even if the reader feels at times that Hübner exaggerates the contrast between the two letters,[34] he has redressed a balance which has for too long been weighted in one direction.

C. T. RHYNE   C. T. Rhyne's *Faith Establishes the Law* (1981), a title in the SBL dissertation series, follows Hübner (and E. Käsemann)[35] in seeing in the statement of Rom 3:31 the transition from the immediately preceding argument to the exposition of the Abraham record in Rom 4:1ff. Paul shows how 'through faith . . . we establish the law' by adducing the example of Abraham who, according to the Torah (Gen 15:6), had his faith, not his works, counted to him for righteousness. This interpretation presupposes an oscillation on Paul's part between two senses of Torah – Torah as law *per se* and Torah as the Pentateuch – but Paul has oscillated between these senses already in Rom 3:19 (cf. Gal 4:21). It is, I think, right to look on Rom 3:31c as introductory to Rom 4:1–25.

If the gospel in this sense 'establishes' the law, then some continuity between law and gospel is implied. Rhyne examines the question of continuity or discontinuity between law and gospel, and finds that, while both continuity and discontinuity are implied by Paul's argument, some of his interpreters stress the one and some the other, while some adopt a mediating position. This appears clearly in their exposition of Rom 10:4. In what sense is Christ 'the end of the law'? Cranfield, as we have seen, insists that 'Christ is the goal to which all along the law has been directed, its true intention and meaning'.[36] Käsemann, on the other hand, insists on discontinuity: law and gospel are for Paul 'mutually exclusive antitheses';[37] Christ and the law belong to different aeons and with the appearance of Christ law has come to an end. What Rhyne would call a mediating position is represented by C. K. Barrett: Christ 'puts an end to

the law, not by destroying all that the law stood for but by realizing it'.[38]
Rhyne defends the interpretation 'goal', which he finds to be in keeping
with Rom 3:31c and also with the statement in Rom 8:4 that what the law
required is fulfilled in the Spirit-led life.

> Whenever someone receives righteousness by faith in Christ, the law's goal
> of righteousness is realized in this act of faith in the work of the resurrected
> and exalted Christ. Thus, the equation, Christ is the goal of the law for
> righteousness, represents the apex of Paul's understanding of the continuity
> between Judaism and Christianity.[39]

H. RÄISÄNEN This is true, but it is not the whole truth. It does not take
sufficient account of Paul's ambivalence on the subject of law – an
ambivalence found even within the argument of Romans, not to speak of
the shift of perspective on the law as between Romans and Galatians. One
writer who does take account of this ambivalence, to the point where he
treats it as an irreconcilable contradiction, is the Finnish scholar Heikki
Räisänen, whose work on *Paul and the Law* was published in 1983.

Räisänen says that he held 'a rather standard Lutheran view' on this
subject until he read the major works on Paul by H.-J. Schoeps and E. P.
Sanders; they compelled him to rethink the whole issue.[40] Like most
students of Paul's thinking about the law, he recognises that it is necessary
to distinguish the various senses in which Paul uses the term 'law'. But even
when the necessary distinctions have been made, Paul's statements on the
subject contain some irreducible contradictions. Those who try to remove
these contradictions by making his attitude to the law wholly positive or
wholly negative do violence to the plain exegesis of inconvenient texts.

The law, according to the natural sense of some of Paul's affirmations
about it, has been abolished, on its moral as well as on its ceremonial side.
Paul conformed to it as a matter of policy when living among Jews, but
when living among Gentiles he treated it as an *adiaphoron*. Yet in some
sense its validity is retained: its just claims on men and women are fulfilled
when they live by the Spirit. It is essential to Paul's argument (in Romans as
well as in Galatians) that no one is able to keep the law; nevertheless some
Gentiles 'do by nature what the law requires' (Rom 2:14) and thus
condemn those who have received the written code and fail to keep it. Paul
cannot deny that the law was designed to lead to life, for God himself says
so in Lev 18:5; in practice, however, he finds that it leads to death, by
increasing the sum total of sinful acts in the world and even by stimulating
people to commit such acts (Rom 7:10). He is alone among NT writers in
seeing the law as a rival principle of salvation to that set forth in the gospel:
none of the others 'sees such a contrast between law and grace or faith'.[41]
In saying this, Räisänen does not overlook John 1:17, but takes its words
to mean that the grace and truth which came through Jesus Christ have
surpassed and outdated the law which was given through Moses.

In Paul's negative arguments about the law Räisänen thinks that
secondary rationalisations have been at work, but what was their primary
cause? Some answers previously given are examined and found wanting.

Paul was not disillusioned about the law before his conversion; far from being defeated in his attempt to achieve 'righteousness under the law', he reckons that he was 'blameless' in that respect (Phil 3:6). As for the view that Paul had been taught to believe that the age of the Messiah would bring the age of law to an end,[42] Räisänen is not persuaded by the arguments brought forward in its support. Paul, he finds, does not appear to have been primarily influenced by meditation on the new-covenant oracle of Jer 31:31–4, or even by the pronouncing of a curse on the person who is hanged in Deut 21:23. Paul nowhere claims dominical authority for the abrogation of the law: 'it seems rather unlikely that he would have attributed a critical attitude to the law to the historical Jesus'.[43] (That is not so certain: Jesus' sovereign freedom in interpreting and applying the law aroused the suspicion that he was setting up his own authority over against that of the law, and Paul, to some extent at least, works out the logic of something that was implicit in Jesus' action and teaching.)

Räisänen is well disposed to the suggestion that Paul adopted and developed a pattern set by the Hellenists among the primitive disciples, but he recognises that our knowledge about those Hellenists is too scanty to allow of any certainty. But, he says, if with this we combine the impact on Paul's mind of his early experiences in the Gentile mission, we may discover the effective motives for the attitude which he later found himself compelled to rationalise in his controversy with judaisers. But, like some others who have grappled with the same problem, Räisänen fails to reckon sufficiently with the logic of Paul's Damascus-road experience – the experience which brought home to him in a flash the 'powerlessness' of the law to accomplish what it was designed to do. Certainly the implications of this sudden insight had to be worked out in the conflict with judaisers and in other controversies: the exigencies of the situation of the moment forced Paul to argue now this way, now that. But in this insight is the coherence which Räisänen cannot find in Paul's theological thought:[44] it justifies Sanders' claim that Paul is 'on the whole a "coherent" though not a "systematic" thinker'.[45]

J. D. G. DUNN   J. D. G. Dunn has recently turned his attention to Paul's relation to the law – notably in his 1983 Manson Memorial Lecture delivered in the University of Manchester and in a paper of 1985, appearing in *New Testament Studies*.[46]

Briefly, Dunn argues that the 'works of law' to which Paul denies any justifying capacity are not works which might lead those who perform them to take pride in their ethical achievement, but 'identity markers' – that is to say, practices which distinguish a Jew from a non-Jew, such as circumcision, the sabbath, food-restrictions and the like.[47]

Crucial to his case is his interpretation of Gal 2:16. 'We know this', says Paul, 'that one is not justified by works of law (*ex ergōn nomou*), but (*ean mē*) through faith in Jesus Christ' (*dia pisteōs Iēsou Christou* where *Iēsou Christou* is objective genitive). There the force of *ean mē* is to exclude the previous option, 'by works of law', and to replace it by the principle of 'faith in Jesus Christ'. But Dunn takes the meaning to be that 'a man is not justified from works of law *except* through faith in Jesus Christ' – such faith being 'the primary identity marker which renders the others superfluous'.[48]

To translate *ean mē* by 'except' in this construction seems to me to run counter to Greek idiom. That apart, Paul's argument throughout Galatians makes it plain that it was not just identity markers that were at issue. Identity markers, for Paul, were optional: if believers in Jesus wished to observe special days or restrict themselves to special kinds of food, then 'let everyone be fully convinced in his own mind' (Rom 14:5). Even in Galatians, circumcision or uncircumcision is a religious irrelevance *per se* (Gal 5:6; 6:15). But if Paul's *Gentile* converts took over Jewish identity markers, like circumcision or the observance of special days (Gal 4:10), they were putting themselves 'under law' (Gal 4:21), and it was their giving any place to law or law-keeping in the matter of salvation that Paul saw as a subversion of the gospel of free grace. The Galatians may have decided to take these practices into their system (as has been said above) as a sort of extra insurance policy, lest faith in Christ should prove insufficient of itself. But for Paul any hope of establishing one's own righteous status in the sight of God, to however limited an extent, was a vain hope, since God's way of righteousness, attested in advance by the law and the prophets, had now been opened to all alike in Christ, and all other ways were barred. 'Christ brings to the believer the righteousness promised in Scripture.'[49]

11

PAUL AND THE LAW IN ROMANS 5–8: AN ACTANTIAL ANALYSIS

BARNABAS LINDARS SSF

INTRODUCTION 'So then, I myself serve the law of God with my mind, but with my flesh I serve the law of sin' (Rom 7:25b). These words sum up the haunting account of Paul's agonising inability to observe the Jewish law, in spite of his honest desire to do so, in Rom 7:7–25. This passage has been the centre of unending controversy, as it is not clear whether it should be taken as strictly autobiographical, or how it relates to Paul's experience before or after his conversion on the road to Damascus. In any case it must have a representative function, because it forms part of Paul's larger argument on the new life that is available to all Christians as a result of the saving act of God in Jesus Christ. The function of law, and in particular the Jewish law, is a crucial issue in this argument. It is, however, difficult to follow Paul's thought, because he keeps changing his terms of reference, and there is no consistent treatment of the issue of the law. His attitude to the law has to be dug out of the argument as a whole, but it would be misleading to take the references out of context. Paul is concerned with the dynamics of religion, and it is from this point of view that he refers to the law. It is thus necessary to see his references to the law in relation to the whole sweep of his argument.

It is now recognised that Paul's attitude to the law in Romans is not quite the same as in his earlier letter to the Galatians.[1] Recent work on Paul has drawn attention to the *ad hoc* nature of his writings, which is bound to lead to differences and inconsistencies.[2] It is not only that Paul has to adjust his expressions to suit the needs of different audiences. Often caught up emotionally in the issues he is dealing with, he cannot be expected to maintain perfect consistency. The way he sees things – even his ideas about his own experience of conversion[3] – is coloured by his involvement in justifying his policy in a controversy fraught with emotion on both sides. This is especially clear in Galatians, in which the question of the law is a burning issue. It is not at all surprising that, in his efforts to prevent the Gentile converts from being compelled by the Judaisers to submit to the law, he uses in that epistle stronger expressions and takes more radical positions than he does in Romans. In Romans, on the other hand, he writes in a much more carefully considered way, in a situation in which he is not under severe pressure, and so can stand back from the controversy and view the issues more objectively.

To some extent it is fair to say that Romans represents a rationalising of Paul's position. He is defending his missionary policy, agreed by the 'pillars' at Jerusalem (Gal 2:9), of admitting Gentiles to Christian fellowship without imposing on them the obligation of circumcision and observance of the law. It is not necessarily inconsistent with the claim that this policy was a direct consequence of his conversion experience[4] to maintain at the same time that he needed to think it through afresh in the light of subsequent events. He could scarcely have foreseen what form the Judaistic controversy would take, or anticipate the particular arguments that would be used in the debate. In Romans he is able to present the issue in the light of the debate that has already taken place. Moreover his purpose is not merely controversial. He wishes to place the law of the Jews within a broader understanding of the nature of religion. He is presenting his views as he wishes them to be known. Though he would, no doubt, stand by everything that he has said previously, he would not necessarily want the extraordinarily negative impression given, for instance, by the Hagar allegory in Gal 4:21–31 to be taken as his last word on the subject. Much of the argument is a careful revision of the argument in Galatians. But Romans sets it in the wider frame of universal religion. In dealing with the law, Paul is conscious that what he says can apply *mutatis mutandis* to sincerely religious people, who are not bound by the Jewish law, but have a comparable sense of moral obligations.

It is customary to refer to this as legalism, but in my view this is a mistake. Legalism suggests a particular mentality, which finds satisfaction in the performance of prescribed laws, and naturally makes much use of casuistry to accommodate the moral dilemmas which such an outlook inevitably encounters. E. P. Sanders has successfully shown that such a mentality is as untrue of the Pharisees in general as it is of Paul.[5] The dilemma which is so graphically described in Romans 7 is not a matter of legalism. Legalism could probably avoid it, because the use of casuistry would enable one to square up one's behaviour with the law or (in the case of a Gentile) with conscience. The real dilemma comes when the law or conscience is treated as a source of guidance, but one fails in spite of all one's goodwill.

If we wish to discover Paul's considered view of the place of the law in religion, it is to Romans that we must turn. The composition is logical, and there are clear breaks between the major sections. Chs. 1–4 deal with the fundamental matter of justification. Chs. 9–11 deal with the special problem of the unbelieving Jews. Between these two sections chs. 5–8 are concerned with the practice of religion in the light of the argument on justification by faith. Ch. 5, with its elaborate contrast between Adam and Christ, sets out God's intention of universal salvation, for which the act of justification in Christ is the decisive step. The coming fulfilment of this universal plan is magnificently described at the conclusion of the section in 8:18-end. The intervening chapters are punctuated by various objections to Paul's position (6:1,15; 7:7,13). It is reasonable to assume that they reflect objections and misunderstandings which Paul has actually encountered in his ministry, and which he has had to take into account in thinking through his position afresh.

Within this section references to the law are spasmodic and subordinate to the main purpose of the argument. But the law is mentioned or referred to in all four objections just referred to, and becomes much more prominent in ch. 7, which is where the difficulties of interpretation are greatest. However, Paul is not dealing with the law as such. We can tell what he thinks about it only by observing the ways in which it figures in his argument. It is therefore necessary to expose the dynamics of the argument, and see how the law functions within it. We need to see it in the context of the axes of power which Paul establishes in the course of his argument, and so determine how it relates to other functioning entities.

Paul's argument in Romans 5–8 is much more like a story than a logical treatise. The story begins in ch. 5 with God's intention of universal salvation, and the reader has the satisfaction of seeing the story reach its happy ending in ch. 8. However, this conclusion is not attained without a variety of incidents in between. These threaten the fulfilment of God's plan, and ways have to be found to overcome their destructive effects. The objections in chs. 6 and 7 are like the obstacles which a hero must surmount before his object is achieved.

The story-like quality of these chapters suggests that the dynamics of the argument might be elucidated by the application of a method which has been successfully employed in the analysis of folk-tales and has been applied very fruitfully to the study of the parables in the Gospels.[6] The methods of structural analysis have in fact been applied to Paul's writings elsewhere.[7] They can be extremely complex, but for our present purpose a simple model will suffice. The model is devised to display the axes of power in the action of the story. It is thus constructed to show the relationships between the *actants* (i.e. the active elements, not just the actors or personalities in the story). This can be illustrated from the Parable of the Lost Sheep (Matt 18:12–14=Luke 15:4–7). Simple as it is, the differences between the two versions show something of the complexity that may be involved in narrative.

In the first table, which gives Matthew's version, the top line gives the overall plot, consisting of the Sender (the originator of the action) leading to the Object (the conclusion of the story) leading to the Receiver (the beneficiary of the action at its conclusion). The lower line has the Subject (the active agent in the story) in the centre. The function of the Subject is to achieve the Object, and this is indicated by the vertical arrow. On the left is the Helper, which is the action taken or experienced by the Subject in order to achieve the Object. On the right is the Opponent, which is an action or circumstance which frustrates the efforts of the Subject. Thus in the first scene the Subject fails to reach the Object. The second scene has a new Helper (in this case the action of the Subject). As there is no Opponent, the Object is gained.

Matt 18:12–13

Sender →	*Object*	→ *Receiver*
Owner of 100 sheep	greater joy	himself
	↑	
Helper →	*Subject*	← *Opponent*
Scene 1. 99 sheep on hills	himself	1. One sheep strays
Scene 2. He seeks straying sheep		2. ——

Matthew then adds the application to the 'little ones' in the form of a statement (18:14).

Luke's version adds two new features. First he reinforces the successful outcome of Scene 2 by adding a third scene, which adds emotional power to the story, but does not alter its basic form. Secondly he rewrites the application to apply to repentant sinners in such a way as to mirror the parable, thus virtually treating it as an allegory.[8] However this in fact involves a change of Subject, as the action is not that of the Sender, but of the persons concerned. The Sender is presumably God, but remains unspecified (but 'heaven' is probably a substitute-word for God).

Luke 15:4–7

Sender →	*Object*	→ *Receiver*
A Owner of 100 sheep	greater joy	A himself
B (God)		B heaven
	↑	
Helper →	*Subject*	← *Opponent*
A 1. 99 sheep in wilderness	A himself	A 1. One sheep strays
2. He seeks straying sheep		2. ——
3. He calls in neighbours		3. ——
B 1. 99 righteous	B 100 persons	B 1. one sinner
2. The sinner repents		2. ——

When this model is applied to Paul's argument in Romans 5–8, the scenes become successive steps in the argument, leading to the desired conclusion (the Object). This will be shown only in a broad way for the earlier part of the argument, but it will be necessary to make a more detailed analysis as we approach the more controversial material in ch. 7.[9]

ADAM AND CHRIST   Romans 5 begins with expressions of heartfelt satisfaction for the benefits procured by God's act of justification (verses 1,

9), or reconciliation (verses 10–11), achieved by the death of Christ. Paul now states the new subject to be treated in what follows by slipping in references to the future. Being 'justified by his [Christ's] blood', we shall be 'saved by him from the wrath of God' (verse 9), or, as he puts it in the next verse, we shall be 'saved by his life'. It is the purpose of the new section to work this out in detail.

The first thing that has to be done is to establish the universal relevance of God's act in Christ. For this purpose Paul introduces his famous contrast between Adam and Christ, taking up a theme which he had already used in 1 Corinthians 15. So here we have two stories, rather like Luke's handling of the Lost Sheep. But Paul has to introduce a third element in order to take account of the law in the divine scheme of things. It is important for our purpose that the function of the law in the scheme should be clearly exposed. The following table gives a simplified analysis of the argument.

Rom 5:12–21

Sender →	Object	→ Receiver
A God: legal figure	life	all people
B God: grace figure		
	↑	
Helper →	Subject	← Opponent
A 1. God's command	A 1. Adam	A 1. disobedience of Adam
2. ⸺	2. people from Adam to Moses	2. they all sinned
3. the law	3. people from Moses to Christ	3. transgressions of the law
B 1. Christ's obedience in dying for us	B 1. Christ	B 1. ⸺
2. Receiving abundance of grace and free gift of righteousness	2. all people	2. ⸺

It will be remembered that, where there is an Opponent, the purpose of the Helper is frustrated, and so the Object cannot be achieved. Thus the result in all the cases under A is death. Paul does not specify the Helper in the case of A2, and his presentation of this item in verses 13–14 may be felt to betray weakness in his argument. But it can be deduced from the fact of death during the A2 period that the people must have sinned, because it has just been stated in verse 12 that death is the result of sin (possibly alluding to Wis 2:24).[10] We shall see later that Paul has not forgotten his contention in 2:12–16 that the good Gentile has an internal law through the promptings of conscience, and this ought to have been included as an alternative Helper alongside both the A2 and A3 periods, though Paul has not felt the need to do so at the present stage in his argument. This permits the conclusion that the implied Helper in A2 is this condition of innate morality.

The law here functions as that which identifies sin (verse 13). This negative view of the law arises from the argument in ch. 2. Though Paul recognises a number of positive aspects of the law (listed in 2:17–20), because he is concerned here with the effects of sin, it is the negative side that is relevant to his argument. Transgression of law is a clear way of identifying sin, and is a normal criterion in judicial action. In fact the whole of Paul's argument is conducted from the point of view of the coming judgement (cf. 1:18).

Moreover, in the progress of his argument Paul tends to use significant words almost as mathematical symbols, condensing a complex set of ideas into a single vocable, which is then available to be placed in relation to a fresh set of considerations in the next stage of the argument.[11] So 'law' in this context means the Jewish law considered as the identifier of sin in a forensic situation. As suggested above in connection with the missing Helper of A2, it should probably be taken to embrace also the innate morality of the good Gentile. I have already pointed out that it is a mistake to refer to this symbolic use of law as 'legalism'.

SIN AND GRACE   Another significant word which Paul uses like a mathematical symbol is 'grace' (*charis*). He has used it in a perfectly normal way, but at a crucial point, in his previous argument to denote the divine favour (3:24). It then began to acquire a quasi-technical sense on the basis of that usage in the argument on faith and works in ch. 4. In 4:4 it means virtually 'unearned income' (RSV 'gift'), and this is carried through in 4:16, leading to the idea of a special status in 5:2 ('the grace in which we stand'). But in 5:17–21 grace has become a commodity which we receive. It has a dynamic quality, comparable to that of sin, but life-giving instead of death-dealing. Thus it is a word that can stand for all that is denoted by the Helper of B2 in the above table of the argument in ch. 5. So Paul uses it as the subject of his concluding sentence in 5:21, which marks a period with its characteristic style of a full and formal phrase ('through Jesus Christ our Lord').

Grace, so understood, is the subject of ch. 6, in which Paul disposes of two objections (really misunderstandings) aroused by his teaching. The first objection ('Are we to continue in sin that grace may abound?') arises directly from 5:20, where he has said that 'where sin increased, grace abounded all the more'. So it is suggested that there might be positive value in sin, inasmuch as it has, as a matter of history, evoked the saving action of God. In reply, Paul points out that the very action whereby one avails oneself of the grace of God itself excludes sin as the method of obtaining it. That action is for his readers already a past event, being their baptism. We may note that Paul here resumes his use of the first-person plural, which he had used in 5:1–11. A simple actantial diagram will suffice to show the point.

Rom 6:1–11

Sender →	Object	→ Receiver
God: grace figure	grace abounding ↑	us
Helper →	Subject	← Opponent
1. continuing in sin	we	1. through baptism we died to sin
2. dying and rising with Christ		2. ——

As a kind of appendix to this first objection Paul adds a much-needed clarification in verses 12–14. He does not want to give the impression that the baptised person is automatically sinless. He thus reasserts the contrast of sin and grace (5:20–1) in such a way as to show that both are operative in the life of the baptised Christian, who is thereby engaged in a continuing moral struggle. At this point he sharpens the relevance of his remarks by changing the subject to 'you'.

Rom 6:12–14

Sender → you	*Object* life ↑	→ *Receiver* yourselves
Helper → A 1. letting sin reign in your mortal bodies	*Subject* you	← *Opponent* A 1. your members as instruments of wickedness
2. yielding yourselves to God, and your members as instruments of righteousness		2. ——
B 1. being under law		B 1. sin has dominion over you
2. being under grace		2. ——

This passage, short as it is, is programmatic. Paul has said in 5:20 that 'law came in, to increase the trespass', and this has associated the law with sin. It can then be argued that it is the law which is the cause of the destructive power of sin, seeing that it is what identifies sin, and so acts as incriminating evidence in a court of law. Without it, sin has no real power. As Paul has been arguing all along that Christians should not be subject to the law, the conclusion may be drawn that what is required for the operation of grace is not preoccupation with sin but freedom from the law. Paul therefore needs to explain that the power of sin is real, and this is what he does in reply to the second objection in 6:15–23. He will then need to expound the real nature of the connection between law and sin, and this will be the subject of ch. 7. So the second objection takes as its presupposition the situation of not being under the law, and the law itself does not enter into the argument. Though Paul uses the 'we' form in the objection in verse 15 ('Are we to sin because we are not under law but under grace?'), the argument which follows continues the more direct 'you'.

Rom 6:15–23

Sender → God: grace figure	*Object* eternal life ↑	→ *Receiver* you
Helper → A 1. ——	*Subject* you	← *Opponent* A 1. enslavement to sin
2. enslavement to God		2. ——
B 1. continuing to sin, because we are not under law but under grace		B 1. enslavement to sin
2. enslavement to God		2. ——

Two stages, A and B, are presupposed, because verses 20–1 explicitly refer to the situation before conversion. Though the Helper under A is not specified, it is obvious that it would have been life under law as opposed to life under grace. Both law and grace have to be understood according to their symbolic meanings, as explained above. In this section of the argument there is an implied correlation between life under law and enslavement to sin on the one hand, and life under grace and enslavement to God on the other. The first will be expounded in ch. 7 and the second in 8:1–17. It is necessary to do this fully and convincingly, because it is the crucial point of the argument. Paul rises to the occasion with immense rhetorical skill.

LAW AND SIN   First Paul takes up the point which he made in reply to the first objection, that Christians do not intentionally continue in sin, because they have died with Christ. This dying with Christ is applied to release from the law. This does not at all mean freedom from restraint in the sense of freedom for licence and lawlessness. It means freedom from the state symbolised by law, in which sin is identified but cannot be brought under control. The point is introduced by means of the analogy of a woman's release from the marriage bond through the death of her husband.

Rom 7:1–6

Sender →	*Object*	→ *Receiver*
A a woman	A freedom to marry another	A herself
B God	B to bear fruit for God	B you/us
	↑	
Helper →	*Subject*	← *Opponent*
A 1. husband is alive	A the woman	A 1. law against adultery
2. husband dies		2. ——
B 1. living under law	B you/we	B 1. not belonging to Christ
2. living in the flesh		2. sinful passions aroused by the law
3. belonging to him who has been raised from the dead		3. ——
4. serving in the new life of the Spirit		4. ——

To help the argument along, Paul here introduces further examples of words which function like mathematical symbols. The Opponent in B is first indicated by the idea of not belonging to Christ, and this corresponds with the terms of reference of the first objection in ch. 6. We should thus expect the Opponent in B2 to be enslavement to sin, but instead Paul is more specific, and refers to sinful passions aroused by the law. This explains his new equivalent for life under the law, i.e. living in the flesh. It denotes a state in which the passions give evidence of the inability to keep control of sin. Paul no doubt means by passions (*pathēmata*) self-will in the broadest sense.[12] The flesh thus becomes a code-word for life without Christ, which is characterised by passions aroused by the law.

Similarly the Helper in B3 corresponds with the terms in 6:1–11, but then in B4 has a new equivalent in the form of serving in the new life of the Spirit. This in its turn replaces the notion of enslavement to God (6:15–23), but we should note the use of the verb 'serving' (*douleuein*), which is maintained at the end of the chapter (7:25). The Spirit thus also acts as a word-symbol, denoting the life of those who belong to Christ, which achieves the Object of bearing fruit for God. This 'new life in the Spirit' is a substitute for the notion of dying with Christ, putting it in positive form. Paul has already prepared the ground for this formulation in 6:4, where he referred to 'newness of life'.

Next Paul has to face another objection. He has now for the first time suggested that the law itself is the Opponent, because he has attributed to it the incitement of passions. It seems, then, that he is asserting that 'the law is sin' (verse 7). So he now has to vindicate the goodness of the law, which he recognises to be the gift of God himself, but without going back on the important observation that the law does play a part in the life of 'the flesh'. For this purpose he composes a narrative in the first person singular, thus relating the issue to his own experience. But the story has a typical quality, and is clearly intended to describe something which the readers can identify from their own experience. Personal details are in fact totally excluded, so that it is impossible to connect it with a known occasion in Paul's life. The choice of the command not to covet is deliberate and tactful, for it gives an example of a situation in which psychological factors operate, but without the complications which might arise if he were to refer to sexual or violent passions. Moreover it is a matter of basic morality, equally applicable to those who observe the Jewish law and to those who are guided by the laws of conscience. The story is told in the past tense, because Paul wishes to expose the situation before and after the introduction of law.

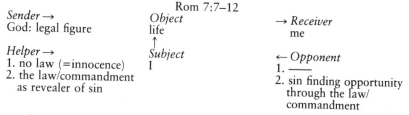

Rom 7:7–12

Sender →	Object	→ Receiver
God: legal figure	life	me
	↑	
Helper →	Subject	← Opponent
1. no law (=innocence)	I	1. ———
2. the law/commandment as revealer of sin		2. sin finding opportunity through the law/ commandment

The remarkable feature of this story is that Paul presupposes a prior situation (Scene 1) when there was no Opponent and the Object was achieved. This can scarcely refer to a period of conscious innocence in his own life, when he was aware of living acceptably without the restraints imposed by a commandment or by the law. The correlation of commandment and law strongly suggests that the real model is the Adam story, which he has already used in ch. 5, as accepted by a number of scholars.[13] This then excludes the idea that Scene 1 corresponds with the time from

Adam to Moses, which was marked by sin on the evidence that death reigned during the period. On the other hand the repeated correlation of commandment and law shows that the scope of Paul's interest is not only the Jewish law, but also the moral law of the good Gentile. Both law and commandment are revealed to be 'holy and just and good' in themselves.

Nevertheless the law appears in this model as instrumental in causing 'death'. It is thus necessary to make a clear distinction between instrument and cause. Even a 'holy and just and good' instrument can prove fatal when employed by a cause bent on destruction. The law has positive value in showing up this destructive force. Paul clarifies this point in verse 13, where he replies to the objection, 'Did that which is good, then, bring death to me?'

Rom 7:13

Sender →	Object	→ Receiver
the law	revelation of sin	me
	↑	
Helper →	Subject	← Opponent
1. no law	I	1. ignorance
2. sin working death in me through what is good		2. ——

Scene 1 is deduced from Paul's earlier statement in verse 7. But here he is not referring to a state of innocence, where ignorance is bliss, but to a state of mind in which there was awareness of the destructive effect of sin, but no means of identifying it correctly. It is, then, more like the situation between Adam and Moses. However, this is no more than the presupposition. Scene 2 is what Paul is actually asserting in this verse, that the law did indeed fulfil its function of revealing sin when tested by the force of sin. Though described as past event, it is in fact a timeless situation. So Paul now changes to timeless present as he explains in detail the dilemma of life under law.

It is indeed a universal experience which Paul now describes, and the readers are expected to identify themselves with Paul and acknowledge that what he says is true in their own experience. But the continuation of the first-person singular form gives a gripping picture of the personal agony which may be involved, which is far more effective than an impersonal account would be. Briefly, it is the dilemma of finding in the law the revelation of sin, but of having no other Helper to give the power to overcome sin. This is explained in a series of statements in verses 14–20.

Rom 7:14–20

Sender →	Object	→ Receiver
I	what I want	my salvation
	↑	
Helper →	Subject	← Opponent
1. the law, which is spiritual	I	1. evil, which lies close at hand
2. I do not understand my own actions		2. the very thing I hate
3. I agree that the law is good		3. sin which dwells with me

Rom 7:14–20

4. I will what is right

5. the good I want
6. myself

4. nothing good in my flesh
5. the evil I do not want
6. sin which dwells within me

The successive descriptions of the Helper show that Paul is thinking of the law, not in a narrow sense, but in line with his symbolic usage to embrace innate morality as well as the Jewish law as such. This explains the larger use of *nomos* in the concluding verses of the chapter, where he brings his presentation of the dilemma to its conclusion.[14] Because 'law' means living under the law, he can by extension use it to refer negatively to living under the power of sin and positively to living under God. 'Law' here, then, virtually means 'regime'. In the concluding summary which now follows Paul's choice of concepts is, of course, geared to the contrasting situation of the life of grace, which is to be the subject of the next chapter. Paul anticipates this in a parenthesis, which expresses relief from unbearable tension, in verse 25a, before condensing the issue of the dilemma into its most basic form in the conclusion to the chapter.

Rom 7:21–5

Sender →	*Object*	*→ Receiver*
I	I want to do right ↑	my salvation
Helper →	*Subject*	*← Opponent*
1. the law, suggesting right	I	1. evil, which is close at hand
2. I delight in the law of God		2. law of sin in my members
(3. God through Jesus Christ		3. ——)
4. I serve law of God with my mind		4. with my flesh I serve law of sin

GRACE AND SPIRIT   The solution to the dilemma has been anticipated in 7:25a. But the subject is too important for such a simple statement. It is the climax of the argument, and Paul treats it with greater fulness than any previous consideration. We shall not need to work through the whole of ch. 8, but it is desirable to continue the actantial model through 8:1–17, so as to see how the successive statements of the solution balance the preceding formulations of the dilemma. Paul announces the solution in verses 1–2.

Rom 8:1–2

Sender →	*Object*	*→ Receiver*
God	No condemnation (i.e. at the judgement) ↑	those who are in Christ Jesus
Helper →	*Subject*	*← Opponent*
1. ——	each one of you	1. the law of sin and death
2. the law of the Spirit of life in Christ Jesus		2. ——

It will be noticed that, though Paul indicates the universal scope by the plural expression for the Receiver, he here uses second person-singular (*se*) for the Subject to apply the solution directly to the readers individually.[15] But *se* is symbolical, and Subject and Receiver are really identical. Similarly Paul continues the symbolical use of law to denote the regime. The 'Spirit of life in Christ Jesus' takes the reader back to 7:6. In Scene 1 the Helper is not specified, because all the alternative possibilities have been excluded by their failure to achieve the Object in 7:14–25.

Paul begins to unpack this opening statement by a series of contrasts between Spirit and flesh. The use of 'flesh' to denote life under the law is also drawn from 7:5, and Paul now reverts to the first-person plural form which he had used at that stage of the argument.

Rom 8:3–4

Sender →	*Object*	*→ Receiver*
God	the just requirement of the law	us
	↑	
Helper →	*Subject*	*← Opponent*
1. the law	We	1. weakened by the flesh
2. sin in the flesh condemned through the sending of his own Son in the likeness of sinful flesh and for sin		2. ——
3. walking not according to the law but according to the Spirit		3. ——

The Object is achieved through two actions, God's redemptive action in Scene 2, and our walking according to the Spirit, which is our response to God's action, in Scene 3. This part of the argument is further elucidated by verses 5–8 on the flesh and verses 9–11 on the Spirit. In verse 5 Paul imagines the theoretical possibility of two groups, which he deals with in the third person.

Rom 8:5–8

Sender →	*Object*	*→ Receiver*
1. those who live by the flesh	life and peace	themselves
2. those who live by the Spirit		
	↑	
Helper →	*Subject*	*← Opponent*
1. minds set on things of the flesh	1. those who live by the flesh	1. hostility to God, making for inability to submit to God's law or to please God
2. minds set on things of the Spirit	2. those who live by the Spirit	2. ——

The next three verses then draw out by contrast the meaning of life in the Spirit. As this accords with Paul's hortatory purpose, he now changes to second-person plural address.

Rom 8:9–11

Sender →	Object	→ Receiver
1. ——	1. belonging to Christ	you
2. Christ in you	2. your spirits alive	
3. he who raised Christ Jesus from the dead	3. life to your mortal bodies ↑	

Helper →	Subject	← Opponent
1a. being in the flesh	you	1a. not having Spirit of Christ
b. being in the Spirit, if the Spirit of God dwells in you		b. ——
2a. your bodies		2a. dead because of sin
b. because of righteousness		b. ——
3a. the Spirit of him who raised Jesus from the dead dwells in you		3a. ——
b. through his Spirit which dwells in you		b. ——

It will be seen that in this section Paul is careful to include the two actions (Scenes 2 and 3) of 8:3–4. He does not wish his readers to forget that the capacity to live in the Spirit is dependent upon the justification which has been achieved through God's action in Christ.

This leads up to the grand statement of verses 12–17, which may be set out in similar fashion. Paul here reverts to the first-person plural, because the statement is indicative rather than hortatory, and he wishes to express his solidarity with his readers. But in verses 13–15 'you' and 'they' are used where the argument corresponds with the above two sections in verses 5–11. Verse 12 is omitted from the following table, because it functions only as the heading to the new paragraph. It picks up the idea of freedom from the law of sin and death in verse 2, now expressed (after resumptive *ara oun*) in terms of not being under obligation to the flesh. This signifies the end of the dilemma described in ch. 7, and in what follows the Helpers now pile up while the Opponents melt away.

Rom 8.13–17

Sender →	Object	→ Receiver
1. the Spirit	1. life	1. you
2. the Spirit of God	2. sons of God	2. them
3. God the giver of Spirit	3. children of God	3. you
4. God the Father	4. children and heirs and glorified together ↑	4. us

Helper →	Subject	← Opponent
1a. living according to flesh	1. you	1a. death
b. putting to death the deeds of the body		b. ——
2. led by the Spirit of God	2. they	2. ——
3a. the spirit of slavery	3. you	3a. fear
b. the spirit of sonship		b. ——

4a. the Spirit bearing witness with our spirit	4. we	4a. ——
b. suffering with Christ		b. ——

The last item (suffering with Christ) has not entered the argument hitherto, but of course it provides the lead into the grand finale which occupies the rest of the chapter.

CONCLUSIONS   The above sections have treated Paul's argument in Romans 5–8 as a whole, using an analytical model which properly belongs to the interpretation of narrative. The justification for this procedure is that the argument does have something of the character of a story, and the axes of power can be appreciated with this method of analysis.

The story tells how God intended to give life to all people (see the first diagram of 5:12–21), and this is splendidly concluded with the final statement of 8:17, where God the Father confers the status of children and heirs and fellow-heirs with Christ and sharers in Christ's glory upon 'us'. It is evident that 'we' are not only Paul and his readers, but potentially all people.

Paul's concept of the function of the law is the negative one of revealing sin. This does not conflict with his positive appreciation of the law as 'holy and just and good' (7:12). The law is at least as valuable as the internal conscience of the good Gentile (2:12–16). Neither of them, however, is capable of ensuring the object which God intends for all people (7:14–20). The reason for this negative way of looking at the law is the forensic framework of Paul's thought. Justification is a concept which belongs to the language of the eschatological judgement (1:17–18). Paul is not here concerned with the educative value of the law (though he showed appreciation of it in Gal 3:24), or with the intrinsic value of its moral precepts, which he never denies. He is concerned with it only as a Helper, i.e. as a means of obtaining the object which God has in store. From this point of view the law is not really different from the self-help of the good Gentile. Both alike have been shown to be subject to sin (1:18–3:20), and both alike are confronted with the same dilemma (7:14–20). The analysis of this last passage shows that the depiction of the Helper is sufficiently broad to apply both to the Jewish law and to innate morality.

The analysis of these chapters also shows that Paul tends to use key words like mathematical symbols. Law and grace, flesh and spirit, are all used in this way. Paul establishes a pattern or nexus of ideas at a certain point in his argument, and then takes up one word from it to carry the whole nexus of ideas into the next stage of the argument. Thus law certainly means the Jewish law, but it is used to denote life under the law and carries with it the comparable conditions of life under innate morality. The much-discussed use of *nomos* in 8:2, where Paul speaks of 'the law of the Spirit of life in Christ Jesus' and 'the law of sin and death', is an extension of this usage, and means life under the conditions of the Spirit and of sin respectively. Thus it virtually means 'regime', though the translation 'law' should be retained to maintain the continuity of the argument. Flesh refers to the selfish passions which belong to life under the power of sin (personified by Paul as an active force), which is also an inevitable feature of life under the law, and so law and flesh become almost interchangeable. It must be stressed that this is entirely due to the dynamic functioning of these words and concepts in Paul's argument, and arises directly from the needs of it. Paul is not drawing in a specialised meaning from outside his normal semantic field.

The changes of person in these chapters often appear quite arbitrary, but can be justified on rhetorical grounds. The use of the first-person singular in 7:7–25 adds great force at a climactic point in the argument. Though Paul speaks out of his own experience, it is experience which he knows to be universal, with which his readers can readily identify. Nothing is said which indicates a particular crisis in his personal history, and the dilemma described in 7:14–25 is not a psychological 'guilt-complex' or neurotic personality disorder. The past tense in 7:7–12 is due to the use of narrative technique. The present tense in the later verses properly expresses a timeless and universal experience.

Paul's argument is primarily aimed at exposing how salvation (the Object) can be achieved for all people (the Receiver). At the same time he has a special interest in the question of whether the Jewish law is a necessary means (Helper) to reach this goal, because the Judaising party is bent on imposing the law on the Gentile converts. Paul shows that neither the Jewish law nor Gentile morality have the power to enable their followers to achieve the object. Both Jew and Gentile alike require the power of the Spirit made available through life in Christ. Consequently insistence on Judaising the Gentiles would be unhelpful, and by introducing an unsatisfactory alternative to their present equally commendable standard of morality would be harmful and misleading.

Law has its proper place in religion, because it provides a moral code by which sin (which is rebellion against God) can be identified. But this can be only an ancillary role in the process of salvation, because law by itself is powerless against the force of sin, backed up by human desires and passions and self-will. Something more is needed to resist these, and that is nothing less than the power of the Spirit of God himself. In his conclusion to the whole argument Paul discloses that this power of the Spirit is the force of divine love in the pattern of redemption: 'We are more than conquerors through him who loved us' (8:37). Only with such strength of love in a vital personal relationship with God can the passion which uses even the law itself for its own ends be turned towards the attainment of salvation.

12
THE STATUS OF LAW IN THE LETTER TO THE EPHESIANS

MARTIN KITCHEN

In his Introduction to *Paul, the Law and the Jewish People*, E. P. Sanders observes that 'the Law had been [Paul's] life before God revealed his Son to him'.[1] By 'life', he means, presumably, the guiding principle, the foundation, and the way in which he both perceived his existence and conducted his affairs. Paul's own claim in Gal 1:14 ('and I advanced in Judaism beyond many of my own age among my people, so zealous was I for the traditions of my fathers'), as well as his more developed testimony in Phil 3:5–6 ('circumcised on the eighth day, of the people of Israel, of the tribe of Benjamin, a Hebrew born of Hebrews; as to the law a Pharisee, as to zeal a persecutor of the church, as to righteousness under the law blameless'), show a degree of pride in his former existence which add to the complexity of establishing the apostle's evaluation of the law in the light of his experience of Christ; for, from this new vantage-point of faith, he finds himself able to say that 'the law – or principle – of the Spirit of life in Christ Jesus has set me free from the law – both "principle" and "precept", as Torah – of sin and death' (Rom 8:2).

The outworking of the relationship between these two conflicting principles is what occupied Paul, presumably, not just because the issue arose in the context of the Galatian churches' desire to 'go over the top', as it were, and be circumcised as well as baptised, just to be on the safe side,[2] and because it then needed further clarification when Paul found himself having to write to Rome in order to raise support for his proposed trip to Spain;[3] but also, and perhaps more importantly, because these problems presented one of the major religious issues for Paul himself, and for his understanding of what it meant to be a worshipper of the one God who had made himself known to the patriarchs and to Moses.

In an article published in 1978,[4] Colin Hickling, in seeking to discover what might constitute the 'centre' of Paul's thought, drew attention to the contradictory ways in which the law is apparently viewed in different epistles. In Galatians the apostle's tone is, he says:

> ... almost unreservedly hostile. Gal 3:19, 'It was added because of transgressions, till the offspring should come to whom the promise had been made; and it was ordained by angels through an intermediary', goes as far as possible towards dissociating the Law altogether from any divine origin.

And in Gal 4:1–11 (the passage concerning the child who is under guardians and trustees, with the reference to elemental spirits, and 'redemption for those who were under the law'), 'acceptance of [the Law's] (here, mainly calendrical) rules by the baptized is asserted to be tantamount to repudiation of baptism'.

In Romans 1–8 Paul softens the contrast between the phrases 'by works of law' and 'by faith', although he is clearly at pains to point out that he does not oppose the law, as his claim in Rom 3:31 makes clear: 'Do we then overthrow the law by this faith? By no means! On the contrary, we uphold the law!' The law is holy (7:12) and fulfilment of what it requires is the purpose of the mission of Jesus (8:4). Yet Hickling points out that, once the argumentation of Romans 1–8 is over, a wider spectrum of Paul's views on the law becomes clearer; indeed, in Rom 13:1–10 'he virtually returns, with some emphasis, to a straightforwardly Jewish understanding: to fulfil the Law is the proper goal of behaviour, and what matters is the correct interpretation of the Law, namely ... its reduction to the love commandment'.

Hickling argues that these 'dissonances' in Paul's view of the law are not to be explained on the basis of the 'familiar synthesis' by which the law is perceived as encountering 'a situation already irretrievably marred ... by sin'. He maintains that it was not simply that the law 'became weak because of the flesh', but rather that the law is perceived in a different way according to the religious standpoint adopted. At this stage he draws attention to a point made by Sanders concerning the plight of human nature in Romans 7, which 'describes ... the pre-Christian or non-Christian life as seen from the perspective of faith'.[5] Thus, says Hickling, the law is viewed 'from the standpoint of [Paul's] personal understanding – and in some degree, perhaps, of his experience – of what it means to be a Christian'.[6]

There exists, therefore, a fundamental ambiguity in Paul's attitude to his Jewish past. Hickling's article concerns itself not only with 'law' as such, but also with Israelite history. In this context, Paul makes a different assessment of Israel's history according to whether he regards the Christian community as continuous with empirical Judaism, 'from whose rejection of the apostolic preaching Paul had himself suffered physically as well as in other ways (2 Cor 1:24; Rom 9:2)' – in which case it is the reverse of "saving history" ' – or whether he regards that history as 'providing the antecedent history of the Christian community' – in which case it is the locus of God's self-disclosure.[7]

In the case of the law, the same applies. What is central for Paul is the necessity to interpret the past from the standpoint of the present, when the present means 'standing at a frontier between the old order and the new, vividly and experientially aware of the life-denying power of everything that precedes initiation into Christ, yet also knowing that "everything is from God" '. In other words, the centre is Christology, in the strict sense of Christ's relation to God, for Christ relativises all that went before, yet he is the Son of the God who created all things and called Abraham as well as Israel and Moses.

Hickling goes on to elaborate this point, first, in the case of eschatology. He notes that a measure of tension exists between futurist and realised understandings[8] with respect to the reference to Paul's conversion in 2 Cor 5:16, to the reservation of the resurrection of Christians until the Last Day in 1 Corinthians 15 and Romans 8, and to the availability of eschatological gifts in Rom 1:17f.; 3:21, and 2 Cor 4:6. In these contexts he suggests that the importance of the present becomes predominant when Paul's basic thought is of 'the gospel as in process of being proclaimed – when, that is, he thinks of the message with which he had been entrusted as itself part of God's saving activity and essentially eschatological work'.

The point is elaborated, secondly, in the case of the status and function of Christ in his pre-existence, and Hickling uses three texts to illustrate this. In Rom 1:3ff., the question is whether the resurrection declared openly a status Jesus had enjoyed from all eternity, or whether it was the moment of his elevation to that status. Hickling maintains that, in view of the fact that Paul clearly left himself open to as wide a variety of interpretations in his own day as in ours, whether he is the author of these verses or endorsed them as he received them from the tradition, we may conclude that he thought the belief in Christ's pre-existence was either not very vulnerable to critical questioning, or not very important. At all events, he could scarcely have laid less stress on Jesus' pre-existence than he does here.

In 1 Cor 8:6, at the opposite extreme, the pre-existent Christ is shown to be mediating God's activity in the creation of the universe. Certainly, there is no temporal reference, and the intention is clearly to attribute to Jesus the divine attributes of uniqueness and of responsibility for the coming into being of all things, and not necessarily that of having existed for ever. However, this is clearly implied, Hickling maintains, in *di' hou ta panta*, and the estimate of his status before history is very high.

In Phil 2:6–11 it is noteworthy that, even though there is here a story about Jesus before he entered human history, which states that he existed before it, and that his decision of self-abasement was made then, there is no reference to his involvement in the act of creation, whereas the level of his glorification – *auton hyperypsōsen* – is measured by his receipt of honour from the whole created order, which is an advance upon a purely Adamic status of being *en morphē theou*. (It is possible that such a concern was, in any case, 'peripheral' to the thought of Paul.)

These are hardly gross inconsistencies, yet they are significant ambiguities, and again, they are to be explained upon the basis of the present standpoint of Paul. Hickling maintains that the common standpoint from which Paul elected to make use of the various statements considered in the article, is 'the concept of a decisive turning point in time . . . that dominates his thought'. Thus in Rom 1:3f., 'it is the declaration of Christ's glory as now known that matters, moreover, of which the recipients are those brought within the sphere of the new order'. In Philippians 2, the stress is entirely upon the second half of the narrative of the Christ-hymn, and this lays fullest possible stress upon the new dignity of Christ acknowledged in the new order. In 2 Cor 8:9, even if the passage appears to speak of a contrast between Christ's former glory and his subsequent abasement, 'a third stage of augmented glory in which Christians participate is obviously implied'.

Hickling proceeds to point out that, consequently, E. P. Sanders' view of Paul's primary convictions, namely, (a) that Jesus Christ is Lord, (b) that Paul was called to be an apostle to the Gentiles, needs supplementing with a rider – that God has brought about a 'decisive and final transformation of time', an *Aeonenwende*, which bears the dualistic colours of apocalyptic. The centre of Paul's thought is thus to be found,

> . . . not simply, or even principally, in the content of his assertions about God and Jesus and his own calling, but in the sense of fundamental and paradoxical contrast, as of one standing at a cosmic frontier, with which this content was perceived.

In a final point, Hickling points out that Paul's knowledge of the redemption and consecration of suffering enabled him to transcend the contrast between the old and new. 'The words he claimed to have heard in ecstasy "power is fully realized – *teleitai* – in weakness" (2 Cor 12:9) point to a supreme reconciliation of opposites'. Elsewhere, the word *astheneia* is characteristic of the state of affairs under the old order apart from Christ, or as it still persists temporarily alongside the new order in Christ. 'Here', Hickling concludes, *astheneia* with all that it implies – both Christ's crucifixion (cf. 2 Cor 13:4), and the apostle's participation in his suffering – are seen to be the locus of God's fullest revelation of himself'.[9] Paul's 'life', then, was changed by his understanding of the intervention of God in history – and, more importantly, into Paul's religious assumptions – by the resurrection of Jesus as the Christ. It was therefore no longer possible for law to be central; yet, not surprisingly, because of its former centrality, it remained a focal issue in the working-out of how the new 'life' was to be understood; and Hickling's analysis of what is central provides a way of looking at the later documents in the continuing Pauline tradition. Of the documents in the Pauline corpus, the Letter to the Ephesians is naturally one of the first to turn to in examining this issue, since it is probably the earliest of the Pauline pseudepigrapha,[10] and, as we shall see, it bridges, to an extent, the even greater gap in ideas which exists between Paul's genuine letters and, say, the Pastoral Letters.

However, upon turning to it, we are immediately struck by the fact that there is only one reference in Ephesians to the law. This in itself is significant, for it shows immediately that the law is not a great issue for the writer of Ephesians, even though his primary theological concern is with the relationship between Jews and Gentiles in the church. The passage in which this one reference is made is Eph 2.15: *ton nomon tōn entolōn en dogmasin katargēsas, hina tous duo ktisē en autǫ eis hena kainon anthrōpon poiōn eirēnēn*. The verse occurs in the context of the writer's call to remembrance of the Gentiles' former state, when, in their so-called 'uncircumcision', they were alienated from the purposes and the grace of God. What has brought about change, says the writer, is the bringing-together of both Jew and Gentile in the one body, Christ, who has, in his flesh, broken down the middle wall of partition and slain the enmity which was the law, in order to create one new *anthrōpos*.

Calvin Roetzel has argued[11] that Eph 2:15a bears an insertion into a hymn of which the writer of Ephesians made use. He takes further the work of G. Schille and J. T. Sanders[12] and, in spite of the difficulties in setting the parameters of the hymn, nevertheless insists that one is to be found here, and argues that the words 'abolishing in his flesh the law of commandments in ordinances' was an addition by the writer. He sees the pleonastic expression 'law of commandments in ordinances' as referring not, as M. Barth thought,[13] to the automatically divisive function of the law, but to a part of the law itself. He also interprets the *mesotoichon tou phragmou* in verse 14 as in apposition to both 'enmity' and 'law', and thus changing the emphasis of the hymn from the cosmos to the law which divides Jews and Gentiles. This leaves him free to assert that, since Eph 2:15a is redactional, this may provide a clue to the purpose of the letter as a whole.

This purpose is to teach that the coming of Christ made the principle of the commandments obsolete when converts were made 'perfect', 'wise', or 'spiritual'; which is evidently what Roetzel understands by 'heavenly'. The writer allegedly found support for this view in the provisional character of the 'law of the commandments' in the letters of Paul, and was convinced that he stood in the mainstream of the Pauline tradition. The question the writer was addressing was, On what terms were Jewish Christians to be accepted in the Church? At the price of the surrender of their legal observance? Or without prejudice, as K. M. Fischer argued,[14] which would thus allow them to continue their distinctive customs and rites?

Roetzel maintains, rather boldly, that the answer to this question depends upon the interpretation of Eph 2:15a. He argues that this verse is crucial to the understanding of the letter, and that what is significant about the law here is that it is the 'law of commandments in ordinances'. He takes Dibelius and Conzelmann to task[15] for fixing attention on *nomos* and for ignoring the qualification which follows. His confession,[16] that no parallel to the peculiar genitival construction, *entolōn en dogmasin*, is known to him does not lead him to take into account the pleonastic nature of the language of the letter. Instead, he makes much of the reading of P[46], '[Jesus] destroyed the law of the commandments' (a reading which has no other support), and seeks to establish, by reference to Philo,[17] that what is advised and desired in Ephesians is 'not the abolition of Torah as Israel's story, but the abrogation of the principle of law seen in the commandments'. He maintains that the text was emended by a later redactor who, though familiar with some of Paul's more positive statements about the law, misunderstood the writer's original intention and, by drawing on Colossians with its negative evaluation of the law, left a confusing text.

The language of Ephesians is notoriously pleonastic. Consequently, the search for hymnic fragments underlying the text is hazardous in the extreme.[18] There would appear to be much stronger grounds for saying that the letter as a whole is to be viewed as a unitary creation, with a deliberately liturgical tone, which consciously sets out to develop Pauline tradition, in the light of changed circumstances, for a particular situation.

Roetzel allows this one verse to bear too much weight. A reading of it in its immediate context makes it quite clear that the writer is saying not very much at all about the law as such. It functions here as the symbol of what has been abolished by the death of Christ. In fact, it is not unreasonable to suppose that Ephesians may have been written as a result of the insight of the writer into the significance of the destruction of Jerusalem in CE 70, and, indeed, soon after that date, in order to re-establish the authority of Paul after his death, and to show how the gospel Paul had preached had been remarkably vindicated by that event.

If Eph 2:14ff. puts forward a view of the death of Christ which has direct theological links with the destruction of the temple, and the *mesotoichon tou phragmou* is to be understood as the dividing fence between the Court of the Gentiles and the Court of Israel, then the construction of the sentence does not demand that *nomon* should be read as in apposition to *mesotoichon*, but rather that the wall was in principle broken down when the sacrifice of Christ was offered. Since one man had died, and the readers knew from their experience of baptism and membership of the Church that both Jew and Gentile had access to God through the sacrifice of Christ, the more recent event of the destruction of Jerusalem, in vindicating the apostle Paul, also underlined the extent to which the law had been rendered of no value. As a system of commandments and ordinances for the people of God, it had been superseded by the life of the new community, the true *politeia* of Israel.[19]

The law, then, is not all that important here; it is a symbol of a passed order, and it is referred to as consisting of commands and ordinances, partly because this is in accordance with the pleonastic tone of the rest of the letter, and partly because it is those very commands and ordinances which have been superseded in the new order. However, Roetzel is right to say that 'what is advised and desired in Ephesians is not the abolition of Torah as Israel's story, but the abrogation of the principle of law seen in the commandments',[20] for the new community, or the new corporate *anthrōpos*, is the antitype of Israel of old; and the language of salvation in Ephesians is the language of the saving acts of God in Israel's history. Moreover, in Ephesians the grace of God is revealed in salvation rather than justification, with its specific reference to law, and in 2:5, 8, 9 the writer refers to *erga agatha*, not *erga nomou*. Yet the religious themes of election in 1:4, 5 and redemption in 1:7 are Jewish, and ethical instructions and lifestyle are expressed in terms of walking – *peripatein* – which presumably has its roots in *halakah*.

In terms of Hickling's article, several striking things emerge from this; for 'centre' and 'periphery' in the thought of Ephesians are also worked out less with reference to law than to the history of Israel, as though these belong together as the yardsticks by which the action of God was to be tested – maybe it would not be too much to say that, for a disciple of Paul, these are the yardsticks by which the action of God had to be measured.

The writer is aware that he stands in a particular relationship with time, but this is a new time, not 'between the times', as for Paul. His theological perception of the destruction of Jerusalem means a 'new time' for the people of God, for God has acted again to bring about the consummation of the plan of human redemption, by making visible the universal access to God implicit in the Pauline understanding of the cross. The focus of what he says is not so much the law, but rather the Gentiles' former state with regard to the sacred history of the people of God. Israel's history thus constitutes the criterion by which closeness and access to God are measured.

Roetzel speaks of a 'spirituality' of Jewish and Gentile unity,[21] and this is not inappropriate. However, the writer is not attempting to present to his readers a solution to the problem of Jewish acceptability in the Church; rather, he is celebrating a new state of affairs, in which the universality of the gospel is clear to all, and the labours and suffering of the apostle openly vindicated. This explains his extended paean to Paul's memory in Ephesians 3. The sufferings of Paul have borne fruit in the actual incorporation of Jews with Gentiles in the Church, and, whatever the circumstances of Paul's death – possibly shameful to the Christian community[22] – God has vindicated him in the events of history.

The writer of Ephesians stands thus as a faithful bearer and reinterpreter of Pauline tradition. He reflects on events of Israel's history and sees saving significance in them. His focus is upon what has happened in recent time, and how God is to be understood in it. The change he makes to Pauline tradition is that human existence is not so much at the intersection of two worlds – this world and the world to come – but that the world to come has, in fact, broken in upon this world with the historical event of Jerusalem's destruction, and that this gives meaning to the apostleship of Paul. The Letter to the Ephesians thus counts among the variety of responses to the fall of Jerusalem to be found in Jewish and Christian thinking in the first century.

13
LAW AND CUSTOM: LUKE–ACTS AND LATE HELLENISM

F. GERALD DOWNING

Unquestionably the Mosaic Law plays a distinctive role in Luke's two-volume work. From the infancy narratives to the closing speeches of Paul, Luke portrays believers in the Christ as faithfully adhering to the Law in a wide variety of ways ... six times in Luke 2, Mary and Joseph perform rites which Luke describes as according to the Law or the custom of the Law ... (and) he depicts Paul worshipping in the synagogue, circumcising Timothy, assuming a private vow, and purifying himself with and paying the expenses for four men who themselves had a vow, for the express purpose of proving to the Jewish Christians in Jerusalem that he lives 'in observance of the Law' (21:23–24). (C. L. Blomberg)[1]

Further, Jesus in Luke seems perhaps to say less in criticism of the law than he does in Mark in particular, while in Acts Paul successfully rebuts charges of offending against the law in any way.[2]

Yet at the same time Luke has two more stories of sabbath healing by Jesus than appear in Mark and Matthew. Luke also allows Jesus to propose according decisive authority to a shared common ethical insight rather than to the law, at least in its apparent customary interpretation.[3] By contrast with his portrayal of Paul, Luke does not seem to allow Stephen to rebut the charges brought against him, of speaking against Moses and the customs he delivered, and the temple. Peter has a vision in which he is encouraged to break Jewish dietary laws and also enjoy table-fellowship with pagans; the possibility of any obligation on Cornelius to accept circumcision is not even raised.[4] Then in ch. 13 of Acts Paul contrasts the remission of sins available through Jesus with that to be had under Moses' law. And in ch. 15 Peter talks of the unbearable yoke of the law, while James agrees that Gentile converts should not be burdened with it. On the one hand there is an observant piety, on the other an apparent freedom to ignore what the law prescribes. As J. L. Houlden also notes, there seems to be an ambivalence that warrants some attention.[5]

Luke (alone in the NT apart from one instance in John) also talks of the 'customs' (*ethē*) of Moses, and S. G. Wilson wonders whether this is not concessive: 'It may be ... that Luke shares the cosmopolitan tone and cultural magnanimity common to Josephus and Philo'.[6] It is 'merely' a matter of local custom, perhaps.

There is also the linked issue of Luke's attitude to Roman law and its representatives, as recently reopened by P. W. Walasky.[7] Jesus' and Paul's encounters with Jewish and Roman courts are closely connected in the narrative, and Paul acknowledges the authority of both with a similar submissiveness. Yet there is more than a hint of lawlessness in Luke's 'Magnificat' (Luke 1:46–55), and alongside this we also notice critical references both to puppet monarchs and to Roman officials.[8]

The half-dozen recent studies I have considered for this essay all attempt to explain Luke's approach with little or no reference to contemporary Hellenistic views which may well have obtained among his intended pagan (or Gentile Christian) readers. I shall argue, however, that all of these apparent tensions or ambivalences really only make sense – or, at least, make better sense, in that context.[9]

A quite different suggestion was made a few years ago by Jacob Jervell. He argued that 'by insisting on Jewish Christians' universal adherence to the law, [Luke] succeeds in showing that they are the restored and true Israel entitled to God's promises and salvation . . . (with) the Gentiles as an associate people'.[10] But Wilson can readily demonstrate that Jervell has not done justice to the more negative and critical responses to the law of which we have noted some instances.[11] He concludes 'Luke stands at a considerable distance from the concerns of Rabbinic Judaism as it developed after 70 CE.'[12] This judgement, I would suggest, remains valid even if we restrict ourselves to Matthew and Josephus for our evidence. Also, and notoriously, two accounts of the faithful performance of Jewish rituals in Luke–Acts – the Purification (Luke 2:22–7) and Paul's vow (Acts 21:17–27) – tally ill with more authoritative accounts available to us of likely contemporary practice.[13] To put it no more strongly, this does not make it easy to see Luke–Acts as a considered defence for Jewish Christians against non-Christian Jews.[14]

Wilson himself prefers a different set of arguments. He suggests (as already noted) that Luke is pleading for the toleration of Jewish customs, practised by Jewish Christians, as the *ethos* of a particular *ethnos*.[15] Wilson does relate the pair 'custom and law' to Hellenistic Jewish usage, but with little or no attention to the wider Gentile context of that usage. Indeed, he argues, any such distinction being made by Luke may as readily be taken to reflect the relation of oral to written law in Judaism after 70 CE, as to any previously debated contrast.[16] 'Law', he urges, constitutes no pressing issue for Gentile Christians, who have accepted the ethical 'spirit' of the Mosaic legislation.[17] Luke, it is said, is mainly concerned to defend Paul against misconceived charges of 'antinomianism' from the side of Jewish Christians, and this is what Luke meant to do by making Paul an example of traditional piety.[18]

Wilson also tries to ease some of the strain between views of the law in Luke–Acts by having Luke freer to respond in 'part two' (Acts) to the new situation after 70 CE, presenting the now dominant Pharisees as tolerant towards, and even occasionally allies of, the Christians (on the non-legal issue of resurrection).[19] And further, Wilson suggests, by stressing the law as prophetic (of Jesus as the Christ), Luke 'may be shifting the terms of the Jewish Christian debate to the less controversial' area of opinion rather than practice.[20] Wilson concludes by again emphasising his impression that Luke–Acts is aimed at Gentile Christians rather than Jewish ones (albeit Gentile Christians in touch with, or concerned about, the views of Christian Jews).[21] Yet there is still no reference to any attitudes to issues of law and custom that such Gentiles are likely to have grown up with.

Blomberg's contribution to the discussion consists in the main in useful surveys of the material in Luke–Acts, and of recent discussion. Beyond that he simply insists that Wilson has not done enough justice to the strand suggesting the irrelevance or supersession of the law in the new age. Blomberg wants to argue that for Luke 'those who continue these customs in the book of Acts do so because the implications of the New Covenant dawned only slowly on them'.[22] Yet this is distinctly odd when Luke's Paul goes on punctiliously observing these customs right up to the final dénouement.

It seems to me that many of the apparently contrasting strands in Luke–Acts to which Wilson and Houlden draw attention must be allowed full weight, but that the explanations offered on the basis of the suggestions canvassed so far are insufficient on their own to deal with the force of the apparent tensions. One side of this tension Blomberg in effect acknowledges, but only to discount other material which Luke himself seems to want to continue to emphasise. So I suggest a closer look at the wider socio-cultural context is worth undertaking, in the hope of achieving some firmer basis for understanding Luke's treatment of these issues.

Issues of law and custom were in fact debated in Greece already before the time of Socrates and Plato, and the discussion continued, often along similar lines, in first-century Hellenism. It is this discussion that is picked up in the Hellenistic Jewish material to which Wilson refers. It may also provide a much richer explanatory context for what we find in Luke–Acts.

An awareness of the variety of common custom, law written down or not, codified or not, enacted or simply common practice, sharpened (or so it is said) men's appreciation of order – its value, and its fragility. How could one achieve an order, essentially coherent, that would be effectively acknowledged on all sides?[23] Initially, in *The Republic*, Plato unfolds his conviction that there 'is' an ideal order which the truly wise man (the philosopher-king) must be aware of and be able to impose on each and every occasion on all others, over-riding any other form of law. This contrasts with his own later admission, in *The Laws*, that only a second-best state is actually feasible, one in which authority (executive power) is itself subject to law. In *The Statesman* Plato wants both the authority of the legislative expert and the informed consent of the governed.

The consent of the governed is yet further stressed by Aristotle, in *The Politics*. For him the collective wisdom of 'the people' (albeit very narrowly defined) may well be wiser than that of any expert. And this of course accords a high value to popular habit, to custom commonly observed in practice (whether written and/or codified or not) and so to the actual – and varying – customs of different cities and peoples. Yet further emphasis falls on this latter (effective custom) among Stoics, convinced that all have access to the order inherent in things as they are, the 'law of nature'. Certainly any common strands among customary laws actually observed must carry considerable weight.

It is the first-century debate of these issues that forms at least an important part of the explanatory context of Luke–Acts, and to that we now turn (accepting that the classical discussion in itself has no particular claim to our attention).[24]

It is worth beginning with two passages from Philo:

> It is a king's duty to command what is right and forbid what is wrong. But to command what should be done and forbid what should not be done is the peculiar function of law; so that it follows at once that the king is a living law and the law a just king. But a king and lawgiver ought to have under his purview not only human but divine matters; for without God's directing care the affairs of kings and subjects cannot go aright. (*De vita Mosis* 2.4–5)

And

> Moses first wished to show that the enacted ordinances are not inconsistent with nature, and secondly, that those who wish to live by the laws have no difficult task. The first generation before any of the statutes were set in writing followed the unwritten law with perfect ease. One might properly say that the enacted laws are nothing else than memorials to the lives of men of old, preserving to a later generation their actual words and deeds. (*De Abrahamo* 5)[25]

Philo, as often, is echoing the Platonic discussion. But in this wider setting, it is clear that Wilson's insistence on an antithetic relationship between 'law' and 'custom' is inadequate.[26] It is not just 'on occasion' that Wilson's contrast collapses. It is occasionally made entirely clear that it is not ever intended. The only contrast is between being written or unwritten. Custom is unwritten law. Unwritten laws may come to be written-down, 'enacted' laws (*tethentas nomous*). Laws commonly observed are also customs, as Wilson's own further quotations show.[27] Unwritten laws are by no means inferior – that they are 'written on men's souls'[28] may well, as we shall see, be an accepted sign of their superiority. The contrast between laws written or unwritten at very least leaves open the question of their value and their effectiveness.

The influence of the contemporary debate also emerges in Wilson's discussion of Josephus,[29] where he notes that in some contexts the terms 'law' and 'custom' can be interchangeable. That Josephus can also at other times stress the value of a written law that is coherently codified[30] only means that he finds more apologetic value in this side of the debate. But that he is using the terms of this debate as conventionally understood is clear among other things from his insistence on Moses having won the people's consent,[31] and then, refusing any despotism, himself having lived subject to the laws he enacted.[32] Josephus proceeds to contrast the varied Greek 'customs and laws' with the one coherent Jewish code (not, *pace* Wilson, Greek custom with Jewish law![33]). But this sort of point is still very much part of the Greek debate.[34]

For the wider, non-Jewish context, some intriguing illustrations may be drawn from Dio Chrysostom. Discourse 75 is in praise of law, as enabling freedom and giving guidance.[35] Law contains 'nothing tortuous or ambiguous', it 'first persuades men and wins their approval'. It is 'Son of Zeus'. To expel law from one's life is madness. Discourse 76 (as conventionally numbered) praises instead custom, 'unwritten law', to the disadvantage of enacted legislation. Custom is constituted by constant appraisal and constant consent, 'preserved in our own souls'.[36] Laws create slaves, custom creates a society of free men; laws have to be learned, custom (by definition) is known; written laws are really only for the wicked.[37] Kings claim to be above law, but even they follow custom. Discourse 80 also disparages written laws and prefers the (internal) 'law of nature' whose following enables freedom.[38]

Not all of this would I claim to be directly relevant; I would only claim to have shown so far that talk of 'laws and customs' would echo a continuing and popular debate,[39] rather than suggest a particular stance such as that suggested by Wilson (a sort of 'anthropologising' tolerance).

The observance of the actual ancestral practices themselves (whether codified or not, whether written or not) was commended on all sides, save only for any that could clearly be shown to harm human flourishing, *eudaimonia*.

One widely accepted negative criterion involved the issue of *superstitio, deisidaimonia*.[40] Cicero (who remains influential throughout the first century) wrote,

> I thought I should be rendering a great service both to myself and to my countrymen if I could tear superstition up by the roots. But I want it distinctly understood that the destruction of superstition does not mean the destruction of religion. For I consider it essential to wisdom to preserve the institutions of our forefathers, retaining their ancient rites and ceremonies. Furthermore, the celestial order and beauty of the universe compel me to confess that there is some excellent and eternal Being who deserves the respect and homage of men. (*De divinatione* 2.148)

The observance of ancestral custom is part of a concern for cosmic order, but also for civic order: 'with piety gone, reverence and religion must soon disappear. And when these are gone life soon becomes a welter of confusion and disorder' (*De natura deorum* 1.3–4).

So Josephus has Nicholas of Damascus argue before Marcus Agrippa,

> If someone should ask [our opponents] which of these things they would
> rather have taken from them, life or their country's customs, including the
> processions, sacrifices and festivals which they observe in honour of the
> gods in whom they believe, I know very well they would rather suffer all
> manner of things than violate any of their country's customs. (*Ant.*
> 16.35–6)[41]

So, in his own name, he insists against Apion, 'A wise man's duty is to be
scrupulously faithful to the religious laws of his country, and to refrain
from the abuse of those of others.'[42] The connection with orderliness is
again explicit: 'Unity and identity of religious belief, perfect uniformity in
habits and customs, produce a very beautiful concord in human character.'[43] 'Innovation' and 'rebellion' are closely connected themes.[44]

This kind of piety provides the main thrust of Philo's letter from Agrippa
I to the Emperor Gaius:

> All men, my emperor, have planted in them a passionate love of their native
> land and a high esteem for their own laws, and on this there is no need to
> instruct you, who love your native city as ardently as you honour your own
> customs. (*Leg. Gaium* 277)

So, again (at *De somniis* 2.123) he complains of Flaccus' attempt

> ... to disturb our ancestral customs and especially to do away with the law
> of the Seventh Day ... thinking if he could destroy the ancestral rule of the
> Sabbath it would lead to irregularity in all other matters and a general
> back-sliding.

Claudius Caesar had sanctioned the observance of Jewish customs in
Alexandria,[45] but also demurred at divine honours for himself on the same
basis of age-old custom. One may compare, again, Dionysius of Hali-
carnassus, on Rome's admirable preservation of its ancient traditions,[46]
and Plutarch's regret at the loss of ancestral rituals.[47] Dio of Prusa defends
himself vigorously against the charge of 'not honouring the gods either
with sacrifices or with hymns, but abolishing the festivals of our fathers',
which leads into further accusations of disturbing the whole pattern and
even tenor of life in Prusa.[48] And as a final example we may recall Pliny
junior writing to Trajan about the Christians. The peace and well-being of
his provinces demands that the temples should be frequented again,
untroubled by 'this contagious superstition.'[49]

No one who lightly abandons the religious customs of his people is
going to be respected: it suggests a general willingness to disturb the
established order of things. Luke's picture of leading Christians maintaining such ancient custom would seem to me to be seeking to commend his
group warmly to any conventional reader of the day: so far from his asking
for indulgence for their pious behaviour, he is inviting warm admiration.

But Luke is also supporting his picture of the movement as responsible
and law-abiding. Though the parents of Jesus are Davidic, they comply at
some cost with Roman taxation law. There is a similar implication in the
response of Pilate to Jesus, and of other Roman officials to Paul in

particular. Walasky is right to challenge the suggestion in Cadbury, Easton and others, that this is 'political' apologetic in any narrow sense. Apologetic it is, however, though much more socio-cultural than directly arguing a case for legal toleration. It attempts to engage the sympathies and interest of enlightened non-members (as I have tried to show elsewhere[50]). Walasky is also probably right to detect a concern to influence church members: an orderly and observant Christian movement can expect reasonable treatment from many representatives of Roman power.

However, Walasky is probably wrong to concentrate on this 'in-group' interest to the exclusion of any other, outward-looking, concern. The analogy of Josephus (for whose relevance for the study of Luke–Acts there are many strong arguments) would clearly suggest otherwise. Josephus certainly first directed his *Jewish War* to his compatriots[51] and for instance describes the Roman army's prowess for the sake of 'others who might be tempted to revolt'.[52] But he then produced a Greek version to engage the sympathies of outsiders.[53] Even though this latter is the explicit aim of the *Antiquities*, yet here, too, he still has an eye on fellow-Jews, encouraging them to a quietist stance and an acceptance of Roman power, as divinely authorised and empowered. Both aims are reinforced by letting each 'audience' overhear what is said to the other.

Against any reading of Luke–Acts as intending to influence important Romans Walasky adduces references to Jesus as a Davidic, as having armed followers, with a Zealot among them, and so forth.[54] I think he unwarrantably assumes a lack of sophistication among Luke's likely readers. Certainly Josephus, again, takes pains to present at least a selection of 'warts' in his picture of Jewish history. He allows the accusation that such rebelliousness is of the essence of Judaism, he presents some of the evidence that might give rise to such a charge; and he then argues that essential Judaism is other, and has been recognised as such by a long succession of pre-Roman and Roman rulers. Luke does just the same for his group; and we may note particularly the deliberate courting of embarrassment in presenting charges against Jesus of 'perverting our nation, forbidding tribute to Caesar, and claiming kingship' (Luke 23:2). The instances of a critical treatment of some Roman officials and Herodian kinglets which somewhat embarrasses Walasky's case[55] also has plenty of parallels in Josephus. No one would take seriously an account which suggested major or minor administrators of law were impeccable. But Paul, like Socrates, acknowledges the court, corrupt though the judge may be.[56]

I would argue, then, that in the light of much contemporary thought, the themes of compliance with ancestral Jewish law and with Roman authority are integrally linked for Luke, and that his narrative both shows the Christians in a good light on these twin counts, and also encourages them to maintain their good order. And yet the account itself is 'realistic' in its acknowledgement of the difficulties such a case involves.

This still leaves the contrasting strand in Luke–Acts to be examined: the parts of the narrative where things are done or said that seem to be critical of the ancient Jewish traditions.

Observance becomes extreme scrupulosity, *superstitio, deisidaimonia* in a pejorative sense, when it suggests that God or the gods demand some action or actions that does or do no good – or even positive harm – to the individual worshipper. A prime example of 'superstition' in the minds of many is afforded by Judaism. In a discussion of this issue, it is here that Seneca starts:

> Let us forbid lamps to be lighted on the Sabbath, since the gods do not need light, nor men take pleasure in soot ... Although a man hear what limit he should observe in sacrifice, and how far he should recoil from burdensome superstition, he will never make sufficient progress until he has conceived the right idea of deity ... one who thinks the gods are unwilling to do harm is wrong: they cannot do harm. (*Epistulae morales* 95.48)

Plutarch also illustrates *deisidaimonia* from Jewish observance of the sabbath, to their own great cost:

> God is brave hope, not cowardly excuse. But the Jews, because it was the Sabbath Day, sat in their places immoveable while the enemy were planting ladders against the walls and capturing the defences, and they did not get up, but remained there, fast bound in the toils of superstition as in one great net. (*De superstitione* (*Moralia* 169c))[57]

The idea that a deity will quickly take offence if the ritual is not punctiliously observed is impious:

> Is not he who believes in such gods as the superstitious believe in a partner to opinions far more unholy [sc. than atheism]? Why, for my part, I should prefer that men should say ... 'there is no Plutarch', rather than that they should say 'Plutarch is an inconstant and fickle person, quick tempered, vindictive over little accidents, pained at trifles. If you invite others to dinner and leave him out, or if you haven't the time and don't go to call on him, or fail to speak to him when you do see him, he will sink his teeth into you ... or get hold of your little child and beat him to death ... or spoil your harvest.' (*De superstitione* (*Moralia* 169f, 170a))[58]

True religion by contrast is an enjoyable enhancement of life (ibid.). The Athenians chided by Luke's Paul with their supposed worry about offending some supposed unknown god are superstitious in this way, worshipping ignorantly.[59]

Jewish sensitivity to possible charges of 'superstitious scrupulosity' appears in Philo. Nothing must be added to or taken away from *eusebeia*. 'Addition will beget superstition and subtraction will beget impiety' (*Spec. Leg.* 4.147). An allegorical reference to divine 'fathering' must not be made too public, 'so strongly does the tide of superstition flow in our minds and drown unmanly and degenerate souls' (*De mutatione nominum* 138); care in naming God must not be allowed to appear 'superstitious';[60] a true understanding of demons will banish *deisidaimonia*;[61] for there are some who suppose they have attained true piety, 'yet have left on it the imprint of superstition' (*De praemiis et poenis* 40).[62]

The Greek term as such, *deisidaimonia*, does not in itself have to be pejorative. Official documents (at least as rendered by Josephus) can use the word neutrally, or at least tolerantly; just once he seems to use it positively, of the penitence of Manasseh.[63]

None the less Josephus himself also has to respond to the adverse overtones of the word in his quotation from Agatharchides, who ridicules first the *deisidaimonia* of a Seleucid queen, Stratonice, and then compares that with the Jews' dreams and traditional irrationality on the subject of law, which allowed Ptolemy son of Lagos to overcome them on a sabbath.[64] What Agatharchides finds ridiculous, others, says Josephus, should admire. But Josephus still cannot himself use *deisidaimonia* admiringly in this context, even though admiration is due to those who value the observance of ancestral law and piety towards God. Religious scrupulosity, and the character of deity that it presupposes, is constantly open to question.[65]

The underlying religious critique is fully accepted by Josephus himself (though without using the word *deisidaimonia*) when, for instance, in response to Apion he contrasts Jewish piety, which acknowledges that God has no needs, with pagan worship of gods who need to be bought off from inflicting serious mischief.[66]

We have touched on one aspect of Jewish supposed 'superstition', the observance of the sabbath. Another, perhaps even more unpopular, was the rite of circumcision. Tacitus ranks it high among the Jews' 'evil and disgusting' customs; it counted as self-mutilation.[67] It was accepted that other nations practised the ritual (but they were equally perverse). The circumcision of those born of Jewish parents might just possibly be tolerated, if contemptuously. The circumcision of other nationals was a superstitious affront. No acceptable deity could demand the adoption of so revolting a practice where it lacked even the slight saving grace of being traditional.[68] It might make sense for Timothy to have been circumcised, as his mother was Jewish;[69] it would have been quite intolerable to suggest any such assault on Cornelius.[70]

Luke in fact makes it doubly clear that Christians are divinely bound to refrain from any 'troublesome' imposition of this Jewish ritual. The issue has been settled by the clearest kind of dream-vision and reinforced by clear signs of divine 'possession'.[71] Only when this story has been told three times, and its implications have been acknowledged and spelled out by a full conclave of the leaders of the Christian way, does Luke get round to allowing for the adult circumcision of someone part-Gentile, though in fact Jewish on his mother's side. At the same time, of course, Luke has Christian Jews accept hospitality from the still non-Jewish Cornelius. A simple ethical basis for continuing table-fellowship is then worked out (Acts 15). Christians clearly escape the third charge against Jews, of misanthropic unsociability.[72]

It is in the light of the widespread critique, then, of superstition, and especially Jewish superstition, that Luke is presenting Christians as properly pious, but without any 'superstitious' scruples that would preclude sabbath healing, suppose God bound to a temple site, demand burdensome or bizarre rituals of those of non-Jewish ancestry, or use such traditions as an excuse for avoiding social contacts. Christians were pious and socially responsible. Their piety had ancient and avowedly Jewish roots, but avoided any of those forms or rigidities that were generally disliked and despised. It was a piety focused on a close and provident deity who cared about conventional morality and orderliness.[73] That could but be acceptable; more than that, it should seem quite admirable.

I would not suggest, however, that Luke's treatment of 'law' and 'custom' was 'merely' a function of the socio-cultural factors here noted. It would seem to me likely that these strands were all of a piece with his own real trust in the close, caring and provident deity of Acts 17, but were also integrated with the rest of his writing.[74]

Before concluding this discussion it would seem only proper to relate it to two of the most debated passages in the Gospel and Acts that relate to matters legal: Luke 16:16–18, and Acts 15:20–1. I would not suppose that the foregoing has solved the problems of interpretation that they pose. But I think it may have afforded some little further support for the conclusions on both passages in this instance argued by Wilson.

On Luke 16:16–18, Wilson says it 'epitomises the ambiguity of Luke's Gospel as a whole, in which the law is both upheld and challenged . . . [maybe] Luke did not intend to offer a consistent view of the law here or elsewhere'.[75] If I am right, and Luke is writing in the context of an ongoing and inconclusive debate, this is perhaps what we might expect. If these pieces of tradition which he included meant anything clear to him – or might to his readers – then it could be something like: Jewish ancestral tradition is complete, all development stops with John; yes, the law is in a real sense 'eternal', changeless; but our approximations to it can be improved (which is what Jesus has done in, for example, tightening marriage laws, which others too saw as an ideal).[76]

On the latter passage, Acts 15:20–1, Wilson argues for an 'ethical' interpretation as being most likely that of the author. 'Would you win over the gods? then be a good man. Whoever imitates them is worshipping them sufficiently' says Seneca (*Epistulae morales* 95.50). 'Never cease honouring the gods with noble deeds and just acts' says Dio (3.52). This is the admired contrary to superstition; and in the case of the decrees, ancient tradition is being accorded an enhanced respect by being understood ethically.

Whether or not my suggestions are persuasive on those two matters of detail, it seems to me necessary to allow that the sorts of readers Luke seems to have been trying to address would read his two-part work in the light that has here been suggested: this two-part work is the tale of an admirable, patient and law-abiding group of contemporaries who maintain an inheritance of ancient piety with pleasure and joy, while by a divinely approved selectivity they effectively avoid any demeaning or fearful restrictions.

It would be hard to imagine how Luke could avoid realising that this is how his story would read, and much easier to suppose that he intended such a response. That it probably represents a very rough approximation

158 /   *The law in Paul and the apostolic tradition*

to the truth of the continuities and divergences between the Gentile Christianity of Luke's day and earlier or contemporary Judaism was in all likelihood not very important. It was the overall impression of an ethically sensitive but not uncritical social and religious conservatism that mattered.[77]

NOTES

I. GOD AS 'JUDGE' IN UGARITIC AND HEBREW THOUGHT

1 Cf. the section 'Textes juridiques' by J. Nougayrol in *Le Palais Royal d'Ugarit III* (*Mission de Ras Shamra VI*) (Paris, 1955).

2 Cf. *CTA* 2 iii 8–9(?), 16(?), 23; 2 iv 14–15(?), 16–17, 22, 24–5(?), 29–30(?).

3 *CTA* 3 E 40; 4 iv 43–4.

4 W. H. Schmidt, *Königtum Gottes in Ugarit und Israel*, BZAW 80 (Berlin, 1966), pp. 36f. Schmidt's arrangement of the lines in three parallel sections has been followed.

5 *CTA* 6 vi 27–9.

6 Cf. H. Donner and W. Röllig, *Kanaanäische und Aramäische Inschriften* (Wiesbaden,[2] 1966–9); the text is given in I, 1, with commentary in II, 2ff. The translation is quoted from F. Rosenthal, 'Canaanite and Aramaic inscriptions', in *ANET*, p. 504.

7 *CTA* 9 rev. 9.

8 Judg 4:4–5. On this passage see, e.g., J. Gray, *Joshua, Judges and Ruth*, NCB (London, 1967), pp. 218f., 268; R. G. Boling, *Judges*, AB (New York, 1975), pp. 94f.; G. F. Moore, *Judges*, ICC (Edinburgh, 1895). For a critique of the view that the 'minor judges' may reflect a pan-Israelite judicial office, and a survey of the use of the verb *špṭ*, see K. W. Whitelam, *The Just King*, JSOTSup 12 (Sheffield, 1979), pp. 47ff.

9 W. Richter, 'Zu den "Richtern Israels"' *ZAW* 77 (N.F. 36) (1965), 40ff.

10 Schmidt, op. cit., p. 38.

11 M. Dahood, *Psalms II*, AB (New York, 1968), pp. 356, 364.

12 M. Dahood, *Psalms I* (1965), pp. 6, 13. He renders *tišpōṭ* as 'you are the ruler' in Ps 67:5 (MT) (*Psalms II*, p. 126).

13 E. A. Speiser, *Genesis*, AB (New York, 1964), p. 134.

14 L. Köhler and W. Baumgartner, *Lexicon in Veteris Testamenti Libros* (Leiden, 1953), pp. 1002f.
15 A. Malamat, 'Aspects of tribal societies in Mari and Israel' in *XVe Recontre Assyriologique: La Civilisation de Mari* (Liège, 1967), p. 133.
16 Köhler–Baumgartner, op. cit., pp. 1002f.
17 A. R. Johnson, *Sacral Kingship in Ancient Israel* (Cardiff,[2] 1967), p. 4. On this theme, cf. Whitelam, op. cit.
18 Cf. J. H. Eaton, *Kingship and the Psalms*, SBT second series 32 (London, 1967), pp. 120, 141f.
19 Exod 22:22. The right of appeal to the king by widows and orphans is instanced in 2 Sam 14:1ff.; cf. also 2 Kgs 8:1–6.
20 F. C. Fensham, 'Widow, orphan, and the poor in ancient Near Eastern legal and wisdom literature', *JNES* 21 (1962), 129ff.
21 Code of Hammurabi, Epilogue, reverse xxiv, 59ff. Translation by T. J. Meek in *ANET*, p. 178.
22 Cf. G. R. Driver and J. C. Miles, *The Babylonian Laws*, vol. i, Legal Commentary (Oxford, 1952), pp. 37ff.
23 *CTA* 16 vi 45–50.
24 Cf. e.g. Deut 21:19; 22:24; Amos 5:10, 15.
25 *CTA* 17 v 7–8.
26 J. R. Porter, *Moses and Monarchy* (Oxford, 1963), p. 24.
27 G. Widengren, *The King and the Tree of Life in Ancient Near Eastern Religion*, King and Saviour 4 (Uppsala Universitets Årsskrift, 1951), pp. 39f.
28 E. I. J. Rosenthal, 'Some aspects of the Hebrew monarchy', *JJS* 9 (1958), 10ff.
29 Whitelam, op. cit.
30 *CTA* 3 v 40–1.
31 F. Gröndahl, *Die Personennamen der Texte aus Ugarit*, Studia Pohl 1 (Rome, 1967), pp. 199f.
32 F. L. Benz, *Personal Names in the Phoenician and Punic Inscriptions*, Studia Pohl 8 (Rome, 1972), pp. 100, 184; cf. p. 215.
33 Gröndahl, op. cit. p. 187.
34 *CTA* 15 ii 7, 11.
35 *CTA* 4 iii 14.
36 *Ugaritica* v, p. 45.
37 *CTA* 2 i 14, 15?, 16–17?
38 G. R. Driver, *Canaanite Myths and Legends* (Edinburgh, [1]1956), p. 79.
39 J. C. L. Gibson *Canaanite Myths and Legends* (Edinburgh, [2]1978), p. 40.
40 R. J. Clifford, *The Cosmic Mountain in Canaan and the Old Testament*, Harvard Semitic Monographs 4 (Cambridge Mass., 1972), pp. 43f.
41 *CTA* 3 v 43ff.
42 *Ugaritica* v, p. 551.
43 ibid., p. 555. The text is as set out in *Ugaritica* v.
44 The transcription suggests that there is a single group of letters *bhdrʿy*.
45 *Ugaritica* v, p. 555.
46 S. B. Parker, 'The feast of *Rāpiʾu*', *UF* 2 (1970), 243.
47 F. M. Cross, *Canaanite Myth and Hebrew Epic* (Cambridge Mass., 1973), p. 21.
48 B. Margulis, 'A Ugaritic psalm (RS 24.252)', *JBL* 89 (1970), 292ff.
49 In Josh 12:4 and 13:12, Ashtaroth and Edrei are mentioned as abodes of Og, king of Bashan, 'one of the remnant of the Rephaim'.
50 A. F. Rainey, 'The Ugaritic texts in *Ugaritica* v, *JAOS* 94 (1974), 187. The view

that *'ttrt* and *hdr'y* are place-names has recently been supported by G. C. Heider, *The Cult of Molek: a Reassessment*, JSOTSup 43 (Sheffield, 1985).

51 J. C. de Moor, 'Studies in the new alphabetic texts from Ras Shamra ɪ', *UF* 1 (1969), 175. De Moor's translation implies that *bhdr'y* is to be divided – see n. 44.

52 Heider, op. cit.

53 A. Jirku, *Der Mythus der Kanaanäer* (Bonn, 1966), p. 15.

54 W. F. Albright, '*Zabûl Yam* and *Thâpiṭ Nahar* in the combat between Baal and the sea', *JPOS* 16 (1936), 19.

55 F. Thureau-Dangin, 'Inscriptions votives sur des statuettes de Ma'eri', *RA* 31 (1934), 142; cf. A. Parrot, 'Les fouilles de Mari', *Syria* 16 (1935), 27.

56 *ANET*, p. 166.

57 Driver and Miles, op. cit., pp. 61ff.

58 Driver, op. cit. p. 12, n. 7.

59 De Moor, op. cit., p. 187.

60 *Ugaritica* v, p. 559.

61 Schmidt, op. cit., p. 37.

62 M. C. Astour, 'Some new divine names from Ugarit', *JAOS* 86 (1966), 282f.

63 *Ugaritica* v, pp. 584f.

64 The transcription suggests that the *n* is visible.

65 Cf. Pss 82; 149.

66 On the Day of Yahweh, cf. e.g. G. von Rad, 'The origin of the concept of the Day of Yahweh', *JSS* 4 (1959), 97ff.; H. H. Rowley, *The Faith of Israel* (London, 1961), pp. 177ff.

67 L. Bronner, *The Stories of Elijah and Elisha as Polemics against Baal Worship*, Pretoria Oriental Series 6 (Leiden, 1968), pp. 13f.

68 1 Kgs 21.

69 1 Kgs 18:17ff.

70 Johnson, op. cit., pp. 67ff.

71 Cf. A. S. Kapelrud, *The Ras Shamra Discoveries and the Old Testament* (Oxford, 1965), p. 72, who suggests that Yahweh's conflict and victory were the basis of his role as judge.

72 So RSV-MT followed by AV has in verse 10 'Ye that love the LORD, hate evil.'

73 So RSV-MT literally 'and the strength of the king'.

74 A. Weiser, *The Psalms* (London, 1962), pp. 45ff.

75 ibid., p. 46.

76 C. J. Labuschagne, *The Incomparability of Yahweh in the Old Testament*, Pretoria Oriental Series 5 (Leiden, 1966), pp. 89ff.

77 J. Gray, 'The kingship of God in the prophets and Psalms', *VT* 11 (1961), 13.

78 *ANET*, p. 165.

2. LAW IN OLD ISRAEL: LAWS CONCERNING ADULTERY

1 Henry McKeating, 'Sanctions against adultery in ancient Israelite society, with some reflections on methodology in the study of Old Testament ethics', *JSOT* 11 (1979), 57–72.

2 Anthony Phillips, 'Another look at adultery', *JSOT* 20 (1981), 3–25; 'The Decalogue – ancient Israel's criminal law', *JJS* 34 (1983), 1–20.

3 This is implied by Deut 22:23f.

4 See M. Fishbane, 'Accusations of adultery: a study of law and scribal practice in Numbers 5:11–31', *HUCA* 45 (1974), 25f.

5 So McKeating, op. cit., p. 63.

6 See A. D. H. Mayes, *Deuteronomy*, NCB (London, 1979), p. 345.
7 Phillips, 'The Decalogue', p. 1.
8 ibid., p. 1.
9 ibid., p. 2.
10 ibid., p. 10.
11 Phillips, 'Another look', p. 19.
12 ibid., p. 4.
13 Phillips, 'The Decalogue', p. 15.
14 McKeating, op. cit., p. 69.
15 ibid., p. 69.
16 ibid., p. 71.
17 Henry McKeating, 'A response to Dr Phillips by Henry McKeating', *JSOT* 20 (1981), 26.
18 E.g. 'wounds and dishonour' (Prov 6:33) or 'compensation' (see Prov 6:35).
19 Anthony Phillips, *Ancient Israel's Criminal Law: A New Approach to the Decalogue* (Oxford, 1970), p. 110.
20 McKeating, 'Response', pp. 25–6.
21 Phillips, 'Another look', p. 15.
22 Phillips, *Ancient Israel's Criminal Law*, p. 110.
23 Gen 12:10–20; 20:1–7; 26:6–11.
24 Gen 39:9.
25 2 Sam 3:7–11.
26 2 Sam 3:14–15.
27 Z. Ben-Barak, 'The legal background to the restoration of Michal to David', VTSup 30 (1979), 15–29.
28 See Deut 22:24.
29 2 Sam 12:14.
30 Cf. 2 Sam 7:14.
31 B. S. Jackson, 'Reflections on biblical criminal law', *JJS* 24 (1973), 34.
32 McKeating, 'Sanctions against adultery', p. 59.
33 Phillips, 'Another look', pp. 17f.

3. 'A PERPETUAL STATUTE THROUGHOUT YOUR GENERATIONS'

1 Philo, *De vita Mosis* 2.14–16; translation in G. F. Moore, *Judaism* (Cambridge MA, 1927), I, 269.
2 'An eternal law for their generations': sabbath (2:33); purification after childbirth (3:14); prohibition of blood (6:12); Feast of Weeks (6:20); circumcision (15:13).

   'Written on the heavenly tablets': purification after childbirth (3:10); prohibition of nakedness (3:31); Feast of Weeks (6:17); circumcision (15:25); Feast of Booths (16:28f); prohibition of intermarriage with foreigners (30:9); second tithe (32:10); prohibition of incest (33:10); Passover (49:8).

   'There is no limit of days for this law': prohibition of blood (6:14); tithe (13:26); Feast of Booths (16:30); prohibition of intermarriage (30:10); second tithe (32:10); prohibition of incest (33:10); Passover (49:8).
3 E. Jenni, 'Das Wort ʿôlām im AT', *ZAW* 64 (1952), 240f.
4 Gen 17:8; 48:4; Lev 25:34.
5 Gen 9:16; 17:1, 13, 19; Exod 31:16; Lev 24:8; cf. *běrît melaḥ* ʿôlām (Num 18:19).
6 Lev 25:32.
7 Gen 9:12.

8 Exod 40:15; Num 25:13.
9 Exod 29:28; 30:21; Lev 6:11, 15 (EVV 18, 22); 7:34; 10:15; 24:9; Num 18:8, 11, 19.
10 Exod 12:14, 17; 27:21; 28:43; 29:9; Lev 3:17; 7:36; 10:9; 16:29, 31, 34; 17:7; 23:14, 21, 31, 41; 24:3; Num 10:8; 15:15; 18:23; 19:20, 21.
11 (a) The person concerned and his descendants (*zera'*) 'after you/him': Gen 17:7, 8, 19; 48:4; Exod 25:43; 30:21; Lev 10:9; Num 18:19; 25:23.
   (b) The person concerned and his sons (and daughters): Exod 29:9, 28; Lev 7:34; 10:15; 24:9; Num 18:8, 11, 19.
   (c) The generations to come (*lĕ-dôrôtām/lĕ-dôrôtēkem*): Exod 12:14, 17; 27:21; 31:16; 40:15; Lev 3:17; 6:11 (EVV 18); 7:36; 17:7; 23:14, 21, 31, 41; 24:9; Num 10:8; 15:15; 18:23.
   (d) The tribe of Levi: Lev 25:32, 34.
12 The phrase 'throughout their/your generations' also occurs on its own, with the same connotation as the fuller phrase: Exod 12:42; 29:42; 30:8, 10, 31; Lev 21:17; 22:3; Num 15:21, 23, 38.
13 G. J. Wenham, *The Book of Leviticus*, New International Commentary on the OT (London/Grand Rapids, 1979), p. 74.
14 ibid., p. 235.
15 E.g. Exod 21:12, 15–17; 22:17–18 (EVV 18–20).
16 E.g. Deut 27:14–26.
17 E.g. Exod 22:20 (EVV 21); 23:9.
18 E.g. Exod 22:22f., 26 (EVV 23f., 27); 23:7.
19 E.g. Lev 19:2; 20:26.
20 E.g. Lev 19 *passim*.
21 Exod 31:14; 35:2; Num 15:32–6.
22 Not being circumcised (Gen 17:14); not observing Passover (Num 9:13); not observing the Day of Atonement (Lev 23:29); not purifying oneself after contact with a corpse (Num 19:13, 20); eating leaven during the Feast of Unleavened Bread (Exod 12:15, 19); eating sacrificial food while unclean (Lev 7:20f.; 22:3); eating the fat (Lev 7:25); consuming the blood (Lev 7:27; 17:10, 14); eating sacrificial meat on the third day (Lev 19:8); counterfeiting the anointing oil or sanctuary incense (Exod 30:33, 38); offering sacrifice anywhere but at the tent of meeting (Lev 17:4, 9); various sexual offences (Lev 18:29; 20:17, 18); working on the sabbath (Exod 31:14); sacrificing a child to Molech (Lev 20:3, 5); practising the occult (Lev 20:6); committing any deliberate sin (Num 15:30f.).
23 'Holy': anointing sacrifice (Exod 29:34); anointing oil (Exod 30:32); incense (Exod 30:37); sabbath (Exod 31:14); tabernacle (Exod 40:9); priests (Lev 21:6–8); priests' portions (Num 18:10); whoever touches holy things (Exod 29:37; 30:29; Lev 6:11, 20 (EVV 18, 27)).
   'Most holy': altar (Exod 29:37); incense altar (Exod 30:10); tabernacle and contents (Exod 30:29); incense (Exod 30:36); altar (Exod 40:10); priests' portion (Lev 2:3, 10; 6:10, 22 (EVV 17, 29); 21:22); sin offering (Lev 6:17 (EVV 24)); guilt offering (Lev 7:1, 6).
24 Gerhard Liedke, *Gestalt und Bezeichnung alttestamentlicher Rechtssätze*, WMANT 39 (Neukirchen, 1971), pp. 174, 178.
25 J. R. Porter, *Leviticus*, Cambridge Bible Commentary (Cambridge, 1976), pp. 58f.; cf. R. Rendtorff, *Die Gesetze in der Priesterschrift*, FRLANT 62 (NF 44) (Göttingen, ²1963), p. 38.
26 Porter, op. cit., p. 132; cf. Rendtorff, op. cit., pp. 59f.

27 P. J. Budd, *Numbers*, Word Biblical Commentary (Waco, Texas, 1984), p. 282.
28 Richard Hentschke, *Satzung und Setzender: ein Beitrag zur israelitischen Rechtsterminologie*, BWANT 83 (5.3) (Stuttgart, 1963), p. 48.
29 M. Noth, *A history of Pentateuchal Traditions* (Englewood Cliffs, 1972), pp. 8–19=*Überlieferungsgeschichte des Pentateuch* (Stuttgart, 1948), pp. 7–19.
30 G. von Rad, *Die Priesterschrift im Hexateuch*, BWANT 65 (4.13) (Leipzig, 1934).
31 F. M. Cross, 'The Priestly work', in *Canaanite Myth and Hebrew Epic* (Cambridge MA/London,1973), pp. 293–325.
32 Rendtorff, op. cit; K.Koch, *Die Priesterschrift von Exodus 25 bis Leviticus 16*, FRLANT 71 (NF 53) (Göttingen, 1959).
33 H. Graf Reventlow, *Das Heiligkeitsgesetz formgeschichtlich untersucht*, WMANT 6 (Neukirchen, 1961); R. Kilian, *Literarkritische und formgeschichtliche Untersuchung des Heiligkeitsgesetzes*, BBB 19 (Bonn, 1963).
34 J. Begrich, 'Die priesterliche Tora', in *Werden und Wesen des Alten Testaments*, BZAW 66 (Giessen, 1936), pp. 63–88=*Gesammelte Studien zum Alten Testament* (München, 1964), pp. 232–60.
35 Variant lists of the passages to be assigned to the Priestly *Grundschrift* are given by Noth, op. cit., and von Rad, op. cit., and by K. Elliger, 'Sinn und Ursprung der Priesterlichen Geschichtserzählung', *ZTK* 49 (1959), 121–43=*Kleine Schriften zum AT* (Müchen, 1966), pp. 174–98.
36 L. E. Browne, *Early Judaism* (Cambridge, 1920), pp. 70–86; P. D. Hanson, *The Dawn of Apocalyptic* (Philadelphia, 1975), pp. 92f.
37 Budd, op. cit.
38 Porter, op. cit.
39 Von Rad, op. cit., and Noth, op. cit., assigned different parts of these chapters to P^g.
40 Num 10:1–10 (silver trumpets); Num 15:37–41 (tassels).
41 F. M. Cross, 'The priestly tabernacle', *BA* 10.3 (1947), 45–68=*The Biblical Archaeologist Reader*, I (Garden City NY, 1961), 201–28.
42 Hentschke, op. cit., p. 69, concludes that the unmistakable hortatory tone, warning the hearers of their duty to obey, must derive from cultic recitation on feast days.
43 Josephus, *Ant.* 11.329ff.; 12.138ff.; V. Tcherikover, *Hellenistic Civilisation and the Jews* (Philadelphia/Jerusalem, 1959), pp. 49, 82f.

4. THE TEMPLE SCROLL: A LAW UNTO ITSELF?

1 Ed. Y. Yadin, *Megillat ha-Miqdaš*, vols. I–III (Jerusalem, 1977); ET, *The Temple Scroll*, vols. I–III (Jerusalem, 1983).
2 Some dispute surrounds the group of fragments, Rockefeller 43.366. It seems that at least Frag. 1 should not be assigned to the Temple Scroll because it explicitly mentions Moses; see B. Levine, 'The Temple Scroll: aspects of its historical provenance and literary character', *BASOR* 232 (1978), 6.
3 Yadin, *The Temple Scroll*, vol. I, ch. 8. E.-M. Laperrousaz has argued for a later date for the Temple Scroll, challenging many of Yadin's archaeological and palaeographical assumptions: 'Notes à propos de la datation du Rouleau du Temple', *RevQ* 10 (1981), 447–52.
4 Yadin, *The Temple Scroll*, I, 418.
5 Y. Yadin, *The Temple Scroll: The Hidden Law of the Dead Sea Sect* (London, 1985), p. 228.
6 H. Stegemann, ' "Das Land" in der Tempelrolle und in anderen Texten aus den

Qumrangefunden', in G. Strecker (ed.), *Das Land Israel in biblischer Zeit* (Göttingen, 1983), p. 157, argues that the Temple Scroll is an extended reworking of Deuteronomy 12–26.

7 For not totally dissimilar apologetic reasons Josephus omits the golden-calf incident as he retells Exodus in *Ant.* 3.

8 It seems better to start with this premise than to search directly for non-biblical sources as A. M. Wilson and L. Wills propose, 'Literary sources of the Temple Scroll', *HTR* 75 (1982), 275–88. Wilson and Wills have recently been challenged in part by P. Callaway, 'Source criticism of the Temple Scroll: the purity laws', *RevQ* 12 (1986), 213–22.

9 Trans. by O. S. Wintermute in J. H. Charlesworth (ed.), *The Old Testament Pseudepigrapha*, II, 54.

10 Trans. by Yadin, *The Temple Scroll*, II, 128–9.

11 ibid., I, 97–8, 103, 114, 124–8, 147; II, 74, 82.

12 Joseph Baumgarten, 'Review' (of *Megillat ha-Miqdaš*), *JBL* 97 (1978), 586. As yet only B.-Z. Wacholder, *The Dawn of Qumran*, HUCM 8 (Cincinnati, 1983), pp. 41–61, has pointed to differences between *Jubilees* and the Temple Scroll; but this he does to show overall how close the two documents lie, *Jubilees* being a later development of the calendric traditions in the Temple Scroll.

13 See, e.g., Yadin, *The Temple Scroll*, I, 44, 52, 76, 78, 111, 151, 160.

14 J. Milgrom, 'Studies in the Temple Scroll', *JBL* 97 (1978), 501–6, has compiled a list of these items involving levitical preferment.

15 Other passages that have parallels in Ezekiel 43–4 include 11QT 12, 15–17 (Ezek 43:13–20), 11QT 13:17–14:? (Ezek 44:24), 11QT 32–3 (Ezek 44:15–19), 11QT 48–51 (Ezek 44:23), 11QT 57:13–15 (Ezek 44:24), 11QT 57:15–18 (Ezek 44:22).

16 Milgrom, op. cit., pp. 503–4.

17 G. Vermes, *The Dead Sea Scrolls in English* (Harmondsworth, ²1975), p. 25.

18 See, e.g., Yadin, *The Temple Scroll*, I, 156, 288, 328, 371–2, 346, 356.

19 J. Maier, *The Temple Scroll*, JSOTSup 34 (Sheffield, 1985), p. 83.

20 Levine, op. cit., p. 13.

21 J. Murphy-O'Connor has written a series of articles in *Revue Biblique*, the latest of which, 'The *Damascus Document* revisited', *RB* 92 (1985), 223–46, contains an appreciation of Davies' work as well as a statement of his own current position. Davies' work is *The Damascus Covenant*, JSOTSup 25 (Sheffield, 1983).

22 E.g. Baumgarten, op. cit., p. 587; D. Dimant, 'Qumran sectarian literature', in M. E. Stone (ed.), *Jewish Writings of the Second Temple Period*, CRINT 2.2 (Assen/Philadelphia, 1984), pp. 526–30; G. Vermes, 'The writings of the Qumran community', in E. Schürer, *The History of the Jewish People in the Age of Jesus Christ*, III.1, rev. and ed. G. Vermes, F. Millar and M. Goodman (Edinburgh, 1986), pp. 406–18.

23 E.g. Levine, op. cit.; L. H. Schiffman, 'The *Temple Scroll* in literary and philological perspective', in W. S. Green (ed.), *Approaches to Ancient Judaism*, II, BJS 9 (Chico, Ca, 1980), 143–55.

24 Schiffman, op. cit., p.149.

25 Wacholder, op. cit., pp. 17–21.

26 Maier, op. cit., p. 6.

27 In this respect it is significant that Y. Thorion has detected phraseology like that of 1 and 2 Chronicles: 'Zur Bedeutung von GBWRY ḤYL LMLḤMH in 11QT LVII, 9', *RevQ* 10 (1981), 597–8.

28 Exod 30:34 may also have influenced the wording concerning the incense in 4QtgLev 1 on Lev 16:12–15.
29 Josephus, *Ant.* 15.390 mentions the training of priests for the rebuilding of the temple; *Ant.* 20.216–23 speaks of the needs of Levites once the building-work had been completed.

5. JEWISH LAW IN THE TIME OF JESUS: TOWARDS A CLARIFICATION OF THE PROBLEM

1 E. P. Sanders, *Jesus and Judaism* (London, 1985), pp. 268–9.
2 E. Käsemann, 'The problem of the historical Jesus', in *Essays on New Testament Themes* (London and Nashville, 1964), pp. 15–47.
3 B. S. Jackson, 'Legalism', *JJS* 30 (1979), 1–22, offers an interesting discussion of the problem. Some *Christian* defenders of Judaism are in danger of distorting it by redefining it as a religion of grace. See my remarks on this in my review of Sanders' *Jesus and Judaism*, in *JJS* 37 (1986), 130ff.
4 On Roman rule in Palestine see the useful survey by M. Stern, 'The province of Judaea', in S. Safrai and M. Stern (eds.), *The Jewish People in the First Century*, I (Assen, 1974), 308–76.
5 Further, S. Safrai, 'Jewish self Government', in Safrai and Stern, op. cit., I, 377–419.
6 See my comments in E. Schürer, *The History of the Jewish People in the Age of Jesus Christ*, rev. G. Vermes, F. Millar and M. Goodman, II (Edinburgh, 1979), 190f.
7 See H. H. Cohn, 'Maimonidean theories of codification', *Jewish Law Annual* 1 (1978), 15–36.
8 B. S. Jackson, 'The concept of religious law in Judaism', in H. Temporini and W. Haase (eds.), *Aufstieg und Niedergang der Römischen Welt*, II.19.1 (Berlin and New York, 1979), pp. 33–52.
9 The legal concepts discussed here may be pursued further by consulting the *Encyclopaedia Judaica* (in English), and the *Talmudic Encyclopedia* (in Hebrew). For orientation on rabbinic law see the admirably clear article by Menachem Elon, 'Mishpat Ivri', in *Encyclopaedia Judaica*, vol. XII, cols. 109–51.
10 Z. W. Falk, *Introduction to Jewish Law of the Second Commonwealth*, Parts I–II (Leiden, 1972–8).
11 For a brief survey see W. D. Davies, 'Law in first century Judaism', in *Jewish and Pauline Studies* (London, 1984), pp. 23f.
12 Further, G. Vermes, 'The Decalogue and the Minim', in *Post-Biblical Jewish Studies* (Leiden, 1975), pp. 169–77.
13 See e.g. the treatment of Moses in Philo's *Vita Moses* and in Josephus' *Ant.* 1.18ff.
14 The *locus classicus* is Philo, *Spec. Leg.* 1.55. Further, Falk, op. cit., Part I, pp. 93ff. Phineas was regarded as the model of such zeal for the law: see 1 Macc 2:26, 54; further: C. T. R. Hayward, ' "Phineas – the same is Elijah": the origins of a Rabbinic tradition', *JJS* 29 (1978), 22–34.
15 Further P. Schäfer, 'Die Torah der messianischen Zeit', in *Studien zur Geschichte und Theologie des Rabbinischen Judentums* (Leiden, 1978), pp. 198–213. In later Judaism some versions of the Qabbalistic doctrine of *šěmittôt* envisaged a Torah for each age! See, G. G. Scholem, *Kabbalah* (Jerusalem, 1974), pp. 121f.
16 Sanders, op. cit., p. 251.

6. ALL FOODS CLEAN: THOUGHTS ON JESUS AND THE LAW

1 The saying forms the climax of the specialist study of W. Paschen, *Rein und Unrein: Untersuchung zur biblischen Wortgeschichte* (München, 1970). For the wider discussion E. P. Sanders, *Jesus and Judaism* (London, 1985; ²1986), is a work of central importance. See also S. Westerholm, *Jesus and Scribal Authority* (Lund, 1978); J. Riches, *Jesus and the Transformation of Judaism* (London, 1980). Mark 7:15 is used as the focus of discussion by H. Räisänen in two articles, 'Zur Herkunft von Markus 7, 15', in J. Delobel (ed.), *Logia: les paroles de Jésus* (Leuven, 1982), pp. 477–84, and 'Jesus and the food laws: reflections on Mark 7.15', *JSNT* 16 (1982), 79–100; and by J. D. G. Dunn, 'Jesus and ritual purity: a study of the tradition history of Mk 7, 15', in *À Cause de l'Évangile: mélanges offerts à Dom Jacques Dupont* (Paris, 1985), pp. 251–76.

2 Räisänen, 'Food laws', p. 87.

3 Commentators who make this claim include Zahn, Jülicher, Lagrange, Leenhardt, Dodd, Bruce and Cranfield. It is considered doubtful by Sanday and Headlam and by Barrett. Käsemann, *Romans* (ET London, 1980), p. 375, regards Rom 14:14 as contributory evidence for the formation of the saying in connection with the Gentile controversy, which implies that it is not an authentic saying of Jesus.

4 Räisänen, 'Food laws', p. 89, following Bultmann and Käsemann.

5 Sanders, op. cit., p. 266.

6 Paschen, op. cit., pp. 173–7.

7 Mark 7:14 has the usual characteristics of a Markan introduction. Verse 16, not found in 'Sin' B 28, etc., is not accepted as a true part of the text in modern critical editions. Verses 17–18a (*hoti*) are typical of Mark; cf. 14a and 4:10–13 and especially 8:17. In verses 19–20 *katharizōn . . . hoti* should also be ascribed to Mark (see further below). Verse 23 is a closing summary based on the saying (cf. 3:30).

8 Westerholm, op. cit., p. 84.

9 I.e. a saying that is easily memorable and so capable of further application; cf. B. Gerhardsson, *The Origins of the Gospel Traditions* (London, 1979), p. 71.

10 Räisänen, 'Food laws', p. 83. So also Dunn, op. cit., p. 262.

11 So V. Taylor, *The Gospel according to St. Mark* (London, ²1966), p. 343, following Lagrange.

12 Matthew's simplified form loses the Semitic idiom *pan . . . ou* (Mark 7:18). Its secondary character is suggested further by the variation of the verb (*eiserchomenon* for *eisporeuomenon*; cf. *exerchetai, exerchontai* in verses 18–19) and by the explanatory *eis to stoma* and *ek tou stomatos* (cf. the explanatory *ek tēs kardias* in verse 18, anticipating 19). Matthew's form is followed closely by *Thomas* 14, which Dunn supposes is based on Q rather than Matthew. It could thus be argued that the differing forms of Matthew and Mark are examples of double attestation. But it is hazardous to assume that so late a document as the Gnostic *Gospel of Thomas* has not been influenced by canonical Matthew during its transmission, even if it is actually developed from Q; cf. B. Chilton, 'The Gospel according to Thomas as a source of Jesus' teaching', in D. Wenham (ed.), *The Jesus Tradition Outside the Gospels*, Gospel Perspectives 5 (Sheffield, 1985), pp. 155–75. For another example of Matthaean simplification leading to a neater couplet, cf. Matt 12:31=Mark 3:28f., conflating also the Q version, Matt 12:32=Luke 12:10.

13 All three details appear in the reconstruction of Paschen, op. cit. p. 177.

Räisänen complains of the reluctance of scholars to publish Aramaic reconstructions of the saying, and takes this to support his view that there never was a Semitic original, as the saying is inauthentic. But it must be said that exact retranslation can never be certain, because we can only guess whether to take the Aramaic of the OT as a model (too early) or the Aramaic of the Targumim (too late). The features mentioned here, however, are constant factors.

14 Cf. Mark 2:21f.; 3:27; 9:39; 10:29. This and the other points militate against the claim of Pesch that verse 15 has been transmitted independently of 18-22; cf. R. Pesch, *Das Markusevangelium* I (Freiburg, 1976), 378.

15 For another example of Mark's use of the plural in place of collective singular, cf. Mark 3:28 (referred to in n. 12 above), where the common Aramaic original behind Mark and Q must have had the singular, which may well have been retained in the Greek used by Mark and altered by him. See the discussion in B. Lindars, *Jesus Son of Man* (London, 1983), pp. 34–8.

16 Though the finite verb *koinoi* is used in verse 20, the participle would certainly be used in the underlying Aramaic. The participle with the article in verse 15, however, does not correspond with this, as it turns the verb into a predicate noun following *estin*.

17 The criterion of dissimilarity is often dismissed as valueless, because it is easily abused, but it has positive value in this case because of the ambiguity of the saying, as will be shown in the next section. Jesus appears to deny the law, but that is not his real intention. Nor can his position be identified with the saying attributed to R. Johanan ben Zakkai (died *c.* 80CE) on defilement from a corpse: 'By your life! It is not the dead that defiles nor the water that purifies! The Holy One, blessed be He, merely says: "I have laid down a statute. I have issued a decree. You are not allowed to transgress my decree"' (*Num. Rab.* 19:8, quoted by N. Perrin, *Rediscovering the Teaching of Jesus* (London, 1967), p. 150). Jesus is not concerned to find reasons why the law should be observed, but to expose the real meaning of defilement.

18 Matt 23:25f., on the cleansing of vessels, is the closest parallel to Mark 7:15 in the Jesus tradition, and well illustrates his attitude. It is excluded from treatment here, because our concern is not with purity customs but with the law itself.

19 For the problem of identifying and defining the Pharisees in the time of Jesus, cf. Sanders, op. cit., pp. 49f., 270–93; J. W. Bowker, *Jesus and the Pharisees* (Cambridge, 1973), pp. 1–15; E. Schürer, *The History of the Jewish People in the Age of Jesus Christ*, II, rev. Vermes, Millar and Black (Edinburgh, 1979), 381–403.

20 For this interpretation of the pericope, cf. Taylor, op. cit., pp. 417–21; C. E. B. Cranfield, *The Gospel according to St. Mark* (Cambridge, rev. edn, 1977), pp. 317–21.

21 I have drawn attention to this feature in connection with the Son of Man problem in Lindars, op. cit., and in 'Response to Richard Bauckham: the idiomatic use of Bar Enasha', *JSNT* 23 (1985), 35–41. See also J. Jónsson, *Humour and Irony in the New Testament* (Reykjavik, 1965).

22 Cf. Taylor, op. cit., p. 344. The classical meaning of *koinos* refers to sharing in common, as opposed to private ownership, but in Hellenistic Judaism it acquired the idea of sharing common life or use over against the separation of that which is sacred or holy (cf. 1 Macc 1:47, 62; *Ep. Arist.* 315). In Acts 10:14 *koinos* is a synonym of *akathartos*, meaning ritually unclean in the sense of profane. But whereas the latter can refer to physical uncleanness, *koinos* is

never used in this sense in the NT and related literature. The verb *koinoō* is used exclusively in the sense of making ritually unclean or profane.

23 The irrational character of the law had become a real difficulty by NT times; cf. *Ep. Arist.* 150 on the distinction of clean and unclean animals for food (Leviticus 11), which is precisely the issue before us in Mark 7:15; also the saying of Johanan ben Zakkai (n. 17), and further references in M. Hengel, *Between Jesus and Paul* (London, 1983), p. 174, n. 50.

24 Cf. Sanders, op. cit., pp. 174–211. His point is that Jesus did not insist on the penalty required for repentance (p. 206). Where ceremonial impurity is concerned this must surely imply that Jesus did not insist on the requirements for restoration of purity. In *Paul and Rabbinic Judaism* (London, 1977), p. 179, Sanders shows that the rabbis held that sins against God were easier to deal with than sins against mankind, which require restitution, because God is merciful to all who repent. Thus Jesus fits in with an observable rabbinic tendency.

25 The word has in the NT the whole range of meanings of the Hebrew *māšāl*, which fundamentally denotes a comparison. It does not necessarily imply an illustrative story.

26 *Chreia*: 'a maxim, often followed by an illustrative story' (Liddell–Scott–Jones). This denotes the use of a saying for regulating moral activity, and so explains the forms in which sayings of Jesus have been preserved, rather than the character of the sayings themselves; cf. K. Berger, *Formgeschichte des Neuen Testaments* (Heidelberg, 1984), pp. 80–92.

27 The concept of 'language-event' is derived from the work of Heidegger; cf. E. Fuchs, 'Was ist ein Sprachereignis?', in his *Zur Frage nach dem historischen Jesus* (Tübingen, 1960), pp. 424–30. Fuchs used it as a hermeneutical key, directed to achieving an existential interpretation of the parables in the present day. But in the hands of his followers, such as Linnemann, Via and Crossan, it has become an exegetical tool, to reach back to the purpose of Jesus in using parables. See A. C. Thiselton, *The Two Horizons* (Exeter, 1980), pp. 335–47.

28 Cf. the well-known *baraitah* in *b. Sanhedrin* 43a: 'On the preparation of the Passover Jesus was hanged, and a crier went before him forty days proclaiming, "He must be led away for stoning because he has practised sorcery and led Israel astray. If anyone knows anything to justify him let him come and declare it." But no one found anything to justify him, and he was hanged on the preparation of the Passover.' The issue is also referred to in Justin, *Dial.* 69; 108.

29 The tendency in Judaism is to stress the necessity of correct *practice*, while permitting considerable freedom in matters of *belief*; cf. A. E. Harvey, 'Forty strokes save one: social aspects of Judaizing and apostasy', in A. E. Harvey (ed.), *Alternative Approaches to New Testament Study* (London, 1985), pp. 79–96.

30 This is recognised as characteristic of vigorous contrastive speech by H. Kruse, 'Die "dialektische Negation" als semitische Idiom', *VT* 4 (1954), 385-400.

31 E. Haenchen, *The Acts of the Apostles* (Oxford, 1971), pp. 361f.

32 Westerholm, op. cit., p. 65. We may add that this is because it was a matter of the law itself, and not just the *halakah* of a particular group. Dunn points out that such practices were valued as 'markers' of Jewish self-definition in Gentile society, 'The new perspective on Paul', *BJRL* 65 (1983), 95–122 (p. 107).

33 So M. Hengel, *Acts and the History of Earliest Christianity* (London, 1979), p. 120.

34 Hengel, ibid., sees it as unworkable in view of the actual situation, so that the extreme interpretation was a response to the frustration which this caused.

35 Jesus prophesied the destruction of the temple as a prelude to *renewal*; cf. Sanders, *Jesus and Judaism*, pp. 70f.

36 Taylor, op. cit. pp. 346f.

37 This has long been the majority view, especially among British scholars, but it has been challenged by J. P. Audet, *La Didachè* (Paris, 1958), followed by W. Rordorf and A. Tuilier, *La Doctrine des douze Apôtres (Didachè)* (Paris, 1978), arguing for a date between 50 and 70 CE. But even this would not exclude knowledge of the pre-Markan *midrash* of Mark 7:21f., which could equally well be the source of the *Didache* list. S. Giet, *L'Énigme de la Didachè* (Paris, 1970), has shown that the sources of the *Didache* themselves span anything up to fifty years, so that a date in the last decades of the first century is preferable.

38 Matthew (15:20b) has seen that it answers the question of Mark 7:5. From this point of view the reference is not to unclean foods as such, but to the risk of making food unclean by touching it with unclean hands; cf. *m. Yadaim* 2:4.

39 The neuter *katharizon* (Κ Γ 33 700 1010 pm) has to agree with *pan to ...
eisporeuomeuon*, but is probably due to itacism. The Western readings (*kai*) *katharizei* (D *l*185 i r), making *aphedrōna* subject (D *ocheton*, perhaps meaning the intestines), and (*kai*) *katharizetai* (1047 syˢ), subject *brōmata*, are attempts to improve the sense.

40 Hence Mark has added *elegen de hoti* at the beginning of verse 20 to resume *oratio recta* after the parenthesis, as is generally recognised; cf. E. J. Pryke, *Redactional Style in Mark* (Cambridge, 1978), pp. 16, 24, 137.

41 For bread as a symbol of participation in the purity of Jewish religion, cf. *Joseph and Asenath* 8 and the notes of C. Burchard in *The Old Testament Pseudepigrapha*, II, ed. J. H. Charlesworth (London, 1985), 211ff.

42 On the text of *Thomas* 14, cf. n. 12 above. The theme of eating is found in the Q version of the Mission Charge, better represented in Luke 10:7f. than in Matt 10:10. The saying has been added to elucidate this point (cf. Luke 10:8: *esthiete ta paratithemena humin*), and is most unlikely to have belonged to the passage originally.

43 Räisänen, 'Zur Herkunft', p. 481.

44 Cf. J. D. Crossan, *In Fragments: The Aphorisms of Jesus* (San Francisco, 1983), for analysis of such changes.

45 C. E. B. Cranfield, *Romans*, II, ICC (Edinburgh, 1979), 690–8, considers six different possibilities for the circumstances which Paul has in mind.

46 So Dunn, 'Jesus and Ritual Purity', pp. 274ff.

47 Hengel, *Acts*, pp. 111–26, takes the view that Gal 2:1–10 refers to private consultation before the main meeting described in Acts 15, at which the concordat was agreed in full assembly, and that the 'decrees' belong to a later directive in the area of Syria and Phoenicia, where the Jewish element was strong. This was worked out after the troubles of Gal 2:11–14, and after Paul had left Antioch, so that Paul 'never acknowledged it or practised it' (p. 117). Hengel suggests that Luke has been confused by his 'Antiochene source' – though he should have known better in view of 21:25, where James informs Paul of the decisions apparently for the first time. Haenchen, however (op. cit., p. 610), thinks that Luke has inserted this verse for the benefit of the reader.

48 Taylor, op. cit., p. 342.

49 Sanders, *Jesus and Judaism*, pp. 270–81.

50 Cf. n. 21 above.

7. JESUS' DEMONSTRATION IN THE TEMPLE

1 E. P. Sanders, *Jesus and Judaism* (London, 1985), p. 251.
2 See ibid., Parts I and III.
3 Cf. L. Gaston, *No Stone on Another: Studies in the Significance of the Fall of Jerusalem in the Synoptic Gospels*, NovTSup 23 (Leiden, 1970), pp. 112–19.
4 Sanders, op. cit., p. 70. For some of the scholars who take this view, see ibid., p. 368, n. 57; cf. also B. F. Meyer, *The Aims of Jesus* (London, 1979), pp. 197–200.
5 R. Bauckham, 'The coin in the fish's mouth', in D. Wenham and C. Blomberg (eds.), *Gospel Perspectives VI: The Miracles of Jesus* (Sheffield, 1986), pp. 219–52.
6 Another recent defence of the authenticity of this saying is W. Horbury, 'The temple tax', in E. Bammel and C. F. D. Moule (eds.), *Jesus and the Politics of His Day* (Cambridge, 1984), pp. 265–86. In my article I have argued also for the authenticity of Matt 17:27, but that is less relevant to our present purposes.
7 The time of origin is debated: for a summary of the evidence suggesting a late post-exilic date, see Horbury, op. cit., p. 279; for an alternative view, see N. J. McEleney, 'Matthew 17:24–27 – who paid the temple tax? A lesson in the avoidance of scandal', *CBQ* 38 (1976), 179–80.
8 Sanders' comment that 'payment of the tax was voluntary' (op. cit., p. 64) is mistaken and has no support in the mishnaic passage he cites as evidence (*m. Šeqalim* 1:3). According to this passage, the tax was voluntary only for those not legally obliged to pay (women, slaves, minors, priests). Cf. K. F. Nickle, *The Collection: A Study in Paul's Strategy*, SBT 48 (London, 1966), pp. 79–80; S. Safrai, 'Relations between the Diaspora and the land of Israel', in S. Safrai and M. Stern (eds.), *The Jewish People in the First Century*, I, CRINT 1 (Assen, 1974), 191.
9 Cf. Josephus, *Ant.* 18.312; and a saying ascribed to Yohanan b. Zakkai, quoted in Horbury, op. cit., p. 280.
10 Cf. H. Montefiore, 'Jesus and the temple tax', *NTS* 11 (1964–5), 68–9.
11 Philo, *Spec. Leg.* 1.76–8; *Leg. Gaium* 156, 315; Josephus, *Ant.* 14.110–13; 16.28, 160–73, 312–13. Cf. Safrai, op. cit., pp. 188–90.
12 For an argument for this interpretation of Matt 17:25–6, against other proposed interpretations, see Bauckham, op. cit. Cf. also Horbury, op. cit., whose interpretation is quite similar to mine.
13 This is the implication of Matt 17:27, as I have interpreted it in Bauckham, op. cit., consistently with Jesus' exposition of God's fatherhood in Matt 6:25–34 par; 7:7–11 par.
14 McEleney, op. cit., p. 187.
15 Cf. Montefiore, op. cit., p. 70. But for a different interpretation, see A. G. Wright, 'The widow's mites: praise or lament? A matter of context', *CBQ* 44 (1982), 256–65.
16 E.g. V. Eppstein, 'The historicity of the Gospel account of the cleansing of the temple', *ZNW* 55 (1964), 42–58, can make no sense of the attack on the moneychangers (pp. 56–7); J. D. M. Derrett, 'The zeal of the house and the cleansing of the temple', *Downside Review* 95 (1977), 79–94, is also least convincing in discussing the moneychangers (p. 83); and Sanders, op. cit., ignores Mark 11:16 (which cannot fit into his interpretation) virtually without explanation (p. 364, n. 1).
17 So also R. E. Brown, *The Gospel according to John (i–xii)*, AB 29 (London, 1971), pp. 118–20; C. H. Dodd, *Historical Tradition in the Fourth Gospel*

(Cambridge, 1963), pp. 156–62; R. Schnackenburg, *The Gospel according to St John*, I (London/New York, 1968), p. 353.

18 Cf. A. Edersheim, *The Life and Times of Jesus the Messiah*, I (London, 1892), p. 369.

19 This would seem to indicate that the Synoptics' chronological scheme of Jesus' last week in Jerusalem is artificial, and that the demonstration in the temple in fact took place more than two weeks before Passover; cf. W. Lane, *The Gospel according to Mark* (London, 1974), p. 405. But we cannot really be sure that payment of tax did not continue at a considerable rate after 1 Nisan.

20 I. Abrahams, *Studies in Pharisaism and the Gospels*, First Series (Cambridge, 1917), p. 86. Abrahams plausibly argues (pp. 85–6) that the opinion, given as one rabbinic opinion among others in *j. Šeqalim* 1, that the moneychangers kept the surcharge as their own profit refers to the arrangements for tax collection in the provinces rather than in the temple.

21 Derrett, op. cit., pp. 82–3.

22 E.g. H. B. Swete, *The Gospel according to St Mark* (London, 1920), p. 255.

23 Probably *peristera* here covers both the 'turtle-dove' (LXX *trugōn*) and the 'pigeon' mentioned in the law.

24 Cf. *m. Ḥullin* 1:5; *Meʿila* 3:4; Derrett, op. cit., p. 84. The complicated rules about bird offerings in Mishnah tractate *Kinnim* are mainly concerned with ways in which the offerings could be invalidated even after the birds were certified fit for sacrifice, but they contributed to the need for careful management of the whole matter. The notorious complexity of the laws on bird offerings (*m. ʿAbot* 3:19) probably explains the comment in *m. Šeqalim* 5:1 about the special skills of Petahiah, the temple treasurer in charge of bird offerings.

25 According to *Lam. Rab.* 2:5 on 2:2 (Soncino 2:2 §4), on the Mount of Olives, which was treated as part of the temple precincts.

26 For reasons for trusting *m. Šeqalim* 5, as an account of the organisation of the temple immediately before the fall of Jerusalem, see J. Jeremias, *Jerusalem in the Time of Jesus* (London, 1969), pp. 170–3. Jeremias' argument (pp. 167–9) makes it likely that the briefer account in *t. Šeqalim* 2:14, which mentions no treasurer in charge of the bird offerings, describes an earlier situation. It is impossible to tell which corresponds more closely to the situation during Jesus' ministry, but in any case it is scarcely conceivable that all the offices mentioned only in the later list did not exist at the time of the earlier list.

27 Sanders, op. cit., p. 65.

28 On this story, see Jeremias, op. cit., pp. 33–4; Abrahams, op. cit., p. 87.

29 Trans. Danby, p. 564.

30 Abrahams, op. cit., p. 84; J. Jeremias, *New Testament Theology: Part 1: The Proclamation of Jesus* (London, 1971), p. 145, n. 1; Derrett, op. cit., p. 85. Josephus, *Ap.* 2.106, which refers only to the prohibition on carrying vessels into the holy place, is not relevant here, since it is incredible that Jesus could have encountered people trying to do this.

31 Lane, op. cit., p. 406; C. Roth, 'The cleansing of the temple and Zechariah xiv 21', *NovT* 4 (1960), 177–8.

32 J. M. Ford, 'Money "bags" in the temple (Mk 11, 16)', *Bib* 57 (1976), 249–53.

33 The disagreement in *m. Šeqalim* 4:3 is not over whether profit was made, but over whether the purchase of wine, oil and flour was a legitimate use of the residue from the temple tax.

34 See Jeremias, *Jerusalem*, p. 49.

35 Cf., at an earlier period, the action of Simon the captain of the temple, in 2 Macc

3:4–6. N. Q. Hamilton, 'Temple cleansing and temple bank', *JBL* 83 (1964), 367, following Abel, interprets his disagreement with the high priest Onias in terms of Simon's determination to pursue the commercial interests of the temple.

36 Cf. E. Schürer, *The History of the Jewish People in the Age of Jesus Christ*, II, rev. and ed. G. Vermes, F. Millar and M. Black (Edinburgh, 1979), pp. 280–1.

37 Jeremias, *Jerusalem*, pp. 25–6.

38 Cf. Hamilton, op. cit.; but I do not know what the evidence is for Derrett's assertion, op. cit., p. 87, that the temple could lend to Jews at interest.

39 Cf. R. A. Horsley, 'Popular prophetic movements at the time of Jesus: their principal features and social origins', *JSNT* 26 (1986), 19.

40 For the evidence for this, see Jeremias, *Jerusalem*, pp. 195–6; cf. the archeological evidence in B. Mazar, *The Mountain of the Lord* (Garden City, New York, 1975), pp. 84–6; N. Avigad, *Discovering Jerusalem* (Nashville, 1983), pp. 129–30.

41 This is not the kind of general allegation against the temple priests which Sanders, op. cit., p. 66, rightly rejects, since there is no evidence to support it. It is an accusation purely against the high-priestly families who actually ran the temple. On generalisations about the priests, see also E. P. Sanders, 'Judaism and the grand "Christian" abstractions: love, mercy, and grace', *Int* 39 (1985), 367–8, where Sanders broaches the important distinction between the priestly aristocracy and the lower clergy.

42 Trans. Jeremias, *Jerusalem*, pp. 195–6.

43 See Schürer, op. cit., II. 234; Jeremias, *Jerusalem*, pp. 194–5. Another family, that of Kamithus, supplied at least three high priests.

44 Apart from Simon Kantheras and his son Elionaeus, only one high priest after 6 CE is known to have belonged to the house of Boethus: Jesus the son of Gamaliel (*c.* 62–3 CE), who was related by marriage to the house of Boethus according to *m. Yebamot* 6:4.

45 The first was high priest *c.* 15–16 CE.

46 Derrett, op. cit., p. 86; cf. Abrahams, op. cit., p. 86.

47 Jeremias, *Jerusalem*, p. 196. Edersheim, op. cit., I, 263, takes the word to refer to perversion of justice.

48 The captain of the temple, who normally belonged to one of the high-priestly families (Jeremias, *Jerusalem*, p. 162), and the other heads of the temple police (*sĕgānîm*) are not mentioned.

49 Jeremias, *Jerusalem*, pp. 165–6.

50 Schürer, op. cit., II. 282–3.

51 It is not clear that 6:7 necessarily presupposes the deposition of Archelaus in CE 6, as E. Brandenburger, 'Himmelfahrt Moses', in *Apokalypsen*, JSHRZ 5 (Gütersloh, 1976), p. 60, supposes.

52 I follow Nickelsburg's and Collins' view of the composition of the *Testament of Moses*: G. W. E. Nickelsburg, 'An Antiochan date for the Testament of Moses', and J. J. Collins, 'The date and provenance of the Testament of Moses', both in G. W. E. Nickelsburg (ed.), *Studies on the Testament of Moses*, SCS 4 (Cambridge, Mass., 1973), pp. 33–43; for a summary, see G. W. E. Nickelsburg, *Jewish Literature Between the Bible and the Mishnah* (London, 1981), pp. 80–3, 212–14. On this view, the original work was composed during the Antiochan persecution, which chs. 5 and 8–9 reflect, but was then updated in the early first century CE by the addition of chs. 6–7, with the effect of pushing chs. 8–9 into the author–reviser's future. Ch. 6 updates the review of history by

describing the Hasmoneans and the reign of Herod the Great, and ch. 7 describes the present situation in the author–reviser's time. But I cannot agree with Nickelsburg (*Jewish Literature*, p. 213) that the 'descriptions in chapter 7 are too stereotyped to be identifiable'. However stereotyped, in the period in question (4 BCE–30 CE) they can apply to no one but the priestly aristocracy. For an argument to this effect, see R. H. Charles, *The Assumption of Moses* (London, 1987), pp. 23–8.

53 Whether the term *archiereus* in Josephus and the NT refers to the members of the high-priestly families, as such, or to the occupants of high offices in the temple hierarchy (see Jeremias, *Jerusalem*, pp. 175–81; Schürer, op. cit., II, 233–6) makes no difference here: in either case it refers to the members of those families who supplied the high priests and monopolised the high offices in the temple.

54 In a general way, this agrees with the interpretation suggested briefly in J. Riches, 'Works and words of Jesus the Jew', *HeyJ* 17 (1986), 57–8, but makes it much more specific.

55 *Contra* Roloff, cited Sanders, *Jesus and Judaism*, p. 367, n. 41.

56 Cf. R. Bultmann, *The History of the Synoptic Tradition* (Oxford, ²1968), pp. 36, 389.

57 ibid., p. 36.

58 E. Trocmé, 'L'expulsion des marchands du temple', *NTS* 15 (1968–9), 6. The future tense is probably a Semitism: cf. Blass–Debrunner §362, and Mark 10:43–5 par Matt 20:26–7.

59 The claim of Dodd, op. cit., pp. 159–60, followed by B. Lindars, *The Gospel of John*, NCB (London, 1977), p. 139; Brown, op. cit., p. 121; A. E. Harvey, *Jesus and the Constraints of History* (London, 1982), p. 133, that John 2:16 alludes to Zech 14:21 seems very uncertain. Cf. Schnackenburg, op. cit., I, 347.

60 E.g. R. H. Hiers, 'Purification of the temple: preparation for the Kingdom of God', *JBL* 90 (1971), 86–9; Hamilton, op. cit., p. 372.

61 Cf. Harvey, op. cit., p. 133; W. W. Watty, 'Jesus and the temple – cleansing or cursing?', *ExpT* 93 (1981–2), 236.

62 Cf. the attribution of a quotation from Hos 6:6 to Jesus in Matt 9:13; 12:7. This seems very likely to be due to Matthew's redaction, but is not a case of Jesus' fulfilment of Old Testament prophecy.

63 Harvey, op. cit., p. 132.

64 Sanders, *Jesus and Judaism*, p. 66.

65 G. W. Buchanan, 'Mark 11.15–19: brigands in the temple', *HUCA* 30 (1959), 169–77; C. K. Barrett, 'The house of prayer and the den of thieves', in E. E. Ellis and E. Grässer (eds.), *Jesus and Paulus* (W. G. Kümmel Festschrift) (Göttingen, ²1978); Gaston, op. cit., p. 85; Harvey, op. cit., p. 132; Sanders, *Jesus and Judaism*, p. 66.

66 Buchanan, op. cit., pp. 176–7; cf. Trocmé, op. cit., p. 8, n. 1.

67 Cf. D. Juel, *Messiah and Temple: The Trial of Jesus in the Gospel of Mark*, SBLDS 31 (Missoula, Montana, 1977), pp. 132–4. But the problem is hardly alleviated by arguing, as Juel does, that Mark is really interested in the *context* of this phrase in Jer 7, rather than in the phrase itself.

68 As do Hiers, op. cit., p. 89; B. Gärtner, *The Temple and the Community in Qumran and the New Testament*, SNTSMS 1 (Cambridge, 1965), pp. 110–11.

69 There is no manuscript evidence for the omission of *pasin tois ethnesin*.

70 *Contra*, e.g., Lohmeyer, quoted *TDNT* v, 121; Hamilton, op. cit., p. 372.

71 See J. Jeremias, *The Prayers of Jesus*, SBT 2.6 (London, 1967), pp. 69–72.

72 This is consistent with Matt 5:23–4, which takes sacrifices as means of atonement seriously, but requires that they should be accompanied by reconciliation.

73 Thus this interpretation is not susceptible to Sanders' criticism of other attempts to distinguish the true purpose of the temple, in Jesus' view, from current abuse of it (*Jesus and Judaism*, pp. 63–4). Sanders envisages such a distinction only in terms of external versus internal worship. In our view Jesus does not oppose the internal (prayer) to the external (sacrifices), but insists that the purpose of the sacrifices is to be the vehicle for prayer, not to maximise profit for the temple and to impose financial burdens on the poor.

74 Buchanan, op. cit. His evidence that *lēstai* as a loanword in rabbinic Hebrew (*lîstîm*) regularly means 'guerrilla warriors' (p. 174, n. 10) does not seem convincing, though the evidence in his subsequent article, 'An additional note to "Mark 11.15–19: brigands in the temple" ', *HUCA* 31 (1960), 103–5, shows that this is sometimes the meaning. Most who think *lēstēs* in Mark 11:17 means 'nationalist rebel (Zealot)' think it is inauthentic (cf. n. 65 above), but Roth, op. cit., pp. 176–7, attributes this meaning to Jesus.

75 Cf. N. Hillyer in *NIDNTT* iii, 380–1: 'robbing the helpless while themselves enjoying the safe refuge of privilege'.

76 J. Jeremias, *Jesus' Promise to the Nations*, SBT 24 (London, 1958), pp. 65–6. For application of Isa 56:7 to the eschatological temple, see *b. Megilla* 18a and further rabbinic references in Strack–Billerbeck i, 852–3.

77 *Contra* W. D. Davies, *The Gospel and the Land* (Berkeley/Los Angeles/London, 1974), pp. 343, 349; R. J. McKelvey, *The New Temple* (London, 1969), pp. 64–5.

78 Cf. *m. Seqalim* 1:5; Josephus, *BJ* 2.408–21. If Gentiles could offer sacrifices, they must presumably have been able to purchase them in the outer court.

79 For proselytes in Jerusalem for festivals, see Acts 2:10; Josephus, *BJ* 2.250; Safrai, op. cit., p. 199.

80 John 12:20; Acts 8:27; Josephus, *BJ* 6:427; Safrai, op. cit., pp. 199–201; cf. 1 Kgs 8:41–3.

81 Sanders, *Jesus and Judaism*, ch. 1.

82 It is not impossible to see the overturning of the tables and chairs as symbolic of the destruction of the temple, as well as denunciation, but since the other two actions of Jesus cannot be so interpreted, it is better to preserve the symbolic unity of Jesus' demonstration by excluding destruction from what is symbolised. Referring to interpretations of the demonstration in the temple as a 'cleansing' and to Jesus' prophecy of the destruction of the temple, Sanders, *Jesus and Judaism*, p. 302, says: 'Jesus probably did not *do* one thing in the temple and *say* another about it during the same brief period without there being some interconnection.' Our interpretation secures a close interconnection, in that the coming destruction of the temple is divine judgement on the abuses Jesus attacks, and this connection is implicit in Jesus' allusion to Jer 7:11.

83 See especially Sanders, *Jesus and Judaism*, chs. 10–11.

84 Cf. Riches, op. cit., p. 57, for a slightly different form of this objection to Sanders' interpretation.

85 *2 Bar.* 32:3–4 is an apparent exception: it seems to describe the destruction of 70 CE purely as a preliminary to the eschatological renewal of the temple. But the whole book, with its implicit treatment of the 586 BCE as typological of the 70 CE destruction, leaves no doubt that the author considered the latter a divine judgement on Israel's sin.

86 Sanders, *Jesus and Judaism*, p. 287.

87 ibid., p. 270.

88 Probably the Sadduccees did not, but Sanders is at pains to stress that Jesus did not offend any particular party: he offended the general Jewish reverence for the temple.

89 ibid., p. 302.

90 ibid., pp. 73–4.

91 ibid., pp. 302–3.

92 D. E. Aune, *Prophecy in Early Christianity and the Ancient Mediterranean World* (Grand Rapids, 1983), p. 137.

93 Hamilton, op. cit., argues that the authority Jesus claimed would have been seen as *royal*; Derrett, op. cit., that it was *prophetic*. But it is not necessary to be so specific.

94 R. A. Horsley, 'High priests and the politics of Roman Palestine: a contextual analysis of the evidence in Josephus', *JSJ* 17 (1986), 36–9.

95 The suitability of Mark 14:58 for this purpose means we must doubt whether this form of the saying ('I will destroy . . .') is what Jesus said. It is more likely a hostile interpretation of what he said.

96 Cf. B. Chilton, 'Jesus *ben David*: reflections on the *Davidssohnfrage*', *JSNT* 14 (1982), 102–3.

8. Q, THE LAW AND JUDAISM

1 Cf. the monographs of D. Lührmann, *Die Redaktion der Logienquelle* (Neukirchen-Vluyn, 1969); P. Hoffmann, *Studien zur Theologie der Logienquelle* (Münster, 1971); S. Schulz, *Q – Die Spruchquelle der Evangelisten* (Zürich, 1972); A. Polag, *Die Christologie der Logienquelle* (Neukirchen-Vluyn, 1977). For surveys of recent study, see R. D. Worden, 'Redaction criticism of Q: a survey', *JBL* 94 (1975), 532–46; F. Neirynck, 'Recent developments in the study of Q', in J. Delobel (ed.), *LOGIA, Les Paroles de Jésus – The Sayings of Jesus*, BETL 59 (Leuven, 1982), pp. 29–75. For a discussion of some of the methodological issues raised, see J. Kloppenborg, 'Tradition and redaction in the synoptic sayings source', *CBQ* 46 (1984), 34–62. All such study must presuppose the two-source theory as the solution to the synoptic problem and this theory will be presupposed here.

2 The abbreviations MattR and LukeR are used here for Matthean redaction and Lukan redaction respectively.

3 See G. Barth, 'Matthew's understanding of the Law', in G. Bornkamm, G. Barth and H. J. Held, *Tradition and Interpretation in Matthew* (London, 1963), p. 66; G. Strecker, *Der Weg der Gerechtigkeit* (Göttingen, 1971), p. 143; J. P. Meier, *Law and History in Matthew's Gospel* (Rome, 1976), p. 58; R. Guelich, *The Sermon on the Mount* (Waco, 1982), p. 145. U. Luz, 'Die Erfüllung des Gesetzes bei Matthäus', *ZTK* 75 (1978), 398–435, on pp. 416f., is unusual in ascribing verse 18d to Matthew's tradition (on the basis of an alleged stereotyped form of an Amen saying as isolated by K. Berger), and verse 18b to MattR. This, however, ignores the possibility that Matthew may have reordered the saying when adding to it. Luz himself admits in his later commentary that the saying with verse 18d could scarcely have existed in isolation, whereas with verse 18b it could: see *Das Evangelium nach Matthäus (Mt 1–7)* (Neukirchen-Vluyn, 1985), p. 230, where in any case Luz seems to indicate some change of mind.

4 There is debate as to whether this means 'never', or whether it is meant to be a

genuinely temporal reference to the apocalyptic consummation of this age. Majority opinion is probably in favour of the latter view: cf. Guelich, op. cit., p. 144; Luz, *Matthäus*, p. 236, with further references.

5 Needless to say, such an interpretation is much disputed, but see Meier, op. cit., pp. 63f.; Guelich, op. cit., pp. 148f., with further references; also C. E. Carlston, 'The things that defile (Mark vii.14) and the law in Matthew and Mark', *NTS* 15 (1968), 75–95.

6 Cf. S. G. Wilson, *Luke and the Law* (Cambridge, 1983), *passim*. This is of course not to deny that Luke regards it as theologically important to show that Christianity is in a line of continuity with Judaism: hence his portrait of Paul in Acts as the law-abiding Jew *par excellence*. But this is probably more of an apologetic ploy to show Christianity as a religion of antiquity, rather than to press observance of the law on the Christian Church.

7 Cf. Wilson, op. cit., pp. 44f., for a full discussion of this verse with further references. Cf. also R. Banks, *Jesus and the Law in the Synoptic Tradition* (Cambridge, 1975), p. 215: 'a rhetorical figure which merely emphasises how hard it is for the Law to pass away'; also Guelich, op. cit., p. 165.

8 See R. Laufen, *Die Doppelüberlieferungen der Logienquelle und des Markusevangeliums* (Bonn, 1980), p. 588, n. 84, for a full list of bibliographical references of those supporting Lukan originality here.

9 For Matthew as more original, see Schulz, op. cit., p. 114; Meier, op. cit., pp. 59f. For the theory of two independent versions here, see Guelich, op. cit., pp. 143f.; also H. Hübner, *Das Gesetz in der synoptischen Tradition* (Witten, 1973), p. 21.

10 Cf. also W. G. Kümmel, 'Jesus und der jüdische Traditionsgedanke', in *Heilsgeschehen und Geschichte* (Marburg, 1965), p. 33; Strecker, op. cit., p. 144; Carlston, op. cit., p. 78; I. H. Marshall, *The Gospel of Luke* (Exeter, 1977), p. 630; Laufen, op. cit., p. 354. The same is the view of those who would see Luke's version as redactional. Thus, for example, Meier too, who claims that Matthew's version (without verse 18d) is more original, agrees that the saying in Q is asserting the abiding validity of the law (op. cit., p. 59). In this context, therefore, the precise reconstruction of the Q wording may not be critical.

11 P. D. Meyer, 'The Community of Q' (Ph.D. dissertation, University of Iowa, 1967), p. 67.

12 For what follows, see my *The Revival of the Griesbach Hypothesis* (Cambridge, 1983), pp. 153f. with further references, especially the earlier discussion of H. Schürmann, '"Wer daher eines dieser geringsten Gebote auflöst . . ." Wo fand Matthäus das Logion Mt 5, 19?', in *Traditionsgeschichtliche Untersuchungen zu den synoptischen Evangelien* (Düsseldorf, 1968), pp. 126ff.; also Laufen, op. cit, pp. 352–4.

13 See Barth, op. cit., p. 63; Strecker, op. cit., p. 167; Schulz, op. cit., pp. 261f.; J. A. Fitzmyer, *The Gospel according to Luke X–XXIV*, AB (New York, 1985), p. 1115, and many others.

14 For a similar view, cf. Polag, op. cit., p. 79, n. 246; also Laufen op. cit., p. 355. H. Schürmann, 'Das Zeugnis der Redenquelle für die Basileia-Verkündigung Jesus', in Delobel, op. cit., pp. 121–200, on pp. 170f., would see Luke 16:16 as modifying and clarifying Luke 16:17 in Q. But the fact that the saying about the eternal validity of the law comes second in both Luke and Matthew, and hence almost certainly in Q as well, suggests that verse 17 is intended to qualify verse 16 and not vice versa.

15 Cf. D. R. Catchpole, 'The synoptic divorce material as a traditio-historical problem', *BJRL* 57 (1974), 92–127; Wilson, op. cit., pp. 46f.

16 Cf. E. P. Sanders, *Jesus and Judaism* (London, 1985), p. 256.

17 See Fitzmyer, op. cit., p. 1121, with further references.

18 So E. Haenchen, 'Matthäus 23', *ZTK* 48 (1951), 38–63, on p. 49; Schulz, op. cit., p. 96; D. E. Garland, *The Intention of Matthew 23* (Leiden, 1979), pp. 41ff., and many others.

19 So Barth, op. cit., p. 80; Schulz, op. cit., p. 100, though it is taken as pre-Matthean by Haenchen, op. cit., p. 39, and by Strecker, op. cit., p. 136.

20 Luke is regarded as secondary by Schulz, op. cit., pp. 100f., Barth, op. cit., p. 80, and Strecker, op. cit., p. 136.

21 So Schulz, op. cit., p. 103; also Schürmann, 'Das Zeugnis der Redenquelle', pp. 174f., who speaks of 'eine Gruppe gesetzestreuer Judenchristen, die aber dem pharisäischen Legalismus gegenüber die ethische Seite der Tora, besonders das Liebesgebot, akzentuieren'. Schürmann would also see within this block of material in Luke 11 several stages of the tradition, with, for example, Luke 11:43 par implying a much more radical break between the Christian and Jewish communities. (See in more detail his 'Die Redekomposition wider "dieses Geschlecht" und seine Führung in der Redequelle (vgl. Mt 23, 1–39 par Lk 11, 37–54)', *SNTU* A 11 (1986), 33–81.) This seems unconvincing, though I have argued that there is a seam visible within Luke 11:42 itself. Multiple stages in the redaction of Q are not *per se* impossible, but such a theory seems an unnecessary complication in this case. A sharp polemic against Pharisees themselves can still be coupled with an acknowledgement of their teaching.

22 See Hoffmann's review of Schulz's book in *BZ* 19 (1975), 104–15, on p. 114: 'Er indiziert eine Rejudaisierungstendenz'; cf. also Polag, op. cit., p. 80; W. Schenk, *Synopse zur Redenquelle der Evangelien* (Düsseldorf, 1981), p. 76. Older interpretations which excised this clause from Luke and regarded it as an interpolation from Matthew (cf. Garland, op. cit., pp. 139f. for details) have clearly missed the facet of Q's ideas about the law being discussed here and have too readily ignored the complex tradition-history which lies between Jesus and our finished Gospels. (The fact that the final clause is missing from some western manuscripts of Luke is easily explained as due to Marcionite influence.)

23 See p. 99 below.

24 Cf. Schulz, op. cit., p. 100; Garland, op. cit., p. 137; Fitzmyer, op. cit., p. 948 and many others.

25 See p. 99 below.

26 J. Jeremias, *The Parables of Jesus* (London, 1963), p. 140.

27 So correctly Schulz, op. cit., p. 101; Garland, op. cit., p. 140.

28 Schulz, op. cit., pp. 96f.

29 ibid., pp. 98f.; also S. Westerholm, *Jesus and Scribal Authority* (Lund, 1978), p. 89.

30 J. Neusner, '"First cleanse the inside". "halakhic" background of a controversy saying', *NTS* 22 (1976), 486–95.

31 For the view that the saying presupposes Shammaite practice, see also A. Finkel, *The Pharisees and the Teacher of Nazareth* (Leiden, 1964), p. 141, though Finkel argues on the basis of *m. Berakot* 8:2 alone. Neusner's argument has been criticised by H. Maccoby, 'The washing of cups', *JSNT* 14 (1982), 3–15. Maccoby argues that, contrary to Neusner, the saying is nothing to do with ritual purification at all. The saying is referring to simple hygienic cleaning and

is metaphorical throughout: the 'cup' is a metaphor for the person of the Pharisee. However, it is not then clear what 'cleaning the outside' refers to. Presumably it is something to do with the Pharisees' practice of worrying about their physical bodies, and, if Neusner is right (cf. p. 99 below), then a crucial part of this would have concerned ritual purification. In any case it is hard to take the whole saying as wholly metaphorical, since one would expect some of the verbs and pronouns to slip into the second person: cf. Garland, op. cit., pp. 145f. Neusner's (and Finkel's) interpretation does have the merit of locating the saying, which is addressed to Pharisees, within the broad contours of pharisaic piety.

32 It is not mentioned by Lührmann or Hoffmann in their monographs, nor is it included by Neirynck in his discussion of Q in his *New Testament Vocabulary* (Leuven, 1984), p. 5. Schulz, op. cit., p. 41, explicitly denies that this is a part of Q, partly on the basis of the difference in wording between Matthew and Luke, partly on the grounds that the view of the sabbath law implied here – that the law can be broken to help other people – is inconsistent with the attitude to the law elsewhere in Q. But if the analysis above is right, then this verse fits very well with a (strict Jewish) casuistic interpretation of the law. Those who would ascribe the verse to Q include Bussmann, Schmid, Schürmann: see A. Polag, *Fragmenta Q* (Neukirchen, 1979), pp. 72f.

33 See Tuckett, op. cit., pp. 98f.

34 See C. G. Montefiore, *The Synoptic Gospels* I (London, 1927), 81f.

35 See Strecker, op. cit., p. 19.

36 However, the appeal to the principle of saving life on the sabbath (cf. Mark 3:4), if it does go back to Jesus, could be seen as an attempt to re-evaluate what constitutes 'saving life': Jesus' miracles of healing on the sabbath illustrate the 'healing' effect of his gospel which strikes at a deeper level than only the physical.

37 Tuckett, op. cit., pp. 125ff.; see also R. H. Fuller, 'The double commandment of love: a test case for the criteria of authenticity', in Fuller (ed.), *Essays on the Love Commandment* (Philadelphia, 1978), pp. 41ff.

38 J. Bowker, *Jesus and the Pharisees* (Cambridge, 1973); cf. also M. Hengel, *The Charismatic Leader and His Followers* (Edinburgh, 1981), p. 56; Westerholm, op. cit., p. 26. Others would argue that 'Pharisees' and 'scribes' are almost synonymous: cf. Sanders, op. cit., p. 198.

39 Fuller, op. cit., pp. 42f.

40 Cf. T. W. Manson, *The Sayings of Jesus* (London, 1949), p. 99, says of the first three woes in Luke 11: 'These three woes are all concerned with character and conduct. There is in them no polemic against Pharisaism as such.'

41 R. A. Wild, 'The encounter between Pharisaic and Christian Judaism: some early gospel evidence', *NovT* 27 (1985), 105–24.

42 J. Neusner, *The Rabbinic Traditions about the Pharisees before 70* (3 vols., Leiden, 1971). For a shorter and more popular account, see his *From Politics to Piety: The Emergence of Pharisaic Judaism* (Engelwood Cliffs, 1973).

43 Wild, op. cit., pp. 110f.; also R. Meyer, '*pharisaios*', in *TDNT*, IX, 28. For the probable situation in Galilee as being little influenced by Pharisism, see also S. Freyne, *Galilee from Alexander the Great to Hadrian: 323 B.C.E. to 135 C.E.* (Wilmington, 1980); Sanders, op. cit., p. 292 (referring to Morton Smith).

44 See, for example, P. Winter, *On the Trial of Jesus* (Berlin, 1961). For other theories that the opposition between Jesus and the Pharisees was considerably less than the Gospels tend to imply, see the survey in Sanders, op. cit., pp. 291f.

45 Cf. Tuckett, op. cit., p. 105, with references cited there. MarkR=Markan redaction.
46 Wild, op. cit., p. 119, appealing to Westerholm, op. cit., p. 83.
47 Clearly the interpretation of the saying depends very heavily on the context in which it is placed: see especially J. D. G. Dunn, 'Jesus and ritual purity: a study of the tradition history of Mk 7,15', in *A Cause de l'Évangile: Mélanges offerts à Dom Jacques Dupont* (Paris, 1985), pp. 251–76.
48 Cf. Carlston, op. cit., p. 95. For further discussion of this saying, see the essay of B. Lindars in this volume.
49 Neusner, *Rabbinic Traditions*, II, 1–5.
50 Most agree that Q stems from a form of Jewish Christianity.
51 Opinions vary: see Laufen, op. cit., pp. 237–9; also U. Wegner, *Der Hauptmann von Kafarnaum* (Tübingen, 1985), pp. 304ff., both with full references.
52 Cf. P. D. Meyer, 'The Gentile mission in Q', *JBL* 89 (1970), 405–17.
53 Lührmann, op. cit., pp. 24ff.
54 Cf. Hoffmann, *Studien*; also his 'Tradition und Situation. Zur "Verbindlichkeit" des Gebots der Feindesliebe in der synoptischen Überlieferung und in der gegenwärtigen Friedensdiskussion', in K. Kertelge (ed.), *Ethik im neuen Testament* (Freiburg, 1984), pp. 50–118, esp. pp. 64–81. See also D. R. Catchpole, 'Jesus and the community of Israel', *BJRL* 68 (1986), 296–316.
55 Cf. n. 22 above. Lührmann, op. cit., pp. 43ff. has argued that the series of woes in Matthew 23 par Luke 11 is broadened by the final woe (Luke 11:49–51 par) to become a polemic against 'this generation', i.e. all Israel, not just against other non-Christian Pharisees. (Though whether the term 'this generation' has quite such a broad reference to Q is uncertain: cf. Hoffmann, *Studien*, p. 169.)
56 A similar claim has been made by R. Hodgson, 'On the Gattung of Q: a dialogue with James M. Robinson', *Bib* 66 (1985), 73–95, with a similar methodology to that offered here but appealing to different Q texts. Hodgson does not go so far as to suggest that the Q community itself claimed to be Pharisees but he does suggest that the Q community should be seen within a context of (hostile) pharisaic Judaism. Hodgson also starts with the theory that the Pharisees were concerned above all with issues of table-fellowship and tithing, and he argues that the same concerns are reflected in Q texts such as Luke 4:4; 10:7; 11:42; 13:29; 17:26f. and pars. However, apart from 11:42 (discussed above), I am not convinced that these texts are really to do with issues of table-fellowship.

9. CHRIST AND THE LAW IN JOHN 7–10

* An earlier form of this paper was read to the British Meeting of the Society for New Testament Studies, Manchester, September 1985.
1 C. K. Barrett, 'The Old Testament in the Fourth Gospel', *JTS* 48 (1947), 155–69.
2 E.g. E. D. Freed, *Old Testament Quotations in the Gospel of John*, NovTSup 11 (Leiden, 1965); G. Reim, *Studien zum alttestamentlichen Hintergrund des Johannesevangeliums*, SNTSMS 22 (Cambridge, 1974).
3 E.g. P. Borgen, *Bread from Heaven: An Exegetical Study of the Concept of Manna in the Gospel of John and the Writings of Philo*, NovTSup 10 (Leiden, 1965); J. J. Enz, 'The book of Exodus as a literary type for the Gospel of John', *JBL* 76 (1957), 208–15; B. Olsson, *Structure and Meaning in the Fourth Gospel*, ConBNT 6 (Lund, 1974); R. H. Smith, 'Exodus typology in the Fourth Gospel', *JBL* 81 (1962), 329–42.

4 E.g. D. G. Bostock, 'Jesus as the new Elisha', *ExpT* 92 (1980–1), 39–41; T. L. Brodie, 'Jesus as the new Elisha: cracking the code', *ExpT* 93 (1981–2), 39–42; R. E. Brown, 'Jesus and Elisha', *Perspective* 12 (1971), 85–104; T. F. Glasson, *Moses in the Fourth Gospel*, SBT 40 (London, 1963); J. L. Martyn, 'We Have Found Elijah', in his *The Gospel of John in Christian History* (New York, 1978), pp. 9–54; W. A. Meeks, *The Prophet-King: Moses Traditions and the Johannine Christology*, NovTSup 14 (Leiden, 1967).

5 On the Gospel's process of compilation and levels of meaning see, e.g., R. E. Brown, *The Gospel According to John I-XII*, AB 29 (Garden City, N.Y., 1966), pp. xxiv-li; J. L. Martyn, *History and Theology in the Fourth Gospel* (Nashville, ²1979), Parts I and II. Martyn describes the two levels in John 5, 7 and 9 in a way that fits with several assertions in this paper.

6 B it read *emenen*; P⁴⁵,⁶⁶,⁷⁵ and most uncials read *emeinen*.

7 M. J. J. Menken, *Numerical Literary Techniques in John*, NovTSup 55 (Leiden, 1985), pp. 189–228.

8 ibid., p. 191.

9 C. H. Dodd, *The Interpretation of the Fourth Gospel* (Cambridge, 1953), pp. 354–62, 400; as also A. Feuillet, *Études Johanniques* (Paris, 1962), pp. 130–51.

10 Brown, *John I-XII*, pp. 402, 404; R. Bultmann, *The Gospel of John: A Commentary* (Oxford, 1971), pp. 285–391, takes 7:1–10:39 together.

11 S. Pancaro, *The Law in the Fourth Gospel*, NovTSup 42 (Leiden, 1975), pp. 56–76, 87–105, 130–92, 263–80.

12 According to J. Mann, *The Bible as Read and Preached in the Old Synagogue I* (Cincinnati, 1940; repr. New York, 1971); C. Perrot, *La Lecture de la Bible*, Collection Massorah Série I: Études Classiques et Textes 1 (Hildesheim, 1973), pp. 271–82.

13 For a discussion of the sabbath healings by Jewish Christians as likely to have incurred the death sentence, see A. B. Kolenkow, 'Healing controversy as a tie between miracle and Passion Material for a Proto-Gospel', *JBL* 95 (1976), 633; Martyn, *History and Theology*, p. 70.

14 As suggested by B. Lindars, *The Gospel of John*, NCB (London, 1972), p. 289; Bo Reicke, *Die zehn Worte in Geschichte und Gegenwart*, BGBE 13 (Tübingen, 1973), p. 56.

15 See the discussion of *wayĕkal* in Gen 2:2 in early Jewish sources in G. J. Brooke, *Exegesis at Qumran: 4Q Florilegium in its Jewish Context*, JSOTSup 29 (Sheffield, 1985), pp. 29–31. Intriguingly Lactantius in Methodius of Olympus (*De conversione* 9.1) connects God's ceasing to work on the sabbath with the Feast of 'our' Tabernacles in the seventh month: see J. Daniélou, *A History of Early Christian Doctrine 1: The Theology of Early Jewish Christianity* (London, 1964), p. 395.

16 On *hamartōlos* in John 9 meaning 'law-breaker' see Pancaro, op. cit., pp. 30–52.

17 Y. Yadin, *Tefillin from Qumran (XQ Phyl 1–4)* (Jerusalem, 1969), p. 41; J. T. Milik, 'Tefillin, Mezuzot et Targums (4Q128–157)', in *Qumrân Grotte 4*, DJD 6 (Oxford, 1977), pp. 48–79.

18 Marriage laws and hence the status of the offspring of mixed marriages were a particular matter of concern in relations between Jews and Samaritans. In some patristic quotations of John 8:48 the charge of being illegitimate is added: see J. Mehlmann, 'John 8, 48 in some patristic quotations', *Bib* 44 (1963), 206–9.

19 Reicke, op. cit., p. 55, links John 5:18 and 10:33 with the third rather than the second commandment.

20 Deut 32:43 in a Greek version may have provided a pentateuchal text; see Deut 32:43 in the *NEB*, where the translation is based on 4QDeut^q: cf. P. Skehan, 'A fragment of the "Song of Moses" (Deut. 32) from Qumran', *BASOR* 136 (1954), 12–15. Ps 82:6 is used in *Mek* 9:79 on Exod 20:19 (ed. Lauterbach, II, 272).

21 A. Guilding, *The Fourth Gospel and Jewish Worship* (Oxford, 1960), p. 96; Brooke, op. cit., p. 323.

22 E. Lohmeyer, *The Lord's Prayer* (London, 1965), p. 69, concludes justifiably that for the first century '"to be hallowed" is to all intents and purposes synonymous with "to be glorified"'.

23 Only elsewhere in the NT at 1 John 3:15.

24 As maintained by Brown, *John I–XII*, p. 316; Lindars, op. cit., p. 289; R. Schnackenburg, *Das Johannesevangelium*, HTKNT 4.3 (Freiburg, 1975), II, 187. An idea rejected recently by R. A. Whitacre, *Johannine Polemic: The Role of Tradition and Theology*, SBLDS 67 (Chico, 1982), p. 34.

25 Probably a reference to the murder of Abel by Cain: Brown, *John I–XII*, p. 358.

26 Pancaro, op. cit., pp. 164, 448–9, 485–7; cf. John 5:19–21.

27 *Mek* 8:51–65 on Exod 20:15 (ed. Lauterbach, II, 260–1). Philo's evidence is ambiguous: he talks of theft which hurts the community, including under this head tyrannical government (*De decalogo* 135–7).

28 See the excellent discussion of the Gospel's use of this technical term by Pancaro, op. cit., pp. 431–51.

29 As Brown, *John I–XII*, p. 340; on the similar case in John 5:31 he cites Deut 17:6 and Num 35:30.

30 C. K. Barrett, *The Gospel According to St. John* (London, ²1978), pp. 336–7, cites *T. Levi* 14:4; *Exod. Rab.* 36:3 amongst other references. See also G. Vermes, '"The Torah is a light"', *VT* 8 (1958), 436–8.

31 See Pancaro, op. cit., pp. 79–91.

32 On this saying see B. Lindars, 'Slave and son in John 8:31–36', in W. C. Weinrich (ed.), *The New Testament Age: Essays in Honor of Bo Reicke* (Macon, 1984), I, 274–86.

33 *Jub.* 16:20–31.

34 *Apoc. Abr.* 1–8.

35 CD 3:2–3.

36 On John 8:41b–47 Brown, *John I–XII*, p. 364, notes generally the equation in the OT of fornication and adultery in relation to Israel's unfaithfulness. B. Malina, 'Does *porneia* mean fornication?' *NovT* 14 (1972), 10–17, argues that *porneia* simply means unlawful sexual conduct or unlawful conduct in general; J. Jensen, 'Does *porneia* mean fornication?' *NovT* 20 (1978), 161–84, argues, against Malina, that the term refers to sexual misconduct alone, though he remains doubtful (p. 181) about the meaning of *porneia* in John 8:41. CD 4:20 uses *zĕnût*, usually translated 'fornication', of a man taking a second wife while the first is still alive.

37 Hos 3:1–3; 4:10–14.

38 Jer 3:9; 5:7; 13:27.

39 Ezek 16:30–9; 23:7–35, 43–5.

40 On the difficulties of Prov. 6:23–6 see W. McKane, *Proverbs*, OTL (London, 1970), pp. 327–30, a section he entitles 'Warnings against adultery'.

41 E.g. Brown, *John I–XII*, pp. cxxii–cxxv, esp. p. cxxiv; B. Lindars, *Behind the*

Fourth Gospel (London, 1971), pp. 48–9, 74. Bar 4:1 and Sir 24:23 are most commonly cited in addition to OT texts. On Wisdom Christology in John 8:12 see Lindars, *The Gospel of John*, pp. 314–16.

42 *Epithumia* occurs several times in Wis 6:11–20, expressing the desire for Wisdom that contrasts well with the desires of the devil in John 8:44. Reim, op. cit., p. 106, sees Wis 6:17–18 behind the allusion to Exod 20:6 in John 14:15, 21; 15:10.

43 John 5:41–4; 12:28–33; 17:5–6, 11–12, 26.

44 Barrett, 'The OT in the Fourth Gospel', p. 161, connects Deut 6:4 with John 10:30.

45 E.g. XQ Phyl 2, 3; 4Q Phyl B (4Q129), 4Q Phyl C (4Q130), 4Q Phyl G–H (4Q134–5); the Nash Papyrus. Cf. S. Safrai, 'The synagogue', in S. Safrai and M. Stern (eds.), *The Jewish People in the First Century*, CRINT 1.2 (Assen, 1976), pp. 926–7; E. Schürer, *The History of the Jewish People in the Age of Jesus Christ* II, rev. G. Vermes, F. Millar and M. Black (Edinburgh, 1979), 454–5.

46 Sabbath 5:9–10, 16–18; idolatry 5:18; honour the father 5:23; false witness 5:31–7; name 5:43. In addition 5:46 may allude to Deut 18:15–18; cf. John 7:40.

47 As elaborated by Barrett, *St John*, p. 292, with references to Wisdom literature.

48 Guilding, op. cit., pp. 95–6.

49 Lev 25:13; Ps 82: 1–2; Isa 61:1–2. See J. A. Sanders, 'The Old Testament in 11Q Melchizedek', *JANESCU* 5 (1973), 374–6.

50 As I have argued in Brooke, op. cit., pp. 319–23.

51 See above n. 17.

52 See the works cited by G. Vermes, 'The decalogue and the Minim', in *Post-Biblical Jewish Studies*, SJLA 8 (Leiden, 1975), p. 175, n. 32.

53 Cf. Mark 10:17–19; Matt 19:16–19; Luke 18:18–20; Rom 13:9–10.

54 As in *Apos. Con.* 7.36.4–5; *Didache* 2:1–7.

55 Reim, op. cit., pp. 125–6.

56 E.g. in *Mek* 7:55–70 on the differences between the sabbath commandment in Exod 20:8 and Deut 5:12 (ed. Lauterbach, II, 252–3); as discussed in J. Neusner, *The Rabbinic Traditions about the Pharisees before 70* (Leiden, 1971), I, 185–6; II, 11.

57 As M. Pamment warns: 'Is there convincing evidence of Samaritan influence on the Fourth Gospel?', *ZNW* 73 (1982), 221–30. Martyn, *History and Theology*, pp. 108–9, aligns the Samaritan ten commandments with the Johannine material concerning the expectation of the prophet like Moses.

58 D. Moody Smith, 'Johannine Christianity: some reflections on its character and delineation', *NTS* 21 (1974–5), 240–2. I share R. E. Brown's unease (*The Community of the Beloved Disciple* (London, 1979), p. 36, n. 52) about Smith's phrase 'less orthodox'.

59 Brown, *The Community of the Beloved Disciple*, pp. 34–54.

60 Martyn, *History and Theology*, pp. 24–62; he focuses particularly on the two levels in John 9 of Jesus' actual ministry and the healing activity of the early Church which led to some being expelled from the synagogue.

61 Martyn, *John in Christian History*, pp. 85–8; *History and Theology*, pp. 38–62, 82–9; this is also elegantly described at the literary level of the final form of the Gospel by A. E. Harvey, *Jesus on Trial: A Study in the Fourth Gospel* (London, 1976).

62 Kolenkow, op. cit., pp. 623–38, reflecting for the Fourth Gospel some aspects

of D. Moody Smith, 'The setting and shape of a Johannine narrative source', *JBL* 95 (1976), 231–41.
63 Most recently W. Rordorf, 'Beobachtungen zum Gebrauch des Dekalogs in der vorkonstantinisch Kirche', in Weinrich, op. cit., II, 431–42 has argued for the catechetical use of the decalogue in the early Church.
64 It is preferable to see Jewish Christians as only part of the target of the *Birkat hamminim*. Vermes, 'The decalogue and the Minim', pp. 176–7, identifies the Minim as the 'progressive, enlightened and intellectual élite of the Mediterranean', the very Jews who may have found the Johannine community's understanding of the decalogue appealing.
65 In this respect Jesus himself stands within this tradition in first-century Judaism; see the Gospel texts cited in n. 53.
66 As recently in J. Gager, *The Origins of Anti-Semitism* (New York, 1985), pp. 151–3.
67 For whom Nicodemus is the type; J. L. Martyn describes him as a secret believer (*History and Theology*, pp. 116–18, 121–2).
68 Rordorf, op. cit., p. 440, links the Jewish discontinuation of the use of the decalogue with the early Christian adoption of it as part of the initiation of new converts at baptism.

10. PAUL AND THE LAW IN RECENT RESEARCH
1 W. D. Davies, 'Law in the New Testament', in *The Interpreter's Dictionary of the Bible*, III (New York/Nashville, 1962), 99.
2 ibid., p. 100.
3 W. D. Davies, 'Paul and the law: reflections on pitfalls in interpretation', *The Hastings Law Journal* 29 (1978), 1459–504, repr. in W. D. Davies, *Jewish and Pauline Studies* (London, 1984), pp. 91–122.
4 M. D. Hooker and S. G. Wilson (eds.), *Paul and Paulinism: Essays in honour of C. K. Barrett* (London, 1982), pp. 4–16.
5 Cf. W. D. Davies, *Torah in the Messianic Age and/or the Age to Come* (Philadelphia, 1952); L. Baeck, 'The faith of Paul', *JJS* 3 (1952), 93–110; H.-J. Schoeps, *Paul: The Theology of the Apostle in the Light of Jewish Religious History* (ET London, 1961), pp. 171–5.
6 Davies, *Jewish and Pauline Studies*, p. 107.
7 ibid., pp. 108–16.
8 C. E. B. Cranfield, 'St. Paul and the law', *SJT* 17 (1964), 43–68.
9 ibid., p. 65.
10 C. F. D. Moule, 'Obligation in the ethic of Paul', in W. R. Farmer, C. F. D. Moule and R. R. Niebuhr (eds.), *Christian History and Interpretation: Studies Presented to John Knox* (Cambridge, 1967), pp. 389–406.
11 Moule, op. cit., p. 391.
12 ibid., p. 392.
13 C. K. Barrett, *The Epistle to the Romans* (London, 1957), p. 129.
14 Moule, op. cit., p. 393; cf. C. K. Barrett, *Freedom and Obligation* (London, 1985), p. 62.
15 Moule, op. cit., p. 393.
16 ibid., p. 394.
17 ibid., pp. 404f.
18 E. P. Sanders, *Paul and Palestinian Judaism* (London, 1977), pp. 75, 236 *et passim*.
19 ibid., pp. 442–7.

20 ibid., p. 549.
21 M. D. Hooker, 'Interchange in Christ', *JTS* n.s. 22 (1971), 349–61; 'Interchange and atonement', *BJRL* 60 (1977–8), 462–81.
22 M. D. Hooker, 'Paul and "covenantal nomism"', in Hooker and Wilson, op. cit., pp. 47–56.
23 Barrett, *Freedom and Obligation*, p. 44.
24 Cf. ibid., p. 115, n. 43.
25 R. H. Gundry, 'Grace, works, and staying saved in Paul', *Bib* 66 (1985), 1–38.
26 E. P. Sanders, *Paul, the Law and the Jewish People* (Philadelphia, 1983), p. 159.
27 Sanders, *Paul and Palestinian Judaism*, p. 552; cf. *Paul, the Law and the Jewish People*, p. 167, n. 38.
28 Cf. Hooker, 'Paul and "covenantal nomism"', p. 54.
29 Hans Hübner, *Law in Paul's Thought* (ET Edinburgh, 1984). Mention should also be made of J. W. Drane, *Paul: Libertine or Legalist?* (London, 1975), where the four capital epistles are seen to conform naturally to a Hegelian *schema*, in which Galatians, with its very negative attitude to the law, represents the thesis, and 1 Corinthians, with its reaction to Corinthian libertinism, represents the antithesis, while 2 Corinthians and Romans mark a synthesis.
30 J. W. MacGorman, 'Problem passages in Galatians', *South West Journal of Theology* 15 (1972), 43, quoted by Hübner, op. cit., p. 13, n. 42.
31 See Davies, *Jewish and Pauline Studies*, pp. 103–8.
32 See also H. Hübner, 'Das ganze und das eine Gesetz', *Kerygma und Dogma* 21 (1975), 239–56.
33 Hübner, *Law in Paul's Thought*, p. 84.
34 H. Räisänen points out (in a discussion of Drane, not of Hübner) that 'several of the contradictions in Paul's thought are already seen in Galatians, and most are still there in Romans' ('Paul's theological difficulties with the law', in *Studia Biblica 1978*, JSNT Sup. 3, III (Sheffield, 1980), p. 302).
35 C. T. Rhyne, *Faith Establishes the Law* (Chico, California, 1981); Hübner, *Law in Paul's Thought*, p. 53; E. Käsemann, *Commentary on Romans* (ET Grand Rapids, 1980), p. 105.
36 C. E. B. Cranfield, *The Epistle to the Romans*, II (Edinburgh, ²1983), 519.
37 Käsemann, *Romans*, p. 282.
38 Barrett, *Romans*, p. 198.
39 Rhyne, op. cit., p. 120.
40 H. Räisänen, *Paul and the Law* (Tübingen, 1983), p. v.
41 ibid., p. 200.
42 See n. 5 above.
43 ibid., p. 248.
44 Full justice is done to the influence of Paul's conversion-experience on this and other aspects of his ministry in S. Kim, *The Origin of Paul's Gospel* (Tübingen, ²1984). In a 'postscript to the second edition' (pp. 336–58), Kim takes account of the criticisms of Räisänen and others.
45 Sanders, *Paul and Palestinian Judaism*, p. 433; *Paul, the Law and the Jewish People*, pp. 147f.
46 J. D. G. Dunn, 'The new perspective on Paul', *BJRL* 65 (1983), 95–122; 'Works of the law and the curse of the law (Galatians 3.10–14)', *NTS* 31 (1985), 523–42.
47 On this interpretation see H. Hübner, 'Was heisst bei Paulus "Werke des Gesetzes"?' in E. Grässer and O. Merk (eds.), *Glaube und Eschatologie:*

Festschrift für W. G. Kümmel zum 80. Geburtstag (Tübingen, 1985), pp. 123–33.

48 Dunn, 'The new perspective on Paul', p. 113.

49 R. Badenas, *Christ the End of the Law: Romans 10.4 in Pauline Perspective* (Sheffield, 1985), p. 148. This monograph comprises a historical survey of the interpretation of Rom 10:4 with a satisfying exegetical 'approach' to its meaning.

11. PAUL AND THE LAW IN ROMANS 5–8: AN ACTANTIAL ANALYSIS

1 Cf. especially H. Hübner, *Law in Paul's Thought* (Edinburgh, 1984).

2 This point has been forcefully presented by H. Räisänen, *Paul and the Law* (Tübingen, 1983).

3 Cf. P. Fredriksen, 'Paul and Augustine: conversion narratives, orthodox traditions, and the retrospective self', *JTS* 37 (1986), 3–34.

4 As strongly asserted by S. Kim, *The Origin of Paul's Gospel* (Tübingen, ²1984).

5 E. P. Sanders, *Paul and Palestinian Judaism* (London, 1977).

6 The actantial model which I use below is a central feature of the narrative analysis of A.-J. Greimas, described by D. Patte, *What is Structural Exegesis?* (Philadelphia, 1976), pp. 35–52. The description includes an analysis of the Parable of the Good Samaritan.

7 Cf. ibid., pp. 68–75.

8 Cf. J. Drury, *The Parables in the Gospels: History and Allegory* (London, 1985), pp. 139f. Drury presupposes that Luke is rewriting Matthew, but recognition of Lukan rewriting is not inconsistent with the Q hypothesis, which Drury rejects.

9 In what follows attention will be confined to the dynamics of the argument, and there will be no discussion of points arising from the vast secondary literature on these chapters. However, it may be pointed out here that the results of the analysis do go some way towards meeting the complaint of Räisänen that 'Paul's thought on the law is full of difficulties and inconsistencies' (op. cit., p. 264).

10 Cf. C. E. B. Cranfield, *Romans*, ICC (Edinburgh, 1975), I, 174. For the vexed question of the date of Wisdom (which might have been written too late to influence Paul) see the discussion of R. M. Springett, 'A suggested historical background to *Sapientia Solomonis*' (unpublished Ph.D. thesis, Manchester, 1984), pp. 41–74, who places it in the first century BCE.

11 So Hübner, op. cit., p. 144, says: 'What is perhaps important for our purpose is to see from them how much Paul makes his formulations on the basis of the situation, and how little Pauline theology may be understood as a firm or even rigid system of fixed and closely defined terms.'

12 *Pathēma* in the NT (always plural except in Heb 2:9) usually refers to sufferings, but means 'passions' here and in Gal 5:24, where it is correlated with 'desires' (*epithumiai*). Thus it has a general application in Gal 5:24 also, including, but not confined to, sexual lust; cf. Cranfield, op. cit., p. 337.

13 Cf. Hübner, op. cit., pp. 72–6.

14 Cf. Cranfield, op. cit., pp. 364f.

15 Reading *se* with most modern editors. The paraphrase 'each one of you' is to bring out the force of the singular (obscured by *NEB* 'you'). This is the hardest reading, as second-person singular does not occur elsewhere in these chapters, though it is not contrary to Paul's style. Other readings can be explained by the unexpectedness of it: *me* (=RSV) shows influence of 7:25; *hēmas* anticipates

verse 4; and omission of the word altogether may be due to haplography after *ēleutherōsen.*

12. THE STATUS OF LAW IN THE LETTER TO THE EPHESIANS
  1 E. P. Sanders, *Paul, the Law and the Jewish People* (London, 1985; originally Fortress Press, 1983), p. 3.
  2 Here I follow J. Munck's understanding of Galatians in 'The Judaizing Gentile Christians', in *Paul and the Salvation of Mankind* (Richmond, Virginia/London, 1959), pp. 87–134.
  3 According to P. S. Minear in *The Obedience of Faith* (London, 1971).
  4 C. J. A. Hickling, 'Centre and periphery in Paul's thought', in *Studia Biblica 1978*, JSNT Sup 3, III (Sheffield, 1980), 199–214.
  5 E. P. Sanders, *Paul and Palestinian Judaism* (London, 1977), p. 443.
  6 Hickling, op. cit., p. 202.
  7 I note the objections of another contributor to this volume, F. G. Downing, to talking of 'revelation' rather than 'salvation' in the context of a Christian theology, but it does seem that God not only acts but also, in some sense, makes himself known.
  8 Hickling, op. cit., p. 204.
  9 ibid., p. 209.
 10 The cumulative arguments amassed by C. L. Mitton, *The Epistle to the Ephesians: its Authorship, Origin and Purpose* (Oxford, 1951), have not been refuted, and a number of scholars (e.g. K. M. Fischer, as in n. 14) are now turning their attention to the resulting question of the consequences of this conclusion, given the shortcomings of the hypothesis of Goodspeed, Knox and Mitton himself.
 11 Calvin J. Roetzel, 'Jewish Christian – Gentile Christian relations: a discussion of Ephesians 2.15a.' *ZNW* 74 (1983), 81–9.
 12 G. Schille, *Frühchristliche Hymnen* (Berlin, 1965), and J. T. Sanders, *The New Testament Christological Hymns* (Cambridge, 1971).
 13 M. Barth, *Ephesians*, AB (Garden City, 1974), *ad loc.*
 14 K. M. Fischer, *Tendenz und Absicht des Epheserbriefes* (Göttingen, 1973).
 15 H. Conzelmann, *Der Brief an die Epheser* (Göttingen, 1965); M. Dibelius, *An die Kolosser, Epheser, und Philemon* (Tübingen, 1953), *ad loc.*
 16 Roetzel, op. cit., p. 84.
 17 He gives no particular reference, but simply appeals to 'the light of Philonic speculation'.
 18 Cf. the comment of M. Hengel on the work of Schille, op. cit.: it 'offers a deterrent example of an early Christian "Panhymnology"' (*Studia Biblica 1978*, III, 196, n. 19).
 19 Cf. the view advanced in much apocalyptic writing that the law was still valid for morality, though the cult was now superseded.
 20 Roetzel, op. cit., p. 87.
 21 ibid., p. 88.
 22 Cf. the view put forward by C. K. Barrett in 'Pauline controversies in the post-Pauline period', *NTS* 20 (1974), 229–45.

13. LAW AND CUSTOM: LUKE–ACTS AND LATE HELLENISM
  1 Craig L. Blomberg, 'The Law in Luke–Acts', *JSNT* 22 (1984), 54–5.
  2 ibid., p. 55.
  3 Luke 13:10–17; 14:1–6.

4 Acts 10.

5 J. L. Houlden, 'The purpose of Luke', *JSNT* 21 (1984), 54–6.

6 S. G. Wilson, *Luke and the Law* (Cambridge, 1983), p. 10.

7 P. W. Walasky, *And So We Came to Rome* (Cambridge, 1983).

8 R. J. Cassidy, *Jesus, Politics and Society* (New York, 1978), rightly notes this strand, but then fails to note the wider context; cf. R. J. Cassidy and P. R. Scharper, *Political Issues in Luke–Acts* (New York, 1983).

9 In addition to Jervell, below, R. Maddox, *The Purpose of Luke–Acts* (Edinburgh, 1983), esp. pp. 36–9. For an impressive analysis of the Hellenistic character of Luke's writing (even in the early chapters of Acts), see P. W. van der Horst 'Hellenistic parallels to the Acts of the Apostles (2.1–47)', *JSNT* 25 (Oct. 1985), 49–60 (and cf. his *ZNW* 74 (1983), 17–26).

10 J. Jervell, *Luke and the People of God* (Minneapolis, 1972), p. 147. R. Banks, *Jesus and the Law in the Synoptic Tradition* (Cambridge, 1975), allows commendably for variety in the material he adduces, but also fails to note the wider context of the Hellenistic discussion.

11 Wilson, op. cit., pp. 55, 57.

12 ibid., p. 57.

13 ibid., pp. 21–2, 65–6.

14 *Contra* Jervell, op. cit., pp. 174–5.

15 Wilson, op. cit., pp. 8–11, 103.

16 ibid, p. 114. This suggestion does not sit comfortably with Wilson's earlier insistence, cited above, that Luke 'stands at a considerable distance from the concerns of Rabbinic Judaism' (ibid., p. 57).

17 Acts 15; Wilson, op. cit., pp. 68–102, 106–7.

18 ibid., pp. 108–11.

19 ibid., pp. 111–12.

20 ibid., p. 113.

21 ibid., pp. 116–17.

22 Blomberg, op. cit., p. 70.

23 G. H. Sabine, *A History of Political Theory* (London, ³1952), pp. 1–159, chs. 1–10; J. W. Jones, *Law and Legal Theory of the Greeks* (Oxford, 1956), especially the first three chapters. F. Schulz, *History of Roman Legal Science* (Oxford, 1946), Part II: 'The Hellenistic period of Roman jurisprudence', and especially pp. 69–75, 'The exclusion of philosophy, rhetoric, and sociology'. A. A. Schiller, *Roman Law* (The Hague/Paris/New York, 1978), especially pp. 569–84, 'Influence of Greek thought upon the Roman jurists', with the conclusion that it was very little. The impact on aristocratic pleaders such as Quintilian and Pliny junior was probably more considerable. It is evidence from them of public views of law and order that are our concern here. G. A. Sabine's views seem largely supported, save that any close link between the *ius gentium* and 'natural law' is rejected by some of the others.

Also worth noting in this connection: E. P. Sanders (ed.), *Jewish and Christian Self-Definition*, vol. I (London, 1980), especially ch. 2, R. M. Grant, 'The social setting of second-century Christianity', pp. 16–29, and particularly pp. 25–6, on the 'apostolic fathers' (cf. also his *Early Christianity and Society* (London, 1978)); also ch. 3, W. R. Schoedel, 'Ignatius of Antioch', pp. 30–56, particularly pp. 50–4. Also E. P. Sanders with A. I. Baumgarten and A. Mendelson (eds.), *Jewish and Christian Self-definition* vol. II (London, 1981), especially ch. 7, B. S. Jackson, 'The problem of Roman influence on the halakah and normative self-definition in Judaism', pp. 157–203: not suggesting very much is discernible, but stressing the likelihood that the working of the pagan courts, and their ethos, would be well known.

24 It is one of the many drawbacks of the discussion of *nomos* in *TDNT* (Kleinknecht) that it concentrates here, and looks primarily for issues germane to its theological systematics – e.g. the law as 'crusher of humanity by guilt'. There are some clearly significant passages quoted from authors around the first century; but even then care is needed: as when, for instance, Dio 3.43 is quoted (A 3 a) on 'monarchy as irresponsible government where the king's will is law', as though expressing Dio's own view of monarchy, when all his Discourses on the topic contrast true kingship with any such autocratic tyranny.

25 Cf. also *De Iosepho* 29–30. The quotations here are from the *Loeb* editions of the texts.

26 Wilson, op. cit., p. 6.

27 ibid., pp. 6–7; noting, e.g., Philo, *Leg. Gaium* 210.

28 Philo, *Spec. Leg.* 4.149.

29 Wilson, op. cit., p. 7.

30 Josephus, *Ap.* 2.155.

31 ibid., 2.153,156.

32 ibid., 2.159–60.

33 Wilson, op. cit., p. 7.

34 Cf. Josephus, *Ap.* 2.176–81.

35 Cf. also Dio 31.142; Philo, quoted above; Plutarch, *Ad principem ineruditum* (*Moralia* 780c).

36 Compare also Dio 3.43–9.

37 Dio 80.3; cf. 1 Tim 1:9!

38 Cf. also Dio 3.43–9, as well as Cicero, *Pro Cluentio* 53; 146; Epictetus, *Dissertations* 1.13.5; 4.3.9–12.

39 For further evidence of its pervasiveness compare also Dionysius, *RA* 2.6.1: 'Romulus established it as a custom to be observed by all his successors'; cf. ibid. 2.73.2: 'the pontifices make laws for the observance of religious rites not established by written law or by custom, but which seem to them worthy of receiving the sanction of law and custom (*nomōn te kai ethismōn*)'; Cicero, *De officiis* 1.148: 'no rules need to be given about what is done in accordance with the established customs and conventions of a community, for these are in themselves rules'; cf. ibid. 2.15; Quintilian, *Institutes* 12.3.6: 'every point of law is based either on written law or accepted custom'; and elements of the debate in Plutarch, *Septem sapientium convivium* (*Moralia* 152A, 154EF); just as Luke talks of *to ethismenon tou nomou* (Luke 2:27), so Plutarch uses *ta nomismata* for 'customary rites': *De genio Socratis* (*Moralia* 585F, 590A).

40 A preliminary sketch of the remainder of the argument appeared in my 'Freedom from the law in Luke–Acts', *JSNT* 26 (1986), 49–52. Although *deisidaimonia* may originally have referred to a commendable respect for divine agencies, in the first-century or so literature surveyed here I note only one such instance, and a few where the term seems to be used in a neutral sense. Mostly it is pejorative. But see further, below.

41 Compare also *Ant.* 16.44.

42 Josephus, *Ap.* 2.144.

43 ibid. 2.179.

44 Josephus, *BJ* 2.414–15, and *Ap.* 2.68–9.

45 P. Lond. 1912, in A. S. Hunt and C. C. Edgar (eds.), *Select Papyri*, LCL (Cambridge MA/London, 1932), vol. II.

46 Dionysius, *RA* 7.70.3.

47 Plutarch, *De cupiditate* (*Moralia* 627D).

48 Dio 43.11.

49 Pliny, *Letters* 10.96.

50 Compare my 'Ethical pagan theism and the speeches in Acts', *NTS* 27 (1981), 455–63; 'Common ground with paganism in Luke and in Josephus', *NTS* 28 (1982), 546–59.

51 Josephus, *BJ* 1.3–6.

52 ibid., 3.108; cf. *BJ* 2.345–7.

53 ibid., 1.11–12.

54 Walasky, op. cit., pp. 16–18.

55 ibid., pp. 22–5.

56 Acts 23:6; 25:10; cf. Epictetus, *Dissertations* 1.29.9–16 and 4.7.33–5.

57 Cf. also Tacitus, *History* 5.1–13; Josephus *Ap* 1.209–12, and *Ant.* 12.5–6, quoted below. Compare also M. Whittaker, *Jews and Christians, Graeco-Roman Views* (Cambridge, 1985); also R. L. Wilkens, *The Christians as the Romans saw Them* (New Haven/London, 1984), pp. 60–7 on 'superstition', pp. 112–17 on tradition. Though Wilkens concentrates mainly on the second century, the issues are mostly similar.

58 Cf. Plutarch, *De Iside et Osiride* (*Moralia* 379E).

59 Acts 17:22; cf. also Plutarch, *Solon* 12.3, on Athenian superstition; though, to be fair, Josephus admires their tradition of piety (*Ap.* 2.130).

60 Philo, *De somniis* 1.230.

61 Philo, *De gigantibus* 16.

62 Cf. Philo, *De cherubim* 42.

63 On the term, see above, n. 40. The references here are to the series of 'documents' referred to by Josephus, *Ant.* 14.228, 232, 234, 237, 240; 12.259 (Samaritans); 19.290 (other nations); cf. Acts 25:19; of Manasseh, *Ant.* 10.42.

64 Josephus, *Ap.* 1.209–12; *Ant.* 12.5–6.

65 Cf. Josephus, again, *BJ* 1.113, on Queen Alexandra, her better judgement overcome by *deisidaimonia*; 2.174, Pilate is overcome by astonishment – not at all by admiration – at the power of the Jews' religious scruples; and cf. also 2.230; *Ant.* 15.277 (Herod).

66 Josephus, *Ap.* 2.192, 249.

67 Tacitus, *History* 5.5,8–9; and compare Whittaker, op. cit., pp. 12–13, 15, 80–5.

68 Cf. the sixth-century *Digest* 48.8.11.1, rescript of Antoninus, in Whittaker, op. cit., p. 85.

69 Acts 16:3.

70 Acts 10:44–8.

71 For the significance of the 'answer' preceding the question (Peter's dream precedes Cornelius' request) see, e.g., Plutarch, *De defectu oraculorum* (*Moralia* 434D–F); for a deity's decent willingness to over-ride a difficult injunction, *De pythiae oraculis* (*Moralia* 403F–404A). For divine possession, Philo, *De somniis* passim; *Spec. leg.* 1.64–5; Josephus, *Ant.* 4.119–22.

72 Josephus, *Ap.* 2.209–10; Whittaker, op. cit., esp. pp. 73–80.

73 The deity (*to theion*) of Acts 17 sounds to many readers very like the God of Seneca, *Epistulae Morales* 95; cf. also Cicero, *Tusculan Disputations* 3.72; *De natura deorum* 1.55; 2.117–18.

74 Agreeing with Leslie Houlden that the overall theological view, of which this may have been a part for Luke, is not easy to discern, I would also agree with

him that it is probably to be found in Luke's trust in 'the definite plan and foreknowledge of God' (Acts 2:23). God's providence has been sufficiently indicated in antiquity for it to be trusted now, and interpreted in the way Luke proposes. Josephus discusses the rather larger issues of Jewish history over the same period in a very similar way: See Downing, 'Ethical pagan theism'.

75 Wilson, op. cit., p. 51.

76 Dionysius, *RA* 2.25–6; Plutarch, *Coniugalia praecepta* (*Moralia* 144A); Musonius Rufus 12,13A, 13B.

77 The pseudo-Clementines and the Letter of Peter show some Christians continuing to pay a deep respect to Jewish tradition. Other Christians, among themselves, are unconcerned or antipathetic. But the underlying concern for order and, concomitantly, for some kind of antiquity, is widely apparent: cf. 1 Clement 37, on the model of military order, followed by 'bishops and deacons, appointed in no new fashion, for indeed, it had been written concerning bishops and deacons from very ancient times' (42); and then cf. 60–1, running from divine creation through to Roman imperial authority, contrasting with the 'sedition' of making superannuated clergy redundant (1). Though Ignatius' sense of his episcopal authority is not unqualified, there is a similar stress on harmony through submission (e.g. Ignatius, *Ephesians* 4–5). This is of course the implication of the 'household' model for the Church (a model Aristotle had rejected as too autocratic. As one philosopher quipped to one espousing 'democracy': 'Have you tried it at home?'). (Cf. also Letter of 'Paul' to Ephesians 6, but also the Pastoral Letters, 1 Peter, Justin and Diognetus. See particularly D. C. Verner, *The Household of God* (Chico, 1983); but also J. H. Elliott, *A Home for the Homeless* (Philadelphia, 1981).

This strand came to dominate; but it must be seen alongside the otherworldliness of second-century Gnosticism on the one hand, and the anarchist radicalism of what I see as Christian Cynicism, from Jesus, or at least from the synoptic tradition, a radicalism which Lucian in the second century saw as the Christians' most obvious characteristic. I take it neither of these has completely disappeared.

Index of References

Index of Modern Authors